SKETCH

OF

THE POLITICAL HISTORY

OF

INDIA

SKETCH

OF

THE POLITICAL HISTORY

OF

INDIA:

FROM THE INTRODUCTION

OF

MR. PITTS BILL, A. D. 1784,

TO THE PRESENT DATE

JOHN MALCOLM

GYAN

Published by

Gyan Publishing House
5, Ansari Road
Daryaganj, New Delhi-110002
Phone: 011-47034999, 9811692060
E-mail: books@gyanbooks.com

Distribution Network
gyanbooks.com
India, USA, Canada, UK, Australia

ISBN: 978-93-6780-066-9 (PB)

First Published, 1811

2nd Impression 2024

Printed at: Gyan Press, Delhi.

SKETCH OF THE POLITICAL HISTORY OF INDIA
Author: JOHN MALCOLM

SKETCH

OF

THE POLITICAL HISTORY

OF

INDIA,

FROM THE INTRODUCTION

OF

MR. PITT'S BILL, A. D. 1784,

TO THE PRESENT DATE.

By JOHN MALCOLM,

LIEUTENANT COLONEL IN THE HONOURABLE EAST INDIA COMPANY'S MADRAS ARMY, RESIDENT AT MYSORE, AND LATE ENVOY TO THE COURT OF PERSIA.

SECOND EDITION.

LONDON:

PRINTED FOR WILLIAM MILLER, ALBEMARLE STREET,

BY JAMES MOYES, GREVILLE STREET, HATTON GARDEN.

1811.

encounter the full force of that active and implacable hostility, which characterizes disputes that involve questions of commercial interest; but the checks which those disputes gave to their success, appear only to have excited their spirit of enterprise.

In the year 1609 they obtained a second Charter, by which this right of exclusive trade was made perpetual; with a proviso, however, like the former, by which the Crown was declared to have the power of resuming the Grant (giving three years' warning), "if it was not "found to promote the interests of the realm."

Though the Company had received the permission of the Emperor of Dehly to form considerable settlements, and establish factories upon the shores of the Empire, they had been hitherto prevented from taking advantage of this indulgence by the intrigues of the Portuguese, and they were ultimately obliged to have recourse to force, to obtain justice from that nation, which claimed, on the ground of prior possession, an exclusive right to the commerce of the Indian seas.

The vessels of the Company were armed, to oppose this arrogant pretension; and in the year 1612, a fleet of them, under Captain Best, defeated the Portuguese in two actions. These victories not only raised the reputation of the English, but enabled them to establish a factory at Surat, under circumstances every way propitious to their success. Anxious to confirm the advantages which they had obtained, the Company solicited the King of England to send an Embassy to the Court of the Emperor Jehaungier, to settle their commerce upon a more secure and liberal basis. King James complied with their request; and Sir Thomas Roe proceeded in the year 1614 to the Imperial Court, which was then residing at Ajmere.

He was received with every honour by Jehaungier, who seemed disposed to accede to all his requests: but the caution of his son and ministers, and the intrigues of the Portuguese missionaries, prevented that success which had been expected.

A confirmation of former grants, and an extended privilege of having resident agents at some of the principal towns in the Empire, were, however, obtained; and having finished this arrangement, the Ambassadour returned to Surat, where he passed some time in settling the new factories at that place, and Baroach, and then sailed for Persia, where he was equally, if not more, successful with Shah Abbas the reigning Sovereign of that nation, from whose friendship he obtained every privilege which could promote the commerce of the Company with the Persian Gulf.

The effort which the Portuguese had made to check the progress of the English on the continent of India, was feeble, and perhaps accelerated their success, by stimulating them to active and decided measures; but it in some degree deranged their finances, as it forced them to the expense of military equipments. Their pecuniary embarrassments were greatly increased by the unfortunate result of an endeavour, which was made at this period, to share with the Dutch in the lucrative trade carried on by that nation with the Spice Islands; where, though the superiority of the English character at first gave them success, and enabled them to conciliate some of the Malay Princes, and to obtain the cession of several valuable settlements, their factories were ultimately destroyed. This was effected by a course of policy, which a sordid cruelty could alone have generated, and a spirit of unfeeling avarice executed; and which, though it attained it's immediate object, has excited lasting feelings of resentment in the British Nation, and left an indelible stain upon the fame of that Country by whom it was adopted.

The Massacre of Amboyna (for such the event, which closed this scene, must ever be termed) had the effect, which the cold calculating foresight of it's perpetrators had anticipated; and from it's occurrence, in 1622, the English may be said to have abandoned the commerce of the Eastern Islands to their rivals.

This catastrophe, some radical defects in the constitution of the Company in England, the smallness of their capital, and their increased expenditure, added to their want of forts, and their consequent reliance on the precarious protection of the native Governments, appear at this period to have brought the affairs of the Company into great distress. Their commerce, which had from the first depended upon lucky adventures, began rapidly to decline; and their history, for a long period, offers nothing but a detail of misfortunes in trade, connected with a series of spirited actions, particularly at sea, where the English invariably asserted their character, and revenged themselves upon the Dutch and Portuguese for the injuries which they suffered on shore.

It was during this moment of distress, that an accident led to the formation of that Settlement in Bengal, which has since proved the source of all their prosperity. The Company were indebted to the professional skill of a physician for this origin of their power and greatness.

This gentleman, whose name was Boughton, had proceeded from Surat to Agrah, and had the good fortune to cure the daughter of the Emperor Shah Jehaun of a severe illness; for which, among other rewards, he received the privilege of carrying on a free trade. He went to Bengal, and there his abilities obtained him equal favour from the Nabob of that Country, who extended the privilege, which had been given to him personally by the Emperor, to all his Nation, and in the year 1696 the Company's servants at Surat built a factory at Hoogley, about one hundred miles from the mouth of the branch of the Ganges, which takes it's name from that town.

But this event, though it opened a new and rich channel of commerce, was not sufficient to arrest the decline of the Company's affairs; and the very existence of that body, as a corporation, would appear to have been nearly annihilated during the civil wars in England.

The trade to India was indeed thrown open from the year 1652 to 1657, in which year Cromwell renewed the privileges of the Company. Nothing can be more opposite, than the accounts given by different authors of the result of this short suspension of the Company's monopoly. One, who wrote in 1681, asserts, that the Nation had nearly lost, during this period, all it's privileges in India; that the value of English commodities was lessened; and that those of India were advanced; while another, whose work appears in 1680, declares, that when the East India trade was laid open, the English merchants afforded the Indian commodities so cheap, as to supply most parts of Europe, and even Amsterdam itself. And the last fact would appear to be confirmed by that passage in the letters of Thurloe, the Secretary to Cromwell, which states, that the merchants of Amsterdam "having heard that the Lord "Protector would dissolve the East India Company at London, and declare the navigation "and commerce to the Indies to be free, and "open, were greatly alarmed; as they considered such a measure would be ruinous to "their own East India Company."*

The death of Cromwell disappointed those expectations, which the Company had latterly cherished, from the support of his Government: but these were more than fulfilled by a new

* These two statements are not at such variance as they may at first sight appear. A sudden and great competition of our merchants in India would produce the effects stated by both writers.

Charter, which they obtained from Charles the Second, dated April 1661.

The Charter of Queen Elizabeth had invested the Company with an exclusive right of commerce for fifteen years; and that Corporation was declared a perpetual body politic by a Charter of James the First: but in that obtained from Charles the Second, the old privileges were not only confirmed, but new ones of great importance added. They were vested with a right of exercising civil jurisdiction and military authority; and with the power of making war or concluding peace with the "Infidels of India;" the State reserving to itself, by this distinction, those prerogatives with respect to European Governments. The clause in the Charter granted by Queen Elizabeth, which stated, that it should become null and void after three years' warning, if the privileges granted proved in any way detrimental to the general interests of the Nation, was, however, inserted in all those subsequently granted.

Charles the Second having married the Infanta of Portugal in 1662, obtained the Island of Bombay, in 1663, as a part of the portion of that Princess; but finding the expense of supporting that possession greater than it's revenue, he ceded it to the Company, in the twentieth year of his reign. Five years afterward he granted to them the Island of St. Helena; and in the same spirit which dictated these important cessions, the whole aid of his Government was applied to promote their interests and prosperity.

This encouragement and protection, combined with the active exertions of the Company, raised them to an apparent state of affluence; which, though it excited attack, gave them great means of resisting it. The Charter granted in 1661, was confirmed by Charles the Second in the twenty-eighth year of his reign, and their privileges were extended by an act passed in the thirty-fifth. But they were still more indebted to James the Second, whose influence had been their chief support during his brother's life, and who, when he ascended the throne, granted them increased immunities, and a still larger portion of the royal power. He authorized them to build fortresses, to levy troops, to determine causes by Courts Martial, and to coin money. By these privileges he raised them into a Power, which they disgraced by a thousand acts of corruption, violence, and tyrannical oppression.

It has been well observed by an able anonymous author, who has written a History of the early period of the East India Company, that "unlimited power in the hands of a single

" person, may be prevented from degenerating " into acts of tyranny, by the terrors of ignominy, or by personal fears. But a body of men " vested with authority, is seldom swayed by " restraint of either kind: as they derive, individually, but little applause from their best " measures; so the portion of infamy, which " may fall from each for the worst public actions, is too small to affect personal character. " Having, therefore, no generous inducement to " follow virtue, the most sordid passions frequently lead them into vice. It is from this " circumstance, that the decisions of public " bodies* sometimes partake of that mortifying " species of tyranny, which is incapable of redress, and yet is beyond revenge. These observations may be applied, without the least " injustice, to the actions of the Indian Company both at home and abroad. Avarice, the " most obstinate and hardened passion of the " human mind, being the first principle of commerce, was the original bond of their union; " and humanity, justice, and even policy, gave " way to the prospect or love of gain."

* Those republics, whose conduct would appear an exception to this rule, have acted under the influence of motives, which could not exist in the minds of men, who had no national feeling for the country they ruled, and only viewed their possessions and power as sources of commercial advantage.

"Besides that want of generous principle," the same author adds in a note upon the above paragraph, "which seems excluded from the "very constitution of a sovereign corporation "of commerce, the great distance of their ad- "ministration in India secured the Company "from a general inspection into their conduct, "and consequently furnished ample opportuni- "ties for a wanton and uncontrolled exercise of "power. All resistance, therefore, to their ar- "bitrary edicts, whether they regarded their "own servants or the natives of the country, "was considered as treason, and punished with "severity. The rulers at home had their fa- "vourites abroad, whom they protected in the "most cruel and oppressive measures by their "authority. Hence it happened, that private "resentments and selfish views were too fre- "quently the only rules of their conduct; and "that their administration had scarce any other "principle of union, than a mutual permission "to commit injustice. Even the exclusive pri- "vilege, which was thought necessary for the "prosperity of their commerce, became an "engine of tyranny against all those whom "they considered as interlopers; and such in- "stances of their barbarity might be produced, "supported by facts, as would excite horror."
This author, who, though neither moderate

nor impartial, is very able, and argumentative, supports this general reasoning with some strong facts. Of these, such only will be adduced, as appear to rest on credible authority. The Company had for a period thrown a veil of secrecy over their affairs, under which those who managed them had no doubt practised many frauds. Though they had doubled their capital in the year 1682, they had not taken in more than one half of the sum at first subscribed: and at the moment they were endeavouring to support an appearance of health in a declining body, by making extravagant dividends to the proprietors of stock, they had incurred a debt of two millions; and, instead of answering the legal demands against them, had affixed a paper to the treasury door, declaring they would pay no more till a certain date, though they pretended at the same time that their affairs were in the most flourishing condition.*

These deceptions at home were supported by iniquities abroad; where the Company's factors, in obedience to the instructions of their employers, first borrowed large sums, and then quarrelled with their creditors.† Sir John Child, one of the most notorious of their Governors, is repre-

* White's 'Account of Indian Trade.'

† Hamilton, Vol. I. page 187. Harris, Vol. II.

sented to have gone still further, and to have seized thirteen large ships at Surat, the property of the merchants of that place, and to have retired with his shameful spoil to Bombay.*

Though the Company had obtained a new Charter from Queen Mary in 1694, several flagrant abuses in the conduct of their affairs were detected by Parliament, in 1695. Their home expenses, it was found, had rapidly increased from the sum of £1200 per annum to that of £90,000; and their Governor, Sir Thomas Cooke, on whose notes this money had been lent, was terrified, by a Bill of Pains and Penalties, to make a discovery, from which it appeared that ten thousand pounds of this cash had gone to the King himself, and other sums to his Ministers and principal servants.† The Duke of Leeds, who was the most obnoxious offender, was impeached for receiving five thousand pounds; but King William put a sudden end to the session; and by that act not only quashed the impeachment, but checked all further inquiry.

The principal, and indeed natural, enemies

* As afterwards appeared on oath, in the Court of Exchequer. The value of £300,000 of this spoil was sent home to the Committee of the Court of Directors, who gave the orders.—White's 'Account of Indian Trade.'

† Journals, April 1695.

of the Company, against whom all their violence both at home and abroad was directed, were those English merchants, who wished to interfere with their monopoly, and who were termed, in the language of the day, interlopers. Their endeavours to check and destroy these, led, no doubt, to many acts of oppression, which have been exaggerated, by the writers of the suffering party, into deeds of the most barbarous tyranny. The interlopers, however, in spite of that violence of which they complained, continued to gain strength; and in 1698 they were able to bring under the cognizance of Parliament the Charter granted to the Company in 1694; and having outbid that Corporation, by offering an advance of two millions* sterling at eight per cent, in consideration of an exclusive right of commerce with the East being vested in the subscribers, a Bill was passed in their favour. But their triumph did not last long, for the old Company obtained a confirmation of their Charter in the ensuing season. On the adoption of this measure, the Nation had two East India Companies by parliamentary authority, instead of one by prerogative.† Nothing could be more violent, than the contests of these Com-

* The old Company offered £700,000, at 4 per cent.

† Ralph, Vol. II. page 845.

panies during the short period that they continued separate. The great efforts of both were directed to the object of gaining power in the House of Commons; and in the general elections of 1700 each was detected in bribery and corruption. The old Company corrupted members, and purchased voices; the other, seats. Thus the one bribed the representatives, the other the constituents. But, tired out at length with a struggle which threatened ruin to both, they united their stock under the Charter which had been granted to the old Company, bearing date the 5th of September 1698; and assumed that name under which they have ever since been incorporated, *The United East India Company.*

During such contentions at home, the state of the Company's affairs abroad may be imagined. The spirit of the principles upon which these were regulated, will be collected from an extract of a letter from their Governor at home to an Officer, who had been appointed Judge for civil affairs in India. "I expect," says this commercial despot, "my will and orders shall "be your rule, and not the laws of England, "which are a heap of nonsense, compiled by a "number of country gentlemen, who hardly "know how to govern their own families, "much less the regulating Companies, and "foreign Commerce. Having now the power "of condemning the Company's enemies, or "such as shall be deemed so, particularly those "that shall question the Company's power over "all the British subjects in India, I expect my "orders from time to time shall be obeyed, and "received as Statute Laws."

The union of the two Companies in England had not an immediate effect in reconciling their servants either at home or abroad; and it was some period before their rooted animosities gave way to a feeling of common interest. It did, at last; and in the year 1708 the united Corporation obtained a Bill most favourable to their commerce and privileges, which was granted, on condition of their lending to Government the sum of £120,000, over and above the two millions which had been lent when the new Company was first established.

That tranquillity, and consequent commercial prosperity, which the Peace of Utrecht brought to Europe, was felt by the British Settlements in the East; and these were about this period (1713) under the rule of men of prudence and ability. But success created enemies. A very general clamour was raised against their monopoly, which was stated to be adverse to the general commercial interests of the Kingdom; and they were obliged to agree to an arrangement.

which was considered advantageous to the State, in order to maintain their right of exclusive trade to India.

The affairs of the united Company continued in the same prosperous condition, both at home and abroad, till war was declared between France and England in the year 1744. The French, who had failed for nearly eighty years in all their attempts to erect and support an East India Company, had succeeded in accomplishing this object about the year 1720; and the regular returns made by this Company from the period of their establishment in India, had been so considerable, that the jealousy of the British Company was raised, and the Government entering with some degree of warmth into that jealousy, turned their attention toward the East, when war was likely to arise between the two Nations. The French, anxious to promote a commerce, still in it's infancy, had proposed a neutrality between the two Companies as early as the year 1742, which the Court of Directors at first accepted, and then rejected. When, therefore, war commenced in Europe in 1744, the flame soon spread to Asia. Their respective Sovereigns assisted each Company. The pursuits of commerce yielded to the occupation of arms; and the strange spectacle was presented, of two European Nations combating with each other on the shores of India, aided by different Native Princes of the Country. These Chiefs, impelled by a short-sighted policy, thus sacrificed their permanent independence, for the attainment of momentary objects of hatred and ambition. For it was early in this contest very obvious, that whether the troops of England or France prevailed, the native Allies must become dependent on the conqueror.

What has been said of the History of the Company, shows in a very strong light, not only the origin, but the character, of their early power; and proves the urgent necessity, which existed, from the earliest period of their association, for the strict and constant interference of the Legislature of the Country, to check excesses, by which the national character of England was so exposed to injury. The Company, or rather the individuals of the Direction by whom the Corporation was governed, were in a great degree dead, as has been shown, to those feelings which urge the mind to good and great actions. They, in fact, recognised no motive, but a desire to enrich themselves, their relations and dependents. Their strength as a community, which was the natural consequence of this system, increased with their means of corruption and oppression: and such was the venality of the times, that it appears that hardly any, however high their station, escaped the contamination.

The occurrence of war, in 1744, between England and France, was the commencement of a new era to British India. The same system of Government remained; but the scene was changed. It had gained importance, from becoming one of national contest, and from the new actors who were introduced. These were no longer unobserved factors, and agents of a trading company, whose obscurity left them without an incentive to virtue, or a dread of shame: but officers of distinction, who not only acted under the control of honourable superiors, but under the observation of their Country, which now began to take a warm interest in Indian affairs.

Though it cannot be supposed that the desire of fame, thus excited, could, by it's operation on the minds of a few individuals, effect a complete change in a system, which was radically bad; it must be acknowledged to have had a wonderful effect. India became a scene, in which character and reputation, as well as wealth, were to be acquired; and many of those, who were employed in distinguished stations in that Country, attained the highest honours, which respect and approbation can bestow, or courage and talents command. The names of Lawrence and Clive (both of whom commenced their career about this period of the History of the Company) will live as long as the annals of England; and be regarded as glorious examples, until the qualities of valour, military skill and elevated genius, shall cease to receive the applause and admiration of mankind.

The Peace of Aix la Chapelle, which was concluded in 1748, terminated those direct hostilities which the French and English Nations had carried on in India; but the armies, which both States maintained at that period on the coast of Coromandel, continued to assist different native Princes, with the object on each side of obtaining, through such policy, a strength that would make their power, at the renewal of a contest, paramount to the other.

Both the English and French had proceeded in this course for some years, with fluctuating success; when the embarrassment, to which it led, induced the Directors of each Company to apply to their Sovereigns, to interpose their power to mediate their differences: and the terms of accommodation were actually agreed upon, when the war of 1756 broke out between the two Nations, and caused their armies in India to enter upon a more extended field of contest than ever. This contest was marked by a series of unparallelled success on the part of the English, who remained, at the peace of 1763, Sovereigns of the rich Provinces of Bengal, Bahar, and Orissa, of the Northern Circars, of part of the Carnatic, and of all their old possessions on the Malabar Coast.

In addition to the strength, which these possessions gave to the Government of the English Company, we may add the resources of it's Allies, the Nabob of the Carnatic, and the Vizier of Oude, whose power it had supported, and over both of whose Courts the English influence was so completely established, that that Nation might be said to command the resources of their dominions.

The rapid aggrandizement of the Company naturally called the observation of the Administration in England to their affairs; and in the year 1767, the House of Commons appointed a Committee to investigate the nature of the Company's Charters, to consider their Treaties and Grants, and to calculate all expenses, civil, naval, and military, which had been incurred by Government on their account.

Their right to any territorial acquisition, was at this period boldly questioned, and their monopoly was a subject of very free discussion; but they found means, as they had on former occasions, to silence opposition from those quarters where they thought it might be dangerous. Their personal and political influence in the State had increased with their fortune and patronage; and too many had become interested in the golden harvest, which about this period opened in the East, to make it easy to control, much less to subvert, a body so strong and so united. The result of this inquiry, therefore, was a compromise between the Company and the Ministers, by which the possessions of the former were confirmed to them for the term of two years, on condition of their paying the public £400,000 per annum. A new engagement, very nearly similar to the former, took place in 1769; but the period of it's duration was extended for five years.

Before this agreement expired, the Company's affairs fell into considerable embarrassment: and in 1773 they petitioned Government for pecuniary aid, which was granted; but the inquiry, that the House of Commons made upon this occasion into their affairs, was followed by an act of the Legislature, which made many important changes in their Government both at home and abroad. The principal of these were:

1st. That the Court of Directors should in future, instead of being chosen annually, be elected for four years; six members annually;

but none to hold their seat for longer than four years.

2d. That the qualification stock should be £1000 instead of £500: £3000, two votes; and £6000, three votes.

3d. That in lieu of the Mayor's Court, the jurisdiction of which was limited to small mercantile causes, a Supreme Court of Judicature, consisting of a Chief Judge and three Puisne Judges, should be appointed by the Crown, with great and extended powers of cognizance over the civil and criminal jurisdiction of the subjects of England, their servants and dependents, residing within the Company's territories in Bengal.

4th. A Governor General, with four Counsellors, were appointed to Fort William, and vested with full powers over the other Presidencies. When any differences occurred, the opinion of the majority was to be decisive; and this Board was directed by the act to transmit regular reports of it's proceedings to the Directors, who were, within fourteen days of the receipt of their despatches, to furnish copies of them to one of his Majesty's Secretaries of State, to whom they were also to send copies of any rules and ordinations which they made; and these were, if disapproved by his Majesty, to become null and void.

This act appointed Warren Hastings, Esquire, Governor General of India; and John Clavering, Esquire, the Honourable George Monson, Richard Barwell, and Phillip Francis, Esquires, the four first Counsellors.

It would be foreign to the intent of this work, to enter into a narrative of Mr. Hastings's Government. It was, from it's commencement till it's termination, marked by events of uncommon magnitude, which ultimately gave rise to a discussion, which not only diffused a more general knowledge of Indian affairs, but awakened the British Nation to a more just sense of the importance of it's interests in India.

Whatever may have been the opinion of contending parties and factions at this period, there are some leading facts relating to this part of the History of British India, upon which all dispassionate minds are now agreed. It is admitted, even by those who condemned part of his conduct, that Mr. Hastings, during a time of unexampled public embarrassment, and at a moment when he had to contend against those from whom he should have derived support, showed all the active energy of a great Statesman; and, by his spirited and extraordinary exertions, saved the interests of his Country in India from that ruin with which they were threatened; and in which they undoubtedly would have been involved, had a man of less resolution, fortitude and genius, held the reigns of Government. This is his praise; and no man could wish higher: but the most strenuous advocates of this distinguished person, while they defend his personal integrity, are forced to acknowledge, that the whole system of the Government over which he presided was corrupt, and full of abuses. The control, or rather right of superintendance, given by the act of 1774 to his Majesty's Ministers, had tended more to increase, than diminish the radical defects of the system. The Ministers were vested with a right of interference, but had little, if any, responsibility with respect to the conduct of the Indian Government. Their favour and aid were indispensable to the Governor General; and, to secure it's continuance, it became necessary, that, in addition to the friends of the Directors of the Company, those of the Ministers of the Crown should be served. Thus the exercise of his patronage in India became the chief, if not the only means, through which the Governor General could expect support in England; and the canvassing nature of the constitution of that Country made it unlikely, that any Minister would cast away such a source of strength as a share in the rich appointments of the East. Consequently, this system, corrupt and inefficient as it was, might have long continued, had not an unwearied spirit of investigation dragged the voluminous records of the Company into light, with the view of criminating their principal agents. The first or Secret Committee of the House of Commons, of which Mr. Dundas was President, commenced the attack; and it's reports were soon followed by those of the Select Committee, which acting under the direction and guidance of Mr. Burke, one of the wisest men and greatest orators England ever boasted, disseminated among all classes a general knowledge of the affairs of the Company.

There can be no doubt, that the promoters of these inquiries (however mixed their motives might have been) became entitled to the gratitude of their Country; as, unless such knowledge had been made general, every attempt to ameliorate and improve a Government, where the temptations to continue a corrupt system were so strong, must have proved vain and abortive.

The extended jurisdiction, given by the act of 1773 to the Supreme Court of Judicature established at Fort William, was found in it's operations so hostile to the prejudices of the Natives of the Company's Provinces, and so likely to destroy that authority, which it was meant to support, that it was limited by a subsequent act, passed in 1781, to the Town and Suburbs of Calcutta.

From the year 1779, when an act was passed, by which the right of the Company to territorial possessions was only extended for one year, till the year 1783 a continual conflict existed between the Directors and his Majesty's Ministers, respecting the terms on which the Company's Charter and exclusive privileges should be prolonged and supported. It is not necessary to dwell upon the various offers, which were made, during this contest, by that Corporation, or to particularize those which were rejected or accepted by his Majesty's Ministers: the great measures, by which this period was followed, have condemned them to oblivion; nor had they any pretensions (for they were avowedly temporary expedients) to escape the fate which they have experienced.

The most serious discussions, regarding Indian affairs, took place in 1783. Mr. Dundas, who had been Chairman of one of the Committees of Inquiry, brought forward in the beginning of this year a Bill, which proposed few great changes, except that of appointing a person, who, under the high title of Governor General and Captain General, should exercise in his own person (under certain checks) complete authority and control over British India.

This high public Officer was to be approved, but not nominated, by the Crown, by whom alone he could be removed. It was proposed by this Bill, that his Majesty's principal Secretary of State should receive copies of all despatches: and to these provisions were added some good general rules with regard to the preservation of the laws, religion and usages, of the Natives. The principle of this Bill, which was the introduction, during the remainder of the Charter, of a more active interference on the part of the executive Government in the administration of the affairs of the Company, was generally approved. It was allowed, that a more efficient and energetic local Government was required; and that a responsibility more defined and more operative on all parties, than that established by the act of 1773, was indispensable to correct the gross abuses of the existing system; but there was a wide difference of opinion in the House of Commons regarding the nature of those checks, which it might be expedient to fix over the controlling powers, which it went to establish; and it was on this ground, that it's utility was chiefly combated. Though this Bill for the Government of India did not succeed, it gave birth to one of a nearly similar character, which was introduced and carried by Mr. Pitt in the next sessions. But as that great measure chiefly owed it's success to the feelings created in the minds of the Directors and Proprietors by the agitation of the plan brought forward by his political rival Mr. Fox, it will be first necessary to take a short view of that measure.

In 1783, Mr. Fox brought forward his celebrated Bills for the better regulation and government of the British possessions in India. These Bills* proceeded on a principle, stated in their preamble, that disorders of an alarming nature and magnitude had long prevailed in the administration of the territorial possessions, revenue and commerce, of British India: that the Natives were reduced to distress, and the public interests in danger of being ruined; a remedy was in consequence become necessary, and the following was proposed:

That the whole power, now vested in the Court of Directors and Proprietors, should be for the space of four years transferred to seven Directors or Commissioners, named in the act; to aid whom, nine Assistant Directors, named also in the act, were selected from Proprietors holding at least £2000 stock each. These, however, were entirely placed under the orders

* They were two; one meant to regulate the home, or, as the Bill termed them, the *domestic* affairs of the Company; the other, their foreign Government.

of the former. On the occurrence of the death, resignation, or removal, (on charges substantiated before the House of Commons,) of one of the seven principal Directors, the vacancy was to be supplied by the King; if one happened among the nine Assistant Directors, the Proprietors of stock (as qualified by the act of 1773) were to elect another.

The principle of these Bills, in regard to the power to be given to the Governor General, was directly opposite to that of Mr. Dundas. It was declared, that the powers of the Governor General in Council should on no occasion be delegated to such Governor alone, or to any person or persons whatever; and the Governor General and Council were restricted in all cases as much as it seemed practicable, but particularly in that of making war. The Governor General was declared not to have the power of entering, or invading with an armed force, the dominion of any Prince of India, except upon intelligence, the credibility of which was to be admitted, and individually recorded by the majority of the Members of his Council, that such Prince was about to make war on the Company or their Allies. The Governor General and Council were not permitted, without orders from the Commissioners, to enter into any offensive alliance for the sharing any Country between the Company and a Native Prince; nor were they to hire out any troops (European or Native) in the territories of any Indian State.

These were the leading provisions of these celebrated Bills, which, though passed with a great majority in the House of Commons, were thrown out by the Lords, and terminated in the expulsion from office of the Statesman by whom they were framed, and the party by whom they were supported. Mr. Fox's measure was declaredly temporary, and adopted as an expedient for the moment. The seven Commissioners, whom he proposed, were to act like Trustees to a Bankrupt House of Commerce, and were to manage the affairs of the East India Company until it was determined what was best and wisest for the future regulation of their concerns. What would have been the ultimate arrangement for the Government of India, had this plan been carried into execution, cannot be known; but it is not probable that the Company would ever have regained their power. It is not, however, intended to enter in this place into any discussion regarding the merits or defects of Mr. Fox's Bills. The wisdom and foresight, which these in some parts displayed, were certainly clouded by strong party-spirit and prejudice; and, from the want of correct and complete information, many of his leading principles were every way inapplicable to the actual state of the Country for which they were framed by that great Statesman.

This scheme, though it was an improvement upon the former administration of India, would probably have been found erroneous in some of it's most fundamental principles; but particularly in that, by which, instead of giving confidence to the ruling authority of India under great and direct responsibility, it multiplied checks upon the local Government; and thus, by the diminution of it's power, lowered and weakened it's means of action; and rendered it more incompetent, than it had been before, to those great, and indeed sovereign, functions, which it has to perform. The clamour against Mr. Fox's Bill was excessive. His scheme of seven Commissioners was represented as a means, which he had devised to perpetuate his own power. His measures went, it was said, to establish an influence in the hands of Ministers, unknown to the Constitution of the Country: and the East India Company, who had been before hated and abused on account of their monopoly and imputed crimes, became the object of pity and commiseration; and were represented by the writers of the day, as an injured and unprotected Body, who were likely to have their privileges violated, and their rights invaded, by a rash and ambitious Minister.

From this violence of party rage, the right of regulating the Company's affairs became a political conflict between two great and nearly equally balanced parties; and the scale was turned by a coalition between Mr. Pitt and the Court of Directors, or rather the great majority of the Proprietors of India Stock; who, though originally adverse to any interference in their concerns, when they found they could not avert that event, naturally chose that side which was least unfavourable to what they considered as their established rights and privileges.

CHAPTER II.

ADMINISTRATION

OF

LORD CORNWALLIS.

CONTENTS.

Mr. Pitt's Bill for the better Administration of India.—Observations upon that Bill.—Lord Cornwallis appointed Governor General.—Account of the Engagements entered into with the Nizam.—Treaty concluded with that Prince.—Treaty with the Mahratta State.—Causes of the War with Tippoo.—Consequences of that War.—Considerations upon the Policy of Lord Cornwallis in commencing War, and concluding Peace.—Connexion between the Nizam and the British Government becomes more intimate.—Consequent Jealousy of the Court of Poonah.—Great Increase of Scindiah's Power.—View of the Affairs of the Carnatic—of Oude.—Lord Cornwallis returns to Europe.—General Reflections upon the State of India at that Time.

It will be useful, in this place, not only to take a view of Mr. Pitt's Bill of 1784, but of the explanatory Act of 1786, and of such Acts as have been subsequently passed; as they collectively form the basis of the present constitution of our Indian Government, the nature of which will be best elucidated by a concise statement of their principal provisions; and this statement will prevent the necessity of interrupting the narrative with any repetitions on this branch of the subject.

Mr. Pitt's Bill of 1784, appointed six Privy Counsellors to be Commissioners for the affairs of India; of whom, one of the Secretaries of State for the time being was President. These Commissioners, who were appointed by his Majesty, and removable at his pleasure, were vested with a control and superintendance over all civil, military and revenue, Officers of the Company; and the Directors of that Corporation were obliged to lay before them all papers relative to the management of their possessions; and to obey all orders which they received from them, on points connected with their civil or military government, or the revenues of their territories.

The Commissioners were obliged to return the copies of papers, which they received from the Directors, in fourteen days, with their approbation; or to state at large their reasons for disapproving of them; and their despatches, so approved or amended, were to be sent to India, unless the Commissioners should attend to any representations of the Court of Directors, respecting further alterations in them.

The Court of Directors had no power to send any orders regarding their civil or military government, without the sanction of the Commissioners; but these might (if the Directors neglected to send true copies of their intended despatches, upon any subject, within fourteen days) send from themselves orders and instructions relative to the civil or military concerns of the Company, to any of the Presidencies of India; and these instructions the Court of Directors were, in such case, bound to forward.

If the Commissioners forwarded any orders to the Court of Directors on points not relating to the civil or military government, or to the revenues of the territorial possessions of the Company, the Directors might appeal to the King and Council.

In all cases of secrecy, and particularly such as related to war or peace with the Native Powers of India, the Commissioners had the power of sending their orders to the local Government of India, through a Secret Committee of the Court of Directors; which Committee, by the act, could in this case only be considered as the vehicle of the instructions to the local authorities in India.

The chief Government in India was by this

act to consist of a Governor General and three Counsellors; and the Commander-in-Chief of the forces for the time being had a voice and precedence next after the Governor General; but was not to succeed, in the event of a vacancy, unless by special appointment of the Directors.

The constitution of the Government of the subordinate Presidencies of Madras and Bombay, was the same as Bengal; and at both, the Governor had, like the Governor General, a casting vote in Council.

These Settlements were by this act placed completely under the rule of the Governor General in Council, on all points connected with negotiations with the Country Powers, peace or war, and the application of their revenues and forces.

The King had a right, by this act, to recall the Governor General, or any Officer of the Company, from India: and if the Court of Directors did not within two months nominate some person to a vacancy, which occurred in any of the principal stations, such as Governor General, Governor, Commander-in-Chief, or Counsellors, to which it was their duty to appoint, the Crown became possessed of the right to make such nomination.

It was declared by this act, that as the pursuit of schemes of conquest was repugnant to the wish, to the honour and the policy, of the British Nation, that it was not lawful for the Governor General in Council of Fort William, without the express authority and concord of the Court of Directors, or of the Secret Committee, either to declare or commence hostilities, or to enter into any treaty for making war against any of the Native Princes or States in India, or any treaty guaranteeing the dominions of such Princes or States, except when hostilities have been commenced, or preparations actually made for the attack of the British Nation in India, or of some of the States and Princes, whose dominions it shall be engaged by subsisting treaties to defend.

The subordinate Presidencies were prohibited by this act from making war or peace, without orders from Fort William, the Court of Directors, or the Secret Committee; except in cases of sudden emergency or imminent danger, when it would be ruinous or unsafe to postpone such hostilities or treaty. The Supreme Government had the power given them of suspending any of the Governors of the subordinate Settlements, who disobeyed their orders.

A new and extraordinary Court was constituted by this act, for the trial of Indian delinquents. It was formed of a specified number of Members of the House of Lords and House of Commons; and had great powers given to it, for the purpose of bringing to justice persons whom it was stated, that common Courts could not reach. But it is needless to dwell upon this part of the Bill, as it was, in consequence of representations from the British subjects in India, completely new-modelled and changed.

An act was passed in 1786, by which several parts of the act of 1784 were explained and amended. The power of appointing a civil servant, of twelve years' standing, on the occurrence of a vacancy, to Councils, was given to the local Governments of India.

The appointment of a Commander-in-Chief to Councils was made an act of option, not of necessity. The Directors were vested with the power of appointing the Commander-in-Chief in India Governor General, &c. of making the Commander-in-Chief at Madras and Bombay President of those Settlements; and, what was more important, the Governor General, and the Governors of Madras and Bombay, were vested by this act with a discretionary right of acting, in extraordinary cases, without the concurrence of their Councils, being held solely and personally responsible for any consequences, which might ensue from the measures adopted under such circumstances.

This great power was only given to such Governor General or Governors, as were specifically appointed to those stations, and did not devolve to their casual successors; and it did not extend to cases of a judicial nature, or to the alteration of any established regulations for the civil government of the British Settlements in India.

In 1797, an act was passed, by which Courts were established at Madras and Bombay with powers nearly similar to those which had been before given to the Supreme Court of Judicature at Bengal. These Courts were made altogether independent of the Company's Governments in India; but they were not competent to try informations against the Governor or Council, unless in cases of felony or treason. The regulations of these Courts were in some respect altered, by an act passed in 1800, when a Chief Judge, and two Puisne Judges, were appointed to the Court of Judicature at Madras.

The intention of Mr. Pitt's Bill for the better administration of Indian affairs, was avowedly more that of temporary reform, than of final establishment. It's object was rather directed to a correction of abuses, and to a control of power, than to the complete removal of admitted evils, or the actual introduction of an efficient system. More could not have been expected, and perhaps was not intended. As his plan proceeded on the avowed ground of maintaining, instead of demolishing, the established constitution of the Company's Government, a great part of the efficiency of the new system was sacrificed to the forms of the old; and much of that embarrassment, which has attended the operation of this measure, may be traced to that spirit of conciliation in which it was originally framed.

The circumstances under which this system commenced, were particularly favourable to it's success and popularity. The admitted abuses which it corrected, the great strength of the Administration in England at the time when it was introduced, the ability and influence of the President of the Board of Control, and the firmness and integrity of the nobleman who was first invested with the high powers, which the amended Bill of 1786 so wisely gave to the Governor General of India; all contributed to cover it's defects, and to bring it's merits into the most prominent point of view. But subsequent events have shown, that it required all these aids to render it successful, and that the failure of any one of them would have had the most serious effect upon it's operation.

In proof of this assertion, it is only necessary to advert to the eagerness with which the Court of Directors have seized every opportunity, which the casual weakness or changes in the Administration of the Country has afforded them, to regain that influence and authority, which they had lost. Since the dissolution of Mr. Pitt's first Administration in 1801, they have been engaged in continual contentions with the Board of Control. During almost the whole period that Lord Dartmouth presided at that Board, these contentions literally prevented the necessary orders being sent to India; and it may be doubted whether the conciliatory policy, which his immediate successor (under nearly similar circumstances) thought it expedient to pursue, was not attended with equally bad effects to the public interests.

The Court of Directors are a highly respectable body of men; and they have acted under this Bill, as all men in their situation would have acted. They have regretted the loss of power, and have desired to regain it. They have been placed in a situation, where they had two interests to promote, which were generally, if not always, opposite in their nature. The one, the general interests of the Nation; the other, the particular interests of the Corporation. Can it be either a subject of surprise or reproach, that the Directors have generally proved true to the latter? or, in other words, that they have supported an interest, which supported them; that they have been faithful to their constituents, and to the vital principles of their constitution, which, though well adapted to the administration of those commercial interests for which it was first framed, was unsuited to the Political Government of a large Empire. This fact, indeed, was admitted by all, that from the theory of Mr. Pitt's Bill the power of the Court of Directors, as a Political Body, should be extinct; but the result has proved otherwise. The influence of the Company in the House of Commons has supported their authority in Leadenhall Street; and when the Administration has not been strong, the control over them has been almost nugatory. There certainly can be no reasonable objection to the Court of Directors, considered as a body of liberal and well-informed men, being intrusted with the administration of the Government of India; but there is an objection, and a strong one, grounded on the nature of their constitution, as the Directors of a commercial company. In the present great scale of our Indian Empire, those intrusted with it's Government should be suited, from their habits and objects in life, to the arduous duties which they have to fulfil: their views should be extended to the general prosperity of the Empire which they rule; and not confined, or rather directed, to a particular branch of it: and they should (into whatever shape the nature of the Government of England required them to be formed) be constituted upon principles, which, while they subjected them to a severe and direct responsibility to their Country, left their exertions in the execution of the great trust committed to them free and unembarrassed.

The failure of Mr. Pitt's Bill in it's operation in this essential point, was foretold by Mr. Burke. "The scheme of reconciling a Direc-"tion really and truly deliberative" (said that great Orator and Statesman) "with an office "really and substantially controlling, is a sort "of machinery, that can be kept in order only "a short time. Either the Directors will "dwindle into clerks, or the Secretary of State, "as has hitherto been the case, will leave "every thing to them, often through design, "and often through neglect. If both should "affect activity; collision, procrastination, "delay, and in the end utter confusion, "must ensue."

The best mode of judging every system of this nature, is by it's practical result; and a cursory view of the principal political events, which have occurred in the Government of India since the introduction of Mr. Pitt's Bill, will be the best comment upon the merits and defects of a measure, which, it never must be forgotten, was deemed, as I have before stated, by it's great author, as an experiment; and one in which, from the difficulty of the task, human wisdom could hardly venture to anticipate success.

The first person to whom the great powers, vested in the Governor General of India by the act of Parliament passed in 1786, were intrusted, was Marquis Cornwallis; and the character of that nobleman was suited to the high charge. Firm in his purposes, possessing unwearied zeal, and unsullied honour, he proceeded toward the objects which he had in view, with a vigour and decision which commanded success. The great reforms and changes, which he effected in the military and civil establishments of India, and the system of internal rule that he introduced into the Provinces of Bengal and Bahar, will ever reflect the highest honour on his name.

The consideration he enjoyed in England greatly promoted that success which attended him in India. His rank and character, while it placed him above the influence of the Ministers of the Crown, or the fear of the Court of Directors, commanded a respect from the civil and military servants of the Company, which, added to the increased powers with which he was vested, freed him from every shadow of opposition. He was enabled, from the same causes, to stimulate to exertion, by the distinction which his personal favour bestowed, the first talents in India; and to combine the efforts of every ambitious and honourable mind in the support of the measures of his Administration.

It is not necessary to enter into any detailed history of Lord Cornwallis's Government. A concise review of the prominent political events, which marked his Administration; and of those principles, which guided his conduct under them; will sufficiently elucidate the subject, and answer the object of this Sketch.

The principal event, which occurred during his Administration, was the war with Tippoo Sultaun. This had it's origin in a violent aggression of that Prince, who, on the 29th of December 1789, stormed the lines of the Rajah of Travancore, a Prince who was acknowledged under the protection of the English Government, by the stipulations of a treaty, which had been concluded with Tippoo in 1784.

To understand the nature and extent of the great political changes which were the consequences of this event, it will be necessary, before I detail the causes of the war with Tippoo Sultaun, to trace, in a succinct manner, the history of the alliances which Lord Cornwallis thought it his duty, on this important occasion, to form with the States of Hyderabad and Poonah.

By a treaty, concluded between the Nizam and the Company in 1766, the latter engaged to furnish that Prince with a subsidiary force, when it was required, to settle the affairs of his Government; with a provision, however, that they should be at liberty to withdraw either a part or the whole of such force, whenever the safety of their own Settlements, or the territories of the Carnatic, rendered such a measure necessary; and by a subsequent article of the same treaty, the Nizam engaged (with a similar provision) to afford the Company, when required, the aid of his troops.

A corps of two battalions joined the Nizam's army under this treaty; but were soon obliged, by the treachery of that Prince, who formed a connexion with Hyder, to return to the Company's territories.

The rupture, which this conduct on the part of the Nizam caused with the Company's Government, terminated in 1768 in another treaty, by which that Prince not only agreed to consider Hyder Naigue as an usurper, and to revoke all sunnuds, or distinctions, which that Chief had received from him or any former Soubahdar of the Deckan; but to aid the Company in obtaining possession of the Dewanee of the Carnatic Balaghaut (or the Country of Hyder), on the condition of their paying him a peishcush of seven lacks of rupees for that Country.

The cession of the Circar of Guntoor to the Company, on the death or misconduct of the Nizam's brother, was an express stipulation of this treaty; and it was also agreed, that the English should furnish the Nizam, on requisition, with a subsidiary corps of two battalions of Sepoys, with guns; on the condition, however, of his defraying the actual expense of such corps, while it remained in his service.

This corps had never been required by the Nizam: and the connexion between that Prince and the Company was, notwithstanding this treaty, of a general and unsettled nature, till the year 1788; when Lord Cornwallis, with a view to obtain the Guntoor Circars, and to effect a settlement of the arrears of peishcush due for the Circars, deputed a British Resident (Sir John Kennaway) to Hyderabad.

The demand of the cession of Guntoor, agreeably to the condition of the treaty of 1768, was accompanied with military preparations, which secured a prompt compliance on the part of the Nizam; who, from the unfortunate issue of a recent contest with Tippoo Sultaun, appeared to be, at the moment when it was made, most anxious for the alliance of the British Government; and, with a view to this object, he had deputed Meer Abdool Cassim to Calcutta, for the purpose of conveying fully his sentiments and wishes to the Governor General.

The mission of Meer Abdool Cassim * was productive of a new engagement, (explanatory of the treaty of 1768,) conveyed in the form of a letter from Lord Cornwallis to the Nizam; but declared by the former to be equally binding upon the British Nation as a regular treaty, which, Lord Cornwallis informed the Nizam, he was prevented entering into (unless just cause should be given) by the laws of his Country, and the injunctions of the King and Company of England.

This public instrument, which was dated the 1st of July 1789, after stating the motives, which regulated the conduct of the English Government in insisting on the cession of the Guntoor Circars, and the objections which existed to giving any farther security, than the pledge of national faith, for the regular payment of the peishcush, (the arrears of which had been settled in a manner satisfactory to both parties,)

* This able man was afterwards better known under his title Meer Allum. He died Prime Minister at Hyderabad in Nov. 1808.

proceeds to explain the 6th article of the treaty of 1768, which, it states, shall be agreed to mean, "That the force engaged for by this article, (two battalions of Sepoys, and six pieces of cannon manned by Europeans,) shall be granted, whenever the Nizam shall apply for it; making only one exception, that it is not to be employed against any Powers in alliance with the Company; viz. Pundit Purdhaun, Madhajee Scindiah, Madhajee Ragojee Bhonslah, and other Mahratta Chiefs, the Nabob of Arcot, Nabob Vizier, or the Rajahs of Tanjore and Travancore."

This explanation altered one very material part of the alliance. The right, which the Company had, under the treaty of 1768, to withhold or withdraw the subsidiary force with which it was bound to aid the Nizam, was abrogated; and the right of that Prince to keep and employ that force in any manner he chose, so long as it was not employed against the above specified Princes and Chiefs in alliance with the Company, was fully recognised and established.

It would appear from subsequent parts of this letter, that Meer Abdool Cassim must have been directed to use his endeavours to persuade the Governor General to adopt measures for the fulfilment of those articles in the treaty of 1768, which related to the vesting of the Dewanee of the Carnatic Balaghaut in the Company, on the condition of paying a sum of seven lacks of rupees annually to the Nizam for that Country; or, in other words, to proceed, on the grounds of the treaty of 1768, to dispossess Tippoo Sultaun of his territories.

The Governor General rejected those propositions, as inadmissible, from the lapse of time which had occurred, and the relations of general amity in which the British Government then stood to the Prince, whose possessions such an engagement would affect.

But, though Tippoo Sultaun had not shown any open indication of hostility against the English Government, or it's Allies, at the period to which we allude, his conduct must have been such, as to make Lord Cornwallis believe, that he cherished hostile projects against the British Government; or his Lordship would hardly, in consequence of the above propositions of the Nizam, have entered into a political engagement with that Prince, which might justly be deemed more than merely defensive against Tippoo Sultaun.

The desire, indeed, of not offending against the letter of the Act of Parliament, would appear on this occasion to have led to a trespass on it's spirit, by the revival of an offensive alliance against Tippoo Sultaun; for such the treaty of 1768 undoubtedly was; because, though Lord Cornwallis, in his letter of the 1st of July 1789, declares, that circumstances have totally prevented the execution of those articles in the treaty of 1768, which go to vest the Company with the Dewanee of the Carnatic Balaghaut; yet he adds, "Should it hereafter happen, that "the Company should obtain possession of the "Country mentioned in those articles with "your Highness's assistance, they (the Com- "pany) will strictly perform the stipulations "in favour of your Highness and the Mah- "rattas."

It is necessary to remark in this place, that two treaties had been concluded, subsequently to the treaty of 1768, between Hyder Ally Khan and the British Government; and the latter State had concluded a treaty of peace with his son Tippoo Sultaun in 1784, by which it had fully recognised his right of sovereignty to the territories which he possessed: and assuredly, under such circumstances, the revival, with any modification, of an offensive alliance against his power, could not but alarm that Prince. Nor was his alarm likely to be dispelled by that qualification in the engagement, which provided, that no immediate operation should be undertaken against his dominions; as the expression, by which that qualification was followed, showed, that the eventual execution of those articles, which went to divest him of his territories, was not deemed an improbable, or, at least, an impossible occurrence by the contracting Powers.

Another part of this engagement, which appeared calculated to excite apprehension in the mind of Tippoo, was, the stipulations which regarded the employment of the subsidiary force granted to the Nizam; which was made discretional, with the exception of not acting against some specified Prince and Chiefs, Allies of the British Government; among whom he was not included.

That such ideas were entertained by Tippoo, from the moment he heard of the conclusion of this engagement, there cannot be a doubt. It would indeed appear, by a letter from the Resident at Poonah, that the Minister of that Court considered this engagement as one of an offensive nature against Tippoo Sultaun.

There is no person acquainted with the nature of the times in which this engagement was formed, but must be sensible that every measure of precautionary policy was then necessary, on the part of the British Government, to counteract and frustrate the ambitious designs of Tippoo Sultaun: but what has been stated will show, that the literal construction of the restrictions of the Act of Parliament had, upon this occasion, the effect of making the Governor General pursue a course, which was perhaps not only questionable in point of faith; but which must have been more offensive to Tippoo Sultaun, and more calculated to produce a war with that Prince, than an avowed contract of a defensive engagement framed for the express and legitimate purpose of limiting his inordinate ambition.

As soon as the actual hostile aggressions of Tippoo Sultaun relieved Lord Cornwallis from the restraints under which he considered himself placed by the letter of the Act of Parliament, he hastened to secure, by every effort within his power, the hearty co-operation of the Nizam, in the war in which that aggression had involved the Company. In his instructions to the Resident at the Court of that Chief, under date the 28th of January 1790, he directs him to inform the Court of Hyderabad of the infraction, by Tippoo, of the treaty of peace between him and the Company; to take every opportunity in his power to expose in it's proper colours the faithless character of that Prince, and to explain to the Nizam and his Ministers the great advantages, which they may derive from forming a close connexion with the British Government.

The Governor General also authorized the

Resident to assure the Nizam, (as an inducement to bring him to an early declaration in favour of the British Government,) that no peace would be concluded with Tippoo, without securing to him a full participation of the advantages which might be obtained by the war; and that as the conduct of Tippoo had placed the English Government at liberty, it was ready to enter into a defensive alliance with the Nizam, for the mutual guarantee against Tippoo of the territories, which might be possessed by the respective parties, when the war should be terminated.

The Governor General, in the same instructions, vested the Resident of Hyderabad with the fullest power to encourage every advance, which might be made by Tippoo Sultaun's tributaries, or subjects, toward forming a connexion with the Company; and directed him to employ persons of rank in obtaining information of Tippoo's designs; or in persuading any of his Ministers or principal Officers to abandon him, and to act under the direction of the English Government in their endeavour to overturn his power; and the Resident was assured, that whatever engagements he might contract with persons of that description, should be punctually fulfilled by Government.

A treaty of offensive and defensive alliance

was, in conformity to these instructions, concluded with the Nizam on the 4th of July 1790, and ratified by the Governor General in Council on the 29th of the same month.

The provisions of this treaty were, that measures should be immediately taken to punish Tippoo Sultaun, and to deprive him of the means of disturbing the general tranquillity. That the Nizam and Paishwah should both vigorously prosecute the war; that the former should send a contingent of ten thousand horse to act with the Company's army, which body were to be paid by the Company; that an equal division of conquests between the contracting parties, was to be made, at the conclusion of the peace, with the exception of such forts and territories as the Honourable Company might take previously to the commencement of hostilities by the other parties.

That particular Zemindars and Polygars, who were specified, having been formerly dependent upon the Nizam and Mahrattas, should (if their forts and territories were taken) be placed upon the same footing, in relation to these Powers, as formerly. That in the event of a peace becoming expedient, it should be settled by mutual consent; and that, after it's conclusion, any attack by Tippoo on one of the parties, was to be punished by all, in the mode, and on the conditions, which the contracting parties might hereafter settle.

It appears from the correspondence of the Resident, that the Nizam throughout this negotiation testified the greatest suspicion of the Mahrattas; and at one conference he asked the British Resident, What this Government would do, if, during the absence of his army, while assisting the Company, the Paishwah, invited by Tippoo, should invade his dominions? "The Company ought to sacrifice them all in "your Highness's defence," replied the Resident, with an honourable warmth, which gave confidence to that Prince; who, however, continued to use his earnest endeavours, during the negotiation of this treaty, to induce the English Government to make, by a specific article, the guarantee of his dominions. And though the Governor General, from a just apprehension of giving offence to the Paishwah, and of losing the benefit of his co-operation in the war, evaded a compliance with his request, he nevertheless authorized the Resident to give the Nizam assurances, which were calculated to confirm his hope of accomplishing this object at a more favourable juncture.

The principle on which Lord Cornwallis resisted the solicitations of the Nizam on this point, is distinctly expressed in his despatch to the Resident, of the 12th April 1790. "I "trust," he states, "that the more that his "Highness reflects upon the nature of his pro- "position, that I should engage to interfere, in "case the Mahrattas should at any time make "unreasonable demands upon him; he will "more clearly see, that as the Mahrattas have "acceded heartily and cordially to the con- "federacy, it would be highly improper in me "to suppose that they would be inclined to "treat one of their own Allies with injustice; "and consequently, that such an assurance "must appear to them in a light highly injuri- "ous and offensive.

"But in order," his Lordship continues, "to prove to his Highness how anxious I am "to go every justifiable length to show my re- "gard to his interests, and to gratify him in his "wishes, you may inform him, that, provided "the Mahrattas do not positively object to it, "I will agree to it's becoming an additional ar- "ticle in the present treaty; that should dif- "ferences arise between any two of the Con- "federates, the third party shall be bound to "interpose his good offices, and to take every "means in his power to bring those differences "to a just and amicable settlement."

The Resident was, in the same despatch, authorized to inform the Nizam and his Ministers, that, should an article to the above effect be assented to by the Poonah Government, and any case should arise, in which Lord Cornwallis's interference should be called upon, in consequence of it, they should always find him in the best disposition to endeavour to save his Highness from the necessity of submitting to mortification or injury.

These assurances appear to have had the effect of giving confidence to the Nizam, and of reconciling him to the treaty in the shape in which it was concluded; and in a despatch to the Resident, under date the 29th July, which accompanied the treaty, Lord Cornwallis confirmed the hopes which his former assurances had led that Prince to entertain upon this point.

" I am perfectly convinced," he informs the Resident in a paragraph of his despatch, " that " you will spare no pains to show the Nizam " how much he is called upon, by considera- " tions of honour and interest, to fulfil his en- " gagements with the strictest punctuality, and " to exert the whole power of his Government " in the most vigorous prosecution of the war: " and although it will be necessary for you to " be constantly upon your guard against en- " couraging his Highness and his Ministers in " too sanguine hopes respecting the value of

" the future connexion, which they may expect to form with this Government, and to avoid making use of any expressions of attention to the Nizam's interests, which could furnish ground for jealousy to the Mahrattas; yet you may constantly assure the Nizam and his Ministers, that they may depend upon receiving the most unequivocal marks of cordiality and friendship from the Company, in return for whatever proofs they shall give of their attention to our interests and wishes in the prosecution of the present war; and that they will find us well disposed, when a proper opportunity offers, to take such further steps for drawing the connexion closer between the two Governments, as may be consistent with good faith and a due attention to subsisting engagements with our other Allies."

Such was the policy, which the Marquis Cornwallis pursued on this critical occasion with the Nizam. He afforded to that Prince immediate security, by the aid of a subsidiary force; he held out prospects to him of great and permanent advantages, by the favourable conditions of the offensive and defensive alliance against Tippoo Sultaun; and by the assurances conveyed to him through the British Resident at his Court, he taught him to expect, in the further happy cultivation and improvement of the alliance, which had been contracted, a complete security, at a more convenient opportunity, against that most serious of all dangers which threatened his power, the restless and insatiable ambition of his Mahratta neighbours.

The wisdom of this policy was seen in it's result. The Nizam co-operated with perfect sincerity in the war against the Sultaun; and though the character of his troops and the habits of his Government, prevented that benefit from his aid, which might have been expected from the numbers of his army, and the extent of his resources, there cannot be a doubt, but that his exertions, however ill conducted, contributed in a considerable degree to the happy termination of a war, which indeed could never have been carried on upon such a scale without his assistance.

The connexion of the British Government with the Court of Poonah subsequent to the treaty of Salbhye, had been of a general though friendly nature. Lord Cornwallis had, on the first appearance of a rupture with Tippoo, directed his attention to an alliance with the Paishwah; and when the conduct of the Sultaun made war unavoidable, he transmitted instructions to the Resident at Poonah, Sir Charles

Mallet, of nearly similar import to those despatched on the same occurrence to the Resident at Hyderabad. There existed no subsidiary engagements with the Court of Poonah: and in these instructions, which were dated the 27th of January 1790, his Lordship expressed a hope, that the Mahrattas would act by themselves in the war, as he apprehended risk, from the composition of their army, (being almost all cavalry,) to any small body of English infantry: he, however, informed the Resident, that if they could not be induced to take an active part without the aid of a British corps, measures should be taken to afford it.

The Poonah State appears to have been, from a variety of causes, perfectly inclined to the proposed alliance: but the emergency of the period made those delays, which are habitual to a Mahratta State, a subject of the most serious anxiety; and it would appear from a despatch from Lord Cornwallis to Sir Charles Mallet, under date the 28th of February, that he felt strongly at this moment the injurious operation of those restrictions, which had prevented his cultivating, at a less urgent and more favourable period, the alliance of the Paishwah.

"Some considerable advantages have, no "doubt, been experienced," his Lordship states, "by the system of neutrality, which the Legis-

" lature required of the Governments in this " Country; but it has at the same time been " attended with the unavoidable inconvenience " of our being constantly exposed to the " necessity of commencing a war, without " having previously secured the assistance of " efficient Allies.

" The late outrageous infraction of the treaty " of peace by Tippoo Sultaun," his Lordship adds, " furnishes a case in point. We could " not suffer the dominions of the Rajah of Tra-" vancore, who was included by name, as our " Ally in that treaty, to be ravaged or insulted, " without being justly charged with pusillani-" mity, or a flagrant breach of faith, and with-" out dishonouring ourselves, by that means, in " the view of all the Powers in India; and as " we have been almost daily obliged, for several " years past, to declare to the Mahrattas, and " to the Nizam, that we were precluded from " contracting any new engagements with them " for affording them aid against the injustice or " ambition of Tippoo, I must acknowledge, " that we cannot claim, as a right, the perform-" ance of these promises which the Mahrattas " have repeatedly made, to co-operate with us " whenever we should be forced into a war " with that Prince."

His Lordship repeats his intention in this

despatch, to offer the Mahrattas a defensive alliance against Tippoo; to which they would, he states, "in reason and equity have a good "title, if they were to take a part with us, "without having made such a previous engagement."

In a despatch to the Resident at Poonah, under date the 22d of March, Lord Cornwallis authorizes the Resident to declare to the Court the objects, which he has in view in the war; the first of which he states to be an indemnification for the expenses and losses sustained by the Company, either in preparations or in military operations. In the event of the Nizam and the Mahrattas joining, Lord Cornwallis declares his next object will be to oblige Tippoo to restore all, which he or his father have usurped or retained from either of these Powers; as well as to force him to surrender that part of the Carnatic, Payen Ghaut, which he now possesses; and, on account of the shocking barbarity with which he treated the Nairs on the Coast of Malabar, he declares it to be his intention, "to "insist upon his setting those people free from "all future dependence upon him."

After some delay, a treaty of offensive and defensive alliance against Tippoo Sultaun, was concluded between the English Government and the Paishwah on the 1st of June, and ratified on the 5th of July, 1790.

The conditions of this treaty were in substance little different from that concluded with the Nizam. It was stipulated, that the Paishwah should have an option, during the war with Tippoo, of the aid of an equal English force to that serving with the Nizam; and that he should, jointly with that Prince, furnish cavalry to serve with the English army, if such aid was required.

The Court of Dowlut Row Scindiah, and of Ragoojee Bhonslah, were solicited by the Governor General to exert their influence to promote the success of this important negotiation: but their efforts, if they even used them, would never have prevailed upon the wary Nanah Furnavese, who then presided over the Paishwah's councils, to adopt such a line of policy, had he and the military Chieftains of the Poonah State not been stimulated by stronger motives; among which may be included, a deep sense of recent injuries sustained from Tippoo Sultaun, an apprehension of the future violence of that Prince, and an expectation of regaining the fine Provinces, which had been wrested from them by him and his father Hyder Ally Khan.

Similar motives had operated on the mind of

the Nizam: and Lord Cornwallis, though he left no expedient untried, which promised to promote the alliance with both that Prince and the Paishwah, was fully sensible that his hopes of success rested entirely upon the grounds which I have stated. His Lordship indeed observes, in his letter to Sir Charles Mallet, under date the 28th of February 1790, "My dependence "upon the support of both those Powers (the "Paishwah and the Nizam), upon the present "occasion, is grounded solely upon the expecta-"tion of their being guided by the common in-"fluence of passions, and by considerations of "evident interest, which ought to dispose them "to seize a favourable opportunity with eager-"ness, to reduce the power of a Prince, whose "ambition knows no bounds, and from whom "both of them have suffered."

It will be now necessary to recur to those events, which immediately produced the war with Tippoo; the conduct observed at the period of their occurrence by the Government of Fort St. George; and the measures which that conduct led Lord Cornwallis to adopt.

The pretext upon which Tippoo Sultaun approached the Country of Travancore, was to recover two places, Cranganore and Jaycotta, which the Rajah had purchased from the Dutch; but which Tippoo alleged were dependent upon him, as forming part of the possessions of his tributary the Rajah of Cochin. The Rajah of Travancore had been desired by the Madras Government (acting under instructions from Bengal) to annul this arrangement; but had remonstrated, on the grounds of Tippoo's assertion being false, the places in question having, he alleged, been obtained by the Dutch from the Portuguese, to whom they had belonged long before the Rajah of Cochin became tributary to the Mysore Government.

In consequence of this remonstrance, which was forwarded to Bengal, the Supreme Government sent detailed instructions to the Government of Fort St. George.

The purport of these instructions, which were dated the 13th of November 1789, was, that if the places in question were found, on full investigation, to have belonged to the Rajah of Cochin subsequently to that Chief's having become a tributary of Mysore, the Rajah of Travancore must be obliged to restore them to the former possessor: If, on the contrary, they had not belonged to the Rajah of Cochin subsequently to the period stated, the claims of Tippoo Sultaun were to be resisted, and the legitimately acquired right of the Rajah of Travancore to those possessions was to be supported. In the event of Tippoo's having obtained possession of them previously to the arrival of the instructions, the Madras Government was directed to open a negotiation with him, with a view to effect, if possible, an amicable adjustment of the point on the above principles. "Of whatever importance" (the Supreme Government observes in a paragraph of this despatch) "the two places in question may appear "to the defence of the territories of the Rajah "of Travancore, it cannot be opposed to the "serious consequences of a war: but we are "equally convinced, that a tame submission to "insult or injury would, in it's effects, prove "the most fatal policy."

The Supreme Government further directed the Government of Fort St. George to take no measures, without it's previous sanction, for dispossessing Tippoo Sultaun of Cranganore and Jaycotta, if he was in actual possession of those places, unless he attacked the other territories of the Rajah of Travancore: but, on such an attack being made, they positively ordered the Government of Fort St. George to deem it an act of hostility, and the commencement of a war, which they were to prosecute with all possible vigour and decision.

These instructions do not appear to have been fully attended to by the Government of Fort St. George; who, indeed, in their letter of the

3d of January, arraigned the reasoning upon which they were grounded, and state their opinion, that the proceeding of the Rajah of Travancore, in purchasing the forts of Cranganore and Jaycotta from the Dutch, was unwarrantable on every principle of policy and justice; and therefore not entitled to the support of the British Government.

Under these impressions, they do not, in the letter they addressed to Tippoo, inform him, agreeably to the instructions of the Supreme Government, that it was the intention of the English Government (if the right of the Dutch to sell these places was established) to resist any attack, which he made upon them; and the letter, which they addressed to the Rajah of Travancore on the same occasion, was not only silent on this point, but, in it's general tenour, calculated to discourage that Prince from entertaining any expectation of support or assistance.

The Government of Fort St. George had also been directed to assemble the army, to suspend the investment, to stop all payments to the Nabob's creditors, and to make no disbursement, which could be avoided, in order that the whole resources of the State might be applied to military preparations: but these instructions seem to have been in a great degree evaded, if not neglected. The military preparations were made in a tardy manner, and on a limited scale, for the declared purpose of saving expense; and the provision of a large proportion of the investment was continued.

These proceedings were early marked by the strongest censure of the Supreme Government; who, in a despatch under date the 8th of February, commented on them with great severity, and demanded, in the most categorical terms, an explanation of the causes, which had, upon this critical occasion, led the Government of Madras to disregard, in the manner in which it had done, their positive and repeated orders and instructions.

After Tippoo was repulsed from the lines of Travancore, he had addressed two letters (under date the 24th of December and 1st of January) to the Government of Fort St. George; in which he attempted to palliate his conduct upon that occasion, and to attribute the attack to the sudden impulse of revenge, which his army felt at the conduct of some of the troops of the Rajah of Travancore. These letters were full of extravagant professions of friendship to the English Government. These professions, though contradicted by the whole tenour of Tippoo's conduct, seem to have been received by the Government of Fort St. George, as strong presumptive proof of the peaceable intentions of that Prince; and in a letter from Mr. John Holland, Governor of Fort St. George, to Lord Cornwallis, under date the 13th of February, in which he advises his Lordship of his intention to proceed to England, he makes use of the following expressions: "As far as I am able to "judge, it is not Tippoo's intention to break "with the Company; he probably feels him-"self injured by the conduct of our tributary, "the Rajah of Travancore; and it rests with "your Lordship to consider how far such con-"duct may have been consistent with the re-"spect which he owed this Government, or "with the laws of Nations. I confess it ap-"pears to me a very important question; and "from the late letters received from Tippoo "Sultaun, there is every reason to think that "he will be disposed to enter into nego-"tiations for the adjustment of the points in "dispute."

The indignation, which the whole tenour of the conduct of the Government of Fort St. George, upon this occasion, had excited in the mind of Lord Cornwallis, was forcibly expressed in his Lordship's letter to Mr. E. J. Holland, the acting Governor of that Presidency, under date the 30th of March 1790; which he concludes with the following passage:

"So far am I from giving credit to the late "Government for economy, in not making the "necessary preparations for war, according to "the positive orders of the Supreme Govern- "ment, after having received the most gross "insults that could be offered to any Nation; "I think it very possible that every cash of that "ill-judged saving may cost to the Company a "crore of rupees: besides which, I still more "sincerely lament the disgraceful sacrifice "which you made, by that delay, of the ho- "nour of your Country, by tamely suffering an "insolent and cruel enemy to overwhelm the "dominions of the Rajah of Travancore, which "we were bound by the most sacred ties of "friendship and good faith to defend."

Lord Cornwallis had determined to proceed immediately to Fort St. George, to prevent the serious dangers, which appeared to him to threaten the public interests from the conduct of the local authority at that Presidency; but the arrival of General Meadows, who was appointed to succeed Mr. Holland, led him to change his resolution, and to intrust to that Officer the conduct of a war, which in a despatch to his address, under date the 8th of March, he describes, as "a measure not less necessary to "vindicate the insulted honour of the Nation, "than to provide for it's future security, by "accomplishing, at a favourable moment, the "reduction of the power of Tippoo Sultaun." The Government of Fort St. George, in a despatch, under date the 8th of March, subsequent to the arrival of General Meadows, transmitted to the Supreme Government a letter, which had been received from Tippoo Sultaun, in reply to the letter addressed to him by Mr. Holland. In this letter Tippoo entered into a long defence of his conduct, both as that related to the Rajah of Travancore, and to the Nabob of the Carnatic; and assented to the suggestion, which had been made by Mr. Holland, of appointing Commissioners, whom, however, he requested might be sent to his Court. No answer was made to his communication by the Government of Fort St. George, who expressed (in this despatch to Bengal) an opinion, that a compliance with his wishes of sending Commissioners to his Court, would be highly derogatory to the dignity of the English Government.

The Supreme Government, in their reply to this communication, stated their having before directed, that the attack of the lines of the Rajah of Travancore should be considered a declaration of war; and they had, they said, concluded, that the Government of Fort St. George were, in obedience to their repeated orders, either busy in making the necessary preparations, or in carrying on the war with vigour; nor did they see how any negotiation could commence with honour, till full reparation was made by Tippoo Sultaun for the outrages which he had already committed.

In concluding this letter they direct, that the Presidency of Fort St. George "should, in "answer to all Tippoo's letters, explicitly in-"form him, that it had incontrovertibly "appeared, that Cranganore and Jaycotta "were held by the Dutch as independent "possessions, and never paid tribute to the "Rajah of Cochin; and therefore that the "Dutch had an undoubted right to dispose "of them to the Rajah of Travancore, or to "any other Power, whom they might think "proper; that they cannot look upon the "attack which Tippoo made upon the Rajah "of Travancore's lines to have happened by "accident, as he was upon the spot, and "conducted it in person; and as the Rajah "has been in possession of those lines upwards "of twenty years, and they were consequently "guaranteed to him by the late treaty of peace; "so violent an act of hostility can be seen in "no other light, than as an infraction of the "treaty with the Company."

General Meadows, on the receipt of these final instructions, proceeded from Madras to join the army, which was assembled on Trichinopoly plain, and reached the camp on the 24th of May. He had informed Tippoo Sultaun of his arrival; and after he had joined the army he received a letter from that Prince, remonstrating against the assembly of troops, which had taken place on the frontier of the Company's dominions, and requesting to be allowed to send a person of rank to make such explanations, as were necessary to restore confidence and friendship between the two States. To this letter General Meadows returned the following short and dignified answer:

" I received yours, and I understand it's con-
" tents. You are a great Prince; and, but for
" your cruelty to your prisoners, I should add,
" an enlightened one. The English, equally
" incapable of offering an insult, as of submit-
" ting to one, have always looked upon war as
" declared from the moment you attacked their
" Ally, the King of Travancore. God does
" not always give the battle to the strong, nor
" the race to the swift; but generally success
" to those, whose cause is just: upon that we
" depend."

On the 12th of June, and a few days subsequent to the despatch of this letter, General Meadows entered the territories of the Sultaun; and commenced a war, which was terminated by Lord Cornwallis in person, on the 23d of February 1792, in a manner most glorious to the British Government, and it's Allies: Tippoo Sultaun having, by the preliminary treaty, which was concluded on the 22d of February 1792, agreed to cede half his territories, and to pay, as a compensation for the expenses incurred by the allied Powers in carrying on the war, the sum of three crores and thirty lacks of rupees.*

It is foreign to my purpose to detail the events of this war, which are indeed sufficiently public; I shall proceed, therefore, to a consideration of the leading features of that policy, which induced Lord Cornwallis to commence the war; and to conclude, at the period when he did, a peace with Tippoo Sultaun.

After the conduct of that Prince showed that he was decidedly hostile to the British Government and it's Allies, the policy of Lord Cornwallis was neither directed to obtain a delay of hostilities; nor limited to the object of repelling the immediate danger with which the State, over whose councils he presided, was threatened. When fully satisfied of the designs of Tippoo, he hastened to attack him. He saw the great advantages which were likely to result from early active offensive operations; and the mo-

* Considerably upwards of three millions sterling.

ment he resolved on war, he contemplated (as appears from the whole tenour of his correspondence previous to the commencement of hostilities) the increase of the Company's territories in the quarters of the Carnatic, and Malabar, as a desirable object of policy; both as it added to the power and resources of the British Government, and as it reduced those of one of it's most formidable rivals. Acting upon the same principles, he held out conquest and increased resources, as incentives to the ambition of the Nizam and the Paishwah in the contest, in which he solicited them to engage, as Allies of the British Government.

The promptness and spirit with which Lord Cornwallis entered into a war, to vindicate the honour of the Company's Government from the insult, which had been offered to it by the attacks on one of it's Allies, raised the reputation of that State for strict adherence to it's engagements.

An event also occurred at the close of the war, which was calculated to improve that impression, and to establish on the strongest grounds the superior firmness, good faith and power, of the British Government.

The Rajah of Coorgh, who bore a hereditary hatred to the family of Tippoo, had during the war with that Prince been most active and zealous in aiding the English Government; and in reward for his faithful services, as well as with a view of placing his Country as a barrier between the dominions of Tippoo and the Company's possessions on the coast of Malabar, Lord Cornwallis included the tribute of Coorgh among the cessions, which were to be made to the English Government, agreeably to the preliminary treaty.

It is difficult to state how far the personal resentment, which the Sultaun entertained against the Rajah, and the importance which he attached to the local position of his territories, might have led him to resist the cession of the tribute of Coorgh, if it had been demanded as an express stipulation of the preliminary treaty. It is evident, that this demand, in the shape it came, was very unexpected, and was considered by the Sultaun as a departure from his preliminary engagement. He argued, and not without the appearance of reason, that the stipulation by which he agreed to cede half of his dominions to the Allies from the Countries adjacent to their own, could never be applied to the cession of this tribute, or of his right as Lord Paramount over a Prince, whose territories were situated within a short distance of his capital, and unconnected (from their being above the Ghauts) with the other cessions made to the

Company. The irritation of the Sultaun upon this question was excessive; and, in his endeavours to carry this point, he was equally impelled by motives of personal resentment against the Rajah, and a just appreciation of the value, from local position, of the Country of Coorgh, which commanded the best approach to his capital, and consequently the best road to Malabar. The same considerations, however, which led him to desire to retain the superiority of Coorgh, determined Lord Cornwallis not to grant it; and the whole settlement, which had been concluded, was brought to issue upon this question: but Lord Cornwallis, though he might have regretted not having earlier made a specific demand of the Coorgh tribute, was too sensible of the degree in which this question involved the national character, to agree to sacrifice to the vengeance of the Sultaun, a Chief, who had been so forward to assist us in the operations of the war. He was not even shaken by the immediate prospect of renewed hostilities, which at one period threatened to be the inevitable result of this difference; and his ultimate success, in obliging Tippoo to resign all claims upon the Country in dispute, not only established the superiority of the British arms, increased the respect and admiration of the Allies; but confirmed in the strongest manner those impressions, which had been made by the grounds on which this war had been undertaken.

The desire of not destroying what has been termed the balance of power in India, is generally stated to have been one of the principal causes, which prevented Lord Cornwallis from prosecuting the war to the total annihilation of Tippoo; which, it is always assumed by those who assert this, he had it completely in his power to do. Without intending to deny that Lord Cornwallis might have destroyed the power of Tippoo, I certainly believe, that he must have been influenced to the line of policy he pursued by more powerful and more proximate causes, than that speculative apprehension of danger from the increase of the dominions of the Nizam and the Mahrattas, which has been so often ascribed as his motive for concluding the peace. It must be remembered, that a division of the territories of Tippoo, though it would have added greatly to the dominions of these States, would have been attended with a more than proportionate increase to the power and resources of the British Government, who, after the destruction of so formidable and inveterate an enemy, would have had less cause than before to dread their hostility. This policy might be disputed, if either the conduct or the character of the Sultaun had justified a hope, that the reduction of his power, by the alienation of half his territories, would have changed his sentiments; or, if the British Government could have placed a reasonable reliance on his good faith or friendship: but it is evident no such expectations were indulged by Lord Cornwallis at the period when he made the peace; for that nobleman, in his letter to the Court of Directors, which accompanied the definitive treaty, describes Tippoo as "a faithless and "violent character, upon whom no dependence "could be placed." With this just impression of his character, added to his knowledge of his ambition, his military habits, and his connexion with the French, Lord Cornwallis must have considered him, even in his reduced state, as much more likely to disturb the tranquillity of the Company's possessions, than either the Nizam or Mahrattas.

The conduct of Lord Cornwallis upon this important occasion, was undoubtedly influenced by more obvious and stronger reasons. The finances of Government were in a very embarrassed state: the general sentiment in England was adverse to any war whatever in India: the Court of Directors had, in several of their despatches, and particularly that under date the 21st of September 1791, which reached his

Lordship previously to the conclusion of the definitive treaty, earnestly called his attention to the conclusion of an early peace, as alike essential to the finances and the interests of the Company: and they declare, in that despatch, their readiness to sacrifice some portion of the advantages, which they might justly expect from the success of the war, rather than risk it's continuance. To these causes may be added the jealousy, which subsisted between the Nizam and the Mahrattas; the difficulty of managing the unwieldy force of the former, and the serious apprehensions which were entertained of the treachery of the latter. These apprehensions were greatly increased at the time when the army was at Seringapatam, by the approach of Madhajee Scindiah towards Poonah, with the rumoured intention of establishing his influence over the Paishwah, and of mixing in the war with no favourable disposition to the interests of the Company's Government.

The accounts, which had arrived in India previously to the conclusion of this peace, of the prospect of an immediate war with Spain, and the probability that such event would involve Great Britain with France, was another strong inducement for Lord Cornwallis to bring the war with Tippoo to a termination; that he might be prepared to repel any attacks of the latter Nation, or to direct the efforts of our arms against it's Settlements in India.

These plain and strong reasons will, without seeking for a general and speculative ground of action, sufficiently account for Lord Cornwallis having concluded a peace with Tippoo at the period he did; as well as for that anxiety and uneasiness with which, from his letter, which accompanied the treaty of peace, he appears to have contemplated the probable renewal of hostilities. He had accomplished all those objects, which he had in view at the commencement of the war; and, under the circumstances in which he was placed, he could not think himself justified in exposing to any hazard, by it's continuance, the great advantages which he had obtained.

The conduct of Lord Cornwallis to Tippoo Sultaun, after the peace, was honourable and dignified; and the affectionate manner in which he treated the hostage Princes, would probably have made an impression on any other Prince. But Tippoo appears to have received such marks of kindness, more as insults to his wounded pride, than as proofs of friendship; and no part of his subsequent conduct gave cause to hope, that he was sincere in his professions of amity; or that the peace, which had been concluded, would be permanent.

Though no specific change was made, after the termination of the war, in the conditions of the alliance with the Nizam; the relations of friendship between that Prince and the Company became more intimate, from the sense of the mutual benefit, which had attended the alliance; and the subsidiary force continued in his service. A contrary feeling, however, appears to have been produced about this period in the Court of Poonah; the causes of which it may not be unuseful to state. A general proposition was made, after the peace with Tippoo Sultaun, to Lord Cornwallis, by Hurry Punt, the Commander of the army of the Paishwah, for eventually subsidizing a British detachment, of the same force and on the same terms as that with the Nizam, to aid the Paishwah; and it was declared, that the purpose for which this force was required, was that of enabling the Paishwah to reduce to obedience any dependent, which might prove refractory. This proposition was rejected by his Lordship on general grounds; but he states in a despatch upon the subject, that the principal cause of objection to the measure, was his conviction, that it was meant to obtain the countenance and support of the British Government against Madhajee Scindiah; of whose design of establishing his influence at Poonah, Nanah Furnavese then entertained the most serious apprehensions.

This occurrence, no doubt, added to that jealousy, which the Poonah State had from the first entertained of our more intimate connexion with the Nizam; and laid the foundation of that contest, which so soon afterwards ensued between those States.

The independent power of Madhajee Scindiah, which was first recognised by the British Government in the treaty of Salbhye, was matured during the Government of Lord Cornwallis; who declaredly governed by that system of neutrality, which the Legislature had so rigidly prescribed, and does not appear to have thought himself at liberty to make even a political effort to prevent that Chief's aggrandizement. The consequence was, the complete establishment of Scindiah's power over the northern parts of Hindoostan; the possession, by that Chief, of the person of the Emperor of Delhi; the formation of a large and formidable corps of regular infantry under European Officers, chiefly French; the erection of founderies and arsenals: in short, the accumulation of those vast military powers and resources, which enabled his immediate successor to carry on a war at the same moment in the Deckan and Hindoostan against the British Government and it's Allies.

Previous to the commencement of the war with Tippoo Sultaun, Scindiah had made overtures to become a party in the confederacy against that Prince, on the condition of an improved alliance with the British Government, of whom he solicited two battalions, to remain with the army with which he at that period proposed to march to Poonah. He also expressed an expectation, that the British Government would engage to defend his possessions in Hindoostan during his absence. In addition to these specific requests, he demanded the general aid of the Company against the Rajpoot Chiefs in Hindoostan, who continued to resist his authority. These conditions were, for a variety of obvious causes, deemed inadmissible; and no alliance of the nature which he wished, was formed. Hence the councils of this Chief were, as I have before stated, suspected, towards the close of the war with Tippoo, of being more of a hostile, than a friendly nature to the British Nation.

The conduct of Madhajee Scindiah, subsequent to the conclusion of the peace with Tippoo, appears to have been viewed with considerable jealousy by Lord Cornwallis; and upon receiving a paper of intelligence, transmitted by the public news-writer of Dehly in July 1792, which stated, that the Emperor of Delhi had written to the Paishwah, and to Scindiah, informing them, that he hoped, through their exertions, to obtain some tribute from Bengal; that nobleman furnished the British Resident at Scindiah's Court with particular instructions upon the subject. In these instructions, which were dated the 9th of August 1792, he states, that though the want of authenticity of the paper of intelligence received from Delhi prevents his making a formal representation upon this point, he is very desirous that his sentiments should be conveyed to Scindiah and his Ministers in the most explicit manner; and he desires the Resident (should he not be able to discover the truth of the statement in a manner that would justify a public representation) to take advantage of any opening, which occurs, to deliver his sentiments. "You will," he observes, "inform Scindiah, that, in the "present situation of the King, I consider all "letters written upon political points in his "name to be by his (Scindiah's) sanction and "authority only; and that you are instructed "by me to add, that an attempt to establish "principles of the above description, by any

"Power whatever, will be warmly resented by "this Government.

"You will," he continues, "in the course of "any conversation or correspondence, which "you may hold with Scindiah upon this point, "take care to recall, in the most forcible "manner, to his recollection, the spirit of "moderation and forbearance, that has been "manifested by the Government during the "long period in which he has been employed "in extending his conquests in the northern "parts of Hindoostan; and that it would give "us pain to be forced to depart from the neu-"tral and pacific system, that we have hitherto "observed in that quarter. You will, at the "same time, inform him, that it is by my "particular directions that you say, that we "have no desire to make any new acquisi-"tions; nor even to interfere in the internal "affairs of the Empire, if we can avoid it with "honour and safety; but that if any of our "neighbours should be rash enough to insult "us by unjust demands, or in any other shape "whatever, we feel ourselves both able and "resolved to exact ample satisfaction."

These instructions were grounded on that proud but just sense of national honour, which will not suffer itself to be approached by the breath of insult, and which keeps danger at a distance by it's alacrity to meet it. They appear to have had at the moment the best effects; Scindiah's Minister having assured the British Resident, that the use which his master wished to make of the Emperor's favour, was to establish his authority over the territories which he held, not to subdue or invade those of others.

No political connexion of any intimacy had ever subsisted between the British Government and Ragojee Bhonslah. The personal character of that Chief, and the local situation of his territories, made it unlikely, that any efficient aid could be obtained from his co-operation in the war with Tippoo. But Lord Cornwallis nevertheless neglected no means to conciliate him to an acquiescence in the justice and policy of that measure, and even invited him to join the confederacy. With a view to those objects, he deputed a Resident to his Court, who was intrusted also with the negotiation of some minor points, connected with the commercial intercourse between the two States; and directed to convey a just impression to the Rajah's mind of the imperious causes, which had obliged the Governor General to march a body of troops through the Province of Cuttack, before he could obtain the Rajah's approbation of that measure.

In order to complete this general view of the political administration of Lord Cornwallis, I shall here shortly refer to those principles of policy, which regulated the conduct of that nobleman in the cultivation of the more intimate alliances, which subsisted between the Company and those native Princes, whom a course of events had rendered immediately dependent upon it's support and protection; and whose interests were, from the nature of their political relation, identified with those of the English Government.

The chief of those Princes, are the Nabob of the Carnatic and the Vizier of Oude. A brief statement of the leading measures, which Lord Cornwallis adopted with these two Princes, will be sufficient to throw every light, which is required, upon this part of the subject.

Subsequently to the arrival of Lord Cornwallis in India, Sir Archibald Campbell (then Governor of Fort St. George) negotiated a treaty with the Nabob of the Carnatic. This treaty, which was concluded on the 24th of February 1787, was framed upon the principle of providing, by an arrangement founded on just and equitable grounds, for the defence of the possessions of the Nabob and the Company in the Carnatic, and Northern Circars.

The principal of it's conditions were, that the

Nabob should contribute an amount of nine lacks of star pagodas annually toward the support of the military peace establishment, which was to be maintained by the Company, for the security of the dominions of the two contracting parties; that, in the event of a failure on the part of the Nabob in the punctual payment of this sum, the Company was to possess a right to appoint it's own Officers, with adequate authority to superintend and receive from the Nabob's Aumildars or Managers, the revenue of certain districts, which were specified, and, by an article of this treaty, made answerable for the regular payment of the annual amount above mentioned. It was further stipulated, that after the amount of the deficiency had been realized, the Officers appointed by the Company were instantly to be recalled. These provisions, however, were only for a state of peace. In the event of war occurring, it was agreed, that the Company should charge themselves with it's conduct, and that four-fifths of the revenue of their possessions in the Carnatic and Circars should be applied to it's prosecution; and by another article the Nabob agreed, that four-fifths of his revenue should be applied to the same purpose; and that his proportion of the debt of the war should be settled at twenty-five fifty-one parts. In the event of the above four-fifths, or any part of it, being diverted from the current expenses of the war, or the debts and expenses incurred thereby, the Company was vested by the treaty with a right of appointing receivers and superintendants, to receive the revenues of all the Nabob's Country from the Nabob's Officers, in the same mode, and upon the same conditions, as had been fixed in the case of districts mortgaged for the security of the annual payment of nine lacks of pagodas, the amount fixed for the military peace establishment.

Such were the leading conditions of an alliance, which, at the period at which it was concluded, was considered as a great improvement of the political relations, which subsisted between the Company and the Nabob of the Carnatic; and such it certainly was in one essential view. It vested the sole military power in the Company; and thereby gave security to the Empire, which had been before exposed to the most serious danger, from it's resources being applied to the support of two armies formed upon opposite principles, and acting under distinct and often distracted opposite authorities.

This was, however, the only view in which this arrangement could be considered beneficial: in every other, it evidently carried the seeds of it's own destruction. The sword was placed in one hand, the purse in another; and to combine both, in order to produce that efficient exertion, which the contracting parties were aware might be required for their mutual safety, it became necessary, unless the Nabob altered the whole principles of his Government, to introduce a complete change into the administration of those Provinces, from which their resources were to be drawn, during the actual existence of a war with a foreign State. In addition to this inconvenience, or rather danger, it must be evident, that the constant changes of authority, to which the territories of the Nabob were by this treaty made eventually subject, were likely to be destructive to every hope of improvement in the Country, or of permanent comfort and prosperity to it's unfortunate inhabitants.

The early result of this treaty, was a failure on the part of the Nabob in the most essential of it's conditions; and when the war occurred with Tippoo Sultaun in 1790, Lord Cornwallis found himself obliged to take possession of all his Highness's Country, to secure the two States against the dangers to which he thought them exposed, from the mismanagement of the Nabob's Officers. This consideration made him direct the actual appointment of the Company's Officers to collect the revenue; contrary to the stipulations of Sir A. Campbell's treaty, which left the collections to be made by the Nabob's

Officers, under the superintendance and authority of the Company's Officers. The Governor General, however, directed that the Nabob might be permitted to appoint Officers to observe the conduct, and inspect the accounts, of the servants of the Company, in order that a satisfactory settlement of accounts, upon the principles prescribed by the alliance, might hereafter be made between his Highness and the British Government.

In a letter, under date the 21st of June 1790, in which Lord Cornwallis directs the Government of Fort St. George to adopt this measure, he states most forcibly the causes, which have led to it's necessity, and gives positive orders for it's immediate execution. He expresses in this despatch great regret, that the Nabob has not been prevailed upon to give his assent to it's adoption. The Government cannot, however, he states, gratify the Nabob's private sensations, by forbearing to take efficient steps to exact the performance of his engagements to the Company, without being guilty of a flagrant neglect of the attention, which was due to the honour and interests of their Country, and to the security of his Highness's own dominions.

Lord Cornwallis also expresses in these instructions his expectation, that the Nabob would ere long become sensible of the interested and criminal motives of those advisers, who had influenced him to resist the solicitations of the Madras Government; and that he would soon see, that while his people were treated with justice and humanity, a liberal fund would be secured for the support of his own dignity, and that of his family; and the remainder of the revenues (to use Lord Cornwallis's own words) "would be rescued from the hands of extortioners and usurers, and honourably applied "to the defence and protection of his subjects "and dominions."

The assumption of the Country of the Nabob facilitated greatly the operations of the war; not only from it's placing the resources of the Carnatic in the hands of the British Government, but from giving that State the undivided power of drawing forth, in the most prompt manner, every military supply, which the Country possessed, to the aid of the public service.

When Lord Cornwallis returned to Fort St. George, after the termination of the war with Tippoo, he opened a negotiation with the Nabob of the Carnatic, which terminated in the conclusion of a new treaty with that Prince on the 12th of July 1792.

The preamble of this engagement annulled the treaty of 1787, concluded by Sir A. Campbell, on the grounds of a representation received from the Nabob under date the 9th of June 1792, addressed to Marquis Cornwallis, which stated, that the resources of the Carnatic were not competent to enable him to perform the stipulations of the above engagement; and that the security which the Nabob had agreed to give to the Company for the regular discharge of the stipulated sums (which he had to pay under that engagement), was not equal to the ends intended: The engagement also, into which the Nabob had entered with the Company for the liquidation of debts due by him to private persons, was annulled; and the treaty entered into by Lord Cornwallis was declared to provide for all cases stated in either of the engagements, which it annulled.

By this treaty, the defence of the territories of both States was (as fixed by Sir A. Campbell's treaty) intrusted to the Company, who were, in the event of war, to assume the management of the Carnatic; which was to remain in their hands during the continuance of such war, and to be returned to the Nabob at it's termination; unless in cases, which were particularly specified. It was also a stipulation of this engagement, that, as long as the Company remained in possession of the Carnatic, they should pay to the Nabob one fifth part of it's revenue.

The Nabob, by an article of this treaty, agreed

to pay nine lacks of pagodas annually, on account of the expenses of the military establishment of the Company during peace; and further to pay the sum of six lacks twenty-one thousand one hundred and five pagodas annually for the liquidation of the debts due by him to his private creditors.

The Company were to be put in possession of the Poligar tribute, as part payment of these sums; and the Nabob was to receive credit for the sum of two lacks sixty-four thousand seven hundred and four pagodas on this account, without the Company's having a right to make any deduction for charges of collection. The amount remaining after this deduction, which the Nabob was to pay annually on account of military expenses, and the liquidation of his private debts, viz. twelve lacks fifty-six thousand and four hundred pagodas, was to be paid in regular instalments; and in the event of any failure on his part, specified districts, yielding revenue to the amount stated, were, under the conditions of this treaty, to be assumed by the Company; and the Nabob was, on this event occurring, to recall all his Officers from the above districts, except one in each, who was to remain, and annually to receive from the Company's Officers attested statements of it's gross revenue and nett receipts.

The revenue of these Countries, when assumed, was to be deducted from the sum to be paid by the Nabob; and they were to remain in the possession of the Company until the arrears due on the instalments were cleared, and the debts due by the Nabob to his private creditors were fully liquidated; after which, those districts were to be restored to his authority. It was, however, stipulated, that on his failure in the regular payment of any of the instalments of the amount of six lacks thirty-five thousand two hundred and ninety-five pagodas, which would remain to be paid annually on account of military expenses exclusively of the paishcush or tribute, the Company possessed a right to reassume such one or more of the specified districts, the revenue of which was equal in value to the amount of the instalments which had fallen in arrear; and, on such event occurring, the district or districts so reassumed were never to be again restored to the Nabob.

Besides these regular and stipulated payments, the Nabob agreed to defray such additional charges, as were incurred in granting him the occasional aid of the Company's troops to support his authority, or preserve internal order in his dominions.

These were the principal conditions of the treaty, which Lord Cornwallis made with the

Nabob of the Carnatic, to whom he restored his Country soon after it's conclusion. Though there can be no doubt this engagement simplified in some points, and greatly ameliorated in others, that which Sir A. Campbell had contracted; it corrected none of it's radical defects. The most material point in which this treaty differed from the one which had been before concluded, was, in that stipulation, which provided for the complete introduction of a new authority in the Government of the Carnatic, on the occurrence of war with any foreign Power. This change of authority, which was conditional in the treaty of 1787, was rendered absolute by that of 1792. By this essential alteration, those faint hopes, which might before have existed, of benefit to the contracting parties from the operation of an efficient administration of the affairs of the Nabob, or any of his successors, were altogether extinguished. This treaty also left the Nabob as much exposed, as the former one, to the destructive intrigues of interested and bad advisers; and to the ruinous arts of usurers and extortioners, who, it was evident, would continue, as they had done before, to stimulate him, by every effort in their power, to the baneful resource of anticipating his revenues, for the purpose of avoiding, or at least protracting, the diminution of his personal authority, by the alienation of any part of his territories.

Lord Cornwallis, however, appears, from the general tenour of his despatches, written at the moment, to have entertained strong hopes of the happy operation of this treaty. But the authorities in England did not partake of this impression, and they early directed an endeavour to modify the whole arrangement, which they apprehended (and, the event proved, with justice) would never yield those advantages, which had been expected from it's conclusion.

It will be necessary, in order to understand the nature of the arrangement which Lord Cornwallis made with the Vizier of Oude, to take a short general view of the connexion, which previously subsisted between the Company and that Prince.

By the treaty of Fyzabad, which was concluded with the Nabob Vizier Asuph ud Dowlah, in the beginning of the year 1775, soon after the accession of that Prince to the Musnud, the Company came into possession of Benares, Ghazipore and Chunar; and it was stipulated, that a regular brigade of the Company's troops should be stationed in the territories of the Nabob for the defence of the Subah of Oude, Corah and Allahabad. The Nabob agreed to pay the monthly amount of two lacks and sixty thousand rupees for the services of this corps, as long as it was stationed with him; and it was also agreed, that if he required further aid to defend other countries than those specified, a sum should be fixed, at the period of the requisition, proportioned to the service.

A few months after this treaty was concluded, Asuph ud Dowlah, in consequence of the great disorders which prevailed in his Country, and the want of discipline and irregularity of his army, applied to the Governor General for the aid of a body of English Officers sufficient for six battalions of Sepoys, a corps of artillery, and a proportion of cavalry. This corps would, he stated in his application, be a complete check upon the remainder of his army, and greatly strengthen his Government. He left the formation entirely to the English Government, engaging, that he would make arrangements, by which it's pay should be regularly discharged.

The corps, which was thus formed, was in 1777 incorporated with the army of the Company, and stationed at Furruckabad. It was termed the temporary brigade, in distinction from the regular brigade in the Nabob's service, which was fixed at Cawnpore. The annual charge to the Vizier for the temporary brigade, was about twenty-three lacks of rupees.

The Vizier was informed by the Governor

General, at the period when the temporary brigade was formed, that it should remain a fixed charge to him for so long a time as he should require it for his service. The Court of Directors, however, appear to have disapproved of this stipulation. "If by this proposition," they state in a despatch upon the subject, "it is in-
"tended to leave the Vizier at liberty to dis-
"charge the troops at his pleasure, we think
"such a stipulation dangerous, and likely to
"operate to our very great inconvenience; and
"if more be meant than is expressed, and you
"intend to exert your influence, first to reduce
"the Vizier to acquiesce in your proposal, and
"afterwards to compel him to keep the troops
"in his pay during your pleasure, your inten-
"tions are unjust, and a correspondent con-
"duct would reflect great dishonour on the
"Company."

The embarrassment, which the Court of Directors anticipated from this arrangement, soon arose. In the year 1779, (two years after the measure had been adopted,) the Vizier, on the ground of a great defalcation of his revenue, caused by a failure of rain, declared his inability to make the advances necessary for the payment of the brigades, and the satisfaction of the other claims of the Company: and, though the estimate of the whole demand of the Company on him for the year was 13,612,188 rupees, he refused to grant orders to the Resident for more than 6,882,000. The Resident, when he reported this proceeding, transmitted a letter from the Vizier, under date the 19th of November 1779, in which he professed his attachment to the Company; but earnestly solicited, that a consideration of his distress might lead the English Government to relieve him from the burden of maintaining the new brigade stationed at Futty Ghur, which he declared was not only useless to his Government, but the cause of great loss in his revenues and customs. He also required the sanction of the Government to the dismission of some other corps in his service, which were commanded by European Officers; and, according to his statement, attended with great expense, and very little utility.

The Government of Bengal considered, that a compliance with the Vizier's wishes would expose both his interests and those of the Company to the greatest danger; as it was evident, that he possessed no immediate means of preserving the internal tranquillity of his own territories, much less of protecting them from the danger with which they were actually threatened by the Mahrattas, with whom a war was at the moment deemed unavoidable. Under this impression, they directed the Resident not only to insist upon a full and prompt performance of his pecuniary engagements to the Company; but to declare to him, that he stood pledged to maintain the armies, which had been formed for his protection; and that in the present circumstances of his Government, and that of the Company, (threatened with immediate war,) to disband any part of those troops which were maintained for his service, was a measure no less improper for him to suggest, than it was for the English Government to adopt.

A letter was written at the same time by the Governor General to the Vizier, in which the dangerous consequences, which were likely to result from a compliance with his requests, were most forcibly stated. It never could have been supposed, the Governor General informed him, that, when he applied for the new brigade, the Company would have been at the pains to raise and discipline so large a body of men, and to augment their establishment by the addition of such an extraordinary number of Officers, as were necessary to command them; if they were liable to be burthened with the sole weight and expense of maintaining these Officers, by a sudden resolution on the part of the Nabob to discharge them, without previous and timely notice, and without their consent. He explicitly informed the Nabob in this letter, that, if he was determined to withdraw himself from the alliance and assistance of the Company, he must give sufficient time and notice of his resolution, in order to prevent the interests of the Company suffering from a hasty execution of it: that he could not consent to the Vizier dismissing the Company's troops at such a distance from home, at such a crisis: and he expected as much time would be given to dispose of the force, when the Vizier had no occasion for it's services, as there had been for raising it. Mr. Hastings concluded this letter, by expressing his conviction, that, notwithstanding the unfortunate failure of the harvest, his Highness's funds were still sufficient to pay a force, which seemed so indispensable for the security of his Country. He therefore insisted on his making good his payment to the Company, even if he was obliged to leave in arrears, or disband, part of his own troops in order to effect that necessary object.

No doubt appeared to have been entertained, at the period of this occurrence, of the imperious necessity, which compelled the British Government to refuse compliance with the requests of the Vizier, but the evils of a subsidiary engagement, the stipulations of which were not absolute, and the dissolution of which depended to a great degree upon the caprice of a native Prince, were never more forcibly experienced; and it perhaps required all that wisdom, firmness, and decision, which marked the character of Mr. Hastings, to save the public interests from the great danger to which they were on this occasion exposed by the conduct of a weak and profligate Prince; who, acting under the influence of wicked and designing men, would have sacrificed, for the gratification of his pleasures, or the attainment of a temporary object, the permanent interests and security of his own Country, and the interests and security of that State with which he had, from a course of events, become completely identified.

Though the Nabob Vizier was obliged to acquiesce, for the moment, in the urgency of the reasons stated by the Governor General, he took the first favourable opportunity of renewing his solicitations upon the subject: and when he had proved his attachment to the British Government in a very unequivocal manner, by his conduct during the rebellion of Cheyt Sing, Rajah of Benares, he again earnestly requested the attention of Mr. Hastings, who, under a more favourable impression of his designs, than he had before entertained, concluded an engagement with him upon the 19th of September, 1781. By this engagement it was agreed, that the temporary brigade should be recalled within the limits of the Company's possessions, that the different corps of Sebundy* in his service under English Officers, should be reduced, and that he should only be charged with the expense of the original brigade, which had been fixed at the rate of 260,000 rupees per month, and one battalion of Sepoys to be stationed with the Resident at Lucknow; the expense of which was fixed at the rate of 25,000 rupees per month.

In the event, however, of the Vizier even requiring a further aid of troops, he was, by the terms of this engagement, to be charged with their actual pay, and allowances, from the date on which they crossed the Carumnassa river.

All the conditions of this engagement appear to have been carried into execution except the most essential, that which related to the recall of the temporary brigade, which Mr. Hastings states (in a general account of his proceedings, published in England), that he was prevented from fulfilling by some political causes, to which the nature of the times obliged him to pay attention. He further states in the same document, that by a subsequent accom-

* Troops employed exclusively in the collection of revenue.

modation, into which he entered with Asuph ud Dowlah in 1784, when he visited Lucknow, he again positively agreed to withdraw the detachment from Furruckabad, and actually left orders with the Resident at Lucknow to that effect; but that, on his return to Calcutta, he found this measure completely at variance with the opinions of the other Members of the Board; and he thought it his duty, from a consideration of his situation, (being on the eve of resigning the Government,) not only to give up all idea of carrying this arrangement into effect, but to make the repeal of his former resolution, upon this subject, an act of his own authority, that it might not appear the effect of opposition, and thereby produce a dangerous influence on the credit of the succeeding Administration.

No material changes in the connexion between the Company and the Vizier occurred during the short Government of Sir John Macpherson: but these delays made the Vizier more anxious for the accomplishment of his object; and, immediately after the arrival of Marquis Cornwallis in India, Asuph ud Dowlah deputed his ablest and most confidential Minister, Hyder Beg Khan, to Fort William, with a view of explaining his situation to that nobleman, and of effecting an arrangement, which would relieve him from some part of the existing burden on his finances.

The nature and result of this negotiation were fully stated by Lord Cornwallis in a minute, which he recorded upon the 20th of April; which document elucidates, in the clearest manner, the principles which regulated the conduct of that nobleman in the final settlement of this difficult and important question.

The Vizier had expressed, through Hyder Beg Khan, his expectations that the English Government would recall the brigade from Furruckabad, agreeably to the stipulations entered into by Mr. Hastings when at Lucknow; but Lord Cornwallis expressed his opinion, that the continuance of that force in the dominions of the Vizier was equally essential to the interests of the Vizier and the Company. His Lordship stated in a letter, which he addressed to the Vizier upon this occasion, the motives which made him desire the continuance of this force in his dominions; and in the minute, which he recorded upon the subject, he sums up the arguments, which had induced him to this line of conduct, by the following remarks: "I shall only observe," he states in that document, "that I by no means considered a single brigade stationed at Cawnpore, as adequate to the defence of the

"Vizier's frontiers; that although it did not "appear to me that there was reason to apprehend any immediate attack upon them, "the recall of so considerable a part of our "force, as the Futty Ghur brigade, might "have precipitated that event; that it is well "known, that the forces in the service of the "Nabob Vizier are under no discipline, and "barely sufficient to preserve the internal "peace of his dominions; that his own immediate subjects are retained within the bounds "of duty and allegiance by the respect inspired "by the Company's troops; that the character "of the Vizier, his inconsiderate profusion in "his expenses, his inattention to provide for "them, and his total disregard to every thing "but momentary gratifications, rendered it "impossible to depend upon his care, either "for the protection of his Country from foreign invasions, or internal commotion; and "that although the charges attending the continuance of the brigade at Futty Ghur exceed "the sum we are authorized to claim from him, "under the orders of the Court of Directors, "the arrangements made by this negotiation "render the additional charge of little importance, when the magnitude of the objects "is considered."

Lord Cornwallis also observes in this minute, that from a general statement of the payments, which the Nabob Vizier had made under different heads to the Company for a period of nine years, those amounted to the average of eighty-four lacks per annum; though, by the treaties of 1775 and 1781, the Nabob had only bound himself to pay to the English Government the sum of 3,121,000 rupees, and 3,420,000 rupees per annum.

His Lordship adds in this document, that by the engagement which he had concluded with Hyder Beg Khan, the annual amount of the Vizier's payment was permanently fixed at fifty lacks of rupees per annum; and he expressed his conviction, that this amount would fully indemnify the Company for all expenses to which they might be exposed from their connexion with the Vizier; and that Prince had, he was assured, perfect ability to make this annual disbursement, without suffering in either his convenience or dignity.

Hyder Beg Khan acquiesced in this arrangement; with a declaration, however, that he relied upon the justice of Government, and it's regard for the interest of his master, to diminish the expenses for the maintenance of the Company's troops in his dominions by a recall of part of them, whenever policy or convenience should warrant such a measure.

Lord Cornwallis, in his letter to the Vizier, made a promise to the effect of the expectation expressed by Hyder Beg Khan; but, in his minute on this subject, his Lordship acknowledges, that he could not foresee a period when such a measure could with prudence be accomplished.

His Lordship in this very able minute took a view of the nature of the connexion between the Company and the Vizier; and the line of conduct, which it was, in his opinion, the duty of the English Government to pursue toward that Prince, with the object of improving and preserving the alliance.

"The connexion," he observes, "between him" (the Vizier) "and the Company now stands "upon the only basis calculated to render it "permanent. We undertake the defence of his "Country; and in return he agrees to defray "the real expenses incurred by an engagement "of so much value to himself. The internal ad-"ministration of his affairs is left to his exclu-"sive management; and my attention will be "constantly directed to the preservation of this "system, whilst the Vizier continues to fulfil "the stipulations into which he has entered.

"By this declaration of a noninterference in "the detail of the Vizier's Government, I do "not mean to preclude myself, or this Board,

" from making representations to him on the " subject of his administration, whenever it " may be essentially necessary; or of propos- " ing to the Vizier any general arrangement, of " importance to the interests of both Govern- " ments: mutual convenience may render such " propositions expedient; and on these grounds " only they ought to be made. The Board will " also, I imagine, see a necessity of giving their " countenance to the Nabob Hyder Beg Khan, " or whoever may be the acting Minister of the " Vizier. At present he possesses the entire " confidence of his master, who is anxious to " procure for him the avowed protection of this " Government. I made no difficulty in assur- " ing the Nabob Hyder Beg Khan, that he " might depend upon the support of this Go- " vernment whilst he served his master with " fidelity; governed the Country with justice " and humanity; and strictly adhered to the " engagements formed with the Honourable " Company."

Lord Cornwallis was too well aware, from the information which he had obtained, of the private character of the Vizier, not to be sensible of the indispensable necessity, which existed, for his giving a decided support to the Minister Hyder Beg Khan, and to those who were, like him, favourable to the friendship which had been established between the two States: and the sentiments he recorded upon this point, prove in the fullest manner, that, if an emergency had happened, he would not have been deterred by any apprehension of the great responsibility, which he incurred, (by a departure from the prescribed system of noninterference and neutrality,) from the adoption of those decided measures of practical policy, which he might have deemed, under the actual condition of affairs at the moment, best calculated to promote the interests and security of the Empire committed to his charge.

His intentions, indeed, upon this point, as well as the reasons upon which they were founded, are explicitly stated in the able minute to which I have before alluded.

"The Board are well informed," he observes, "that the administration of affairs in the Oude "Government depends entirely upon the Mi-"nister; that the Vizier himself takes no far-"ther concern in it, than to give the sanction "of his name and authority to the acts of his "servants; and that such is his disinclination "to every thing that has the appearance of "business, that even this formality is not com-"plied with, on his part, without reluctance. "The Vizier himself being profuse to an ex-"treme, and little solicitous concerning the "mode of obtaining funds to supply his habits "of dissipation; the Company must rather look "to the Minister, than to him, for the punctual "performance of his engagement. Exposed as "he is to the effects of caprice and intrigue, it "is impossible to determine how long the "Nabob Hyder Beg Khan may continue to "possess the confidence of the Vizier.

"The embarrassments attending his situation "are many; as he will find it difficult, if the "idea which I have formed of his master's cha- "racter is just, to combine the two objects, of "conciliating the esteem and affection of the "Nabob, and establishing a system of Govern- "ment calculated to promote his true interests. "I forbear to expatiate further on this subject, "and only hope, that no occurrence will ever "happen to compel this Government to inter- "fere between the Vizier and his acting Mi- "nister, or to give countenance to the latter "against the approbation of the former."

These were the principal features of the only arrangement of political importance, which took place with the Vizier of Oude during Lord Cornwallis's administration of the Company's affairs in India. It's operation was perhaps as happy, as the personal character of Asuph u Dowlah admitted of it's being; but the indolence, dissipation, and extravagance of that

Prince, created a constant embarrassment in his affairs, and rendered it often difficult for him to fulfil his engagements with the Company; of the value of whose aid and protection he appears always to have become least sensible, when the tranquil state of his dominions proved most forcibly the benefits of the alliance.

Until the last year of Lord Cornwallis's administration, a peace existed between Great Britain and France, which enabled his Lordship to employ the whole of the British force in India against Tippoo Sultaun, during the war with that Prince; and to avoid that increase of military establishment, which must have been made, if it had been requisite to provide for the defence of the exposed parts of our possessions against the possible attacks of France, or to have equipped armaments against the colonies and possessions of that State, or it's Allies.

When the account of war between France and England reached India, Pondicherry was immediately attacked, and taken, by an army from Fort St. George, under the Commander of the forces of that Presidency, Major General Sir John Brathwaite. Lord Cornwallis had hastened from Fort William, to take the direction of this service; but did not reach the coast till it was accomplished. He did not return to Bengal, but sailed for England in the month of August 1793.

The extraordinary success, which attended Lord Cornwallis's administration of the affairs of British India, is no doubt in a considerable degree to be attributed to the manly spirit, sound judgment, and unshaken firmness, which distinguished the character of that respectable nobleman. But a retrospect to the former history of India will enable us to discover a still more powerful cause of that success, in the exercise of those great civil and military powers, which were, by the confidence of his King and Country, vested in his person. It was the possession of these powers, which enabled him to unite, with such effect to the promotion of every object in his administration, the hitherto divided and distracted local authorities of British India; and the active control, and direction, which he assumed over the subordinate Presidencies of Fort St. George and Bombay, during the whole of his Government, placed their means and resources as much at his immediate command as those of Bengal.

The impression originally made upon the minds of the native Princes of India by the rank and character of Lord Cornwallis, was confirmed by their observation of his extended powers.

Their attention was directed to the supreme authority of the British Nation in India with an awe and respect, which they had never before paid it. The manner in which Lord Cornwallis drew forth the strength and resources of the British Government to the reduction of Tippoo Sultaun, excited sentiments of equal astonishment and alarm; and the success of that war, combined with the great addition of strength, of territory, and of reputation, which it's termination brought to the English Government, while it extorted the admiration of all the native Powers of India, raised their fears; nor was it possible that these, which were the result of actual events, could be removed by any display of moderation, which in itself implied a sense of that superiority, which formed the just ground of all their apprehensions.

The Indian Government in England could not be insensible to the probable effects of the great changes, which had taken place in the state of British India. They had seen (perhaps with regret), that events, which they had no power of controlling, had forced Lord Cornwallis to an actual departure from that pacific system of forbearance and neutrality, which they had believed practicable, and which they had so earnestly recommended to his attention; and that in opposition to those views, which they had taken of their interests, their territories had been greatly increased, and their political relations much extended, during his administration.

The admission of that necessity, which forced Lord Cornwallis into a course of measures so contrary to their wishes and policy, does not appear to have been followed by a conclusion, that the same causes might again produce the same effect; and a general impression would appear at this period to have been received in England, that the exertions of that nobleman had placed the affairs of the Company on the true footing of security and strength, which had been so long desired; and that nothing was requisite, but mild, moderate, and conciliatory councils, in the local authorities, to secure the lasting tranquillity and prosperity of the British possessions in India. And this errour seems more extraordinary, when we consider the actual state of every native Power in India, as represented in those authentic public documents, which have been referred to in this concise narrative of Lord Cornwallis's Administration.

CHAPTER III.

ADMINISTRATION

OF

SIR JOHN SHORE.

CONTENTS.

State of Affairs favourable to the Security of the British Government.—Great political Changes during this Administration.—Retrospect of the Guarantee Treaty proposed by Marquis Cornwallis.—Court of Poonah refuses to accede to this.—The Nizam anxious for a separate Treaty of Guarantee.—Reasons of Sir John Shore against this.—Hostile Disposition of the Court of Poonah.—Causes of the Quarrel between that Court and the Nizam.—Tippoo threatens to attack the Nizam.—The Governor General resolves not to assist this Prince.—View of the Policy pursued by him on this Occasion.—Convention of Kurdlah.—British Influence at the Court of Hyderabad greatly impaired.—Rebellion of the Son of the Nizam.—French Corps in the Nizam's Service much encouraged at this Time.—Death of the Paishwah.—Consequences of this Event.—Failure of the Treaty with the Nabob of the Carnatic.—Proposed Modification of that Treaty rejected by the Nabob.—View of the Affairs of Oude.—New Treaty with the Vizier.—Invasion of Zemaun Shah.—Consi-

derations upon the Probability and Danger of Invasion from the Northern Tribes.—Concluding Remarks on the System of Policy pursued by the British Government during this Administration.

Sir John Shore, a most respectable civil servant of the Company, who had, by a series of important services in India, recommended himself to the favour and notice of the Court of Directors, was appointed to succeed the Marquis Cornwallis as Governor General of India; and it appears to have been expected by the authorities in England, that all those great advantages, which Lord Cornwallis had obtained, would be confirmed and improved by the ability, local knowledge, and industry, of his successor.

The state of the different native Powers of India at the period when Sir John Shore took charge of the Supreme Government, has been described. The condition of affairs certainly did not promise a very long exemption from hostilities; but it was, on the other hand, in every respect free from danger. The English Government had at no period been so strong in actual military force and resources. It's principal enemy, Tippoo, was much reduced. The Soubahdar of the Deckan, the most important of all it's Allies, was firm to his engagements, and disposed to the cultivation and improvement of the friendship which had been established between him and the Company: and the Mahrattas, though their jealousy had evidently been greatly excited by the success of it's arms, and the extension of it's territories and political relations, regarded that State with a respect and apprehension, which was likely to make them cautious how they offended it.

In taking a general view of the leading political transactions of Sir John Shore's Government, it appears of great consequence to observe, how far that course of policy, which he thought it his duty to pursue, affected this state of affairs; and to what extent those favourable impressions, which I have described, as existing among the native Powers, and which, in an Empire like that of British India, have a value beyond force, were changed by the measures of his Administration.

Though no war with a foreign Power occurred during the Administration of Sir John Shore, that period was marked by political changes in the state of India of great importance; and these merit particular attention, as it is impossible to form any just opinion of the events, which have since happened, without a clear and distinct knowledge of those occurrences by which they were immediately preceded and produced.

The political event of most consequence, which happened during his Administration, was the rupture, which took place between the Nizam and Mahrattas. In order to understand the causes of this rupture, and the nature of that interference by which the British Government attempted to prevent it's occurrence, it will be necessary to trace in a cursory manner the changes, which took place in the Courts of Hyderabad and Poonah, from the period of the conclusion of the peace at Seringapatam, till the period of the disgraceful convention of Kurdlah, which may be considered as having annihilated, for the moment, the independence of the Nizam Government.

The Marquis Cornwallis, soon after the conclusion of the war with Tippoo Sultaun, made an endeavour, in fulfilment of the 10th and 13th articles of the treaty of offensive and defensive alliance with the Nizam and Paishwah, to reduce into the form of an explicit and definite treaty of guarantee, those articles in the subsisting treaties, by which it was generally agreed, that the contracting Powers should guarantee to each other, against any future attacks of the Sultaun, those territories, which they actually possessed at the termination of the war with that Prince.

His Lordship, in his letter under date the 7th of August 1792, to the Resident at Poonah, states his opinion respecting the great importance of this arrangement, for the common security of the respective parties; and he also defines, in that despatch, the principle upon which he conceives this treaty should be framed.

"The Allies," he observes, "are bound to "guarantee against Tippoo the territories that "each of them might possess at the conclusion "of the war; but it must always be adverted "to, that the stipulation is merely defensive, "and cannot operate unless Tippoo should at-"tack either of them without just provoca-"tion.

"It must therefore be clearly expressed in "the treaty of guarantee, that in case any dif-"ference should arise between one of the latter "and Tippoo, the other Allies are to have a "right to expect that the nature and circum-"stances of such difference shall be fully "communicated to them, in order that they "may give their opinion and advice, and en-"deavour to settle it by a temperate negotia-"tion, and that they shall not be considered as "bound to take up arms in his favour, until "they are convinced that he has justice on his "side, and all measures of conciliation shall "have proved fruitless.

"Should a rupture become unavoidable, the "interest and safety of the contracting Powers

" will be so evidently and deeply involved in " the event, that it would be highly injudi- " cious in them to limit their exertions in " endeavouring to bring it to a speedy and " honourable conclusion; and it must, con- " sequently, be stipulated, that the whole " force of each State is to be employed for " that purpose.

" The distress and danger of the party, that " may be attacked, being entitled to the great- " est attention from the other members of the " alliance; it ought to be understood and " settled, that, whilst no time should be lost " in preparing their whole force to take the " field, every immediate assistance, that may " be practicable, should be afforded with such " troops as may be in actual readiness for " service."

Lord Cornwallis subsequently framed a schedule of a treaty upon these principles, which he transmitted to the Courts of Hyderabad and Poonah. It is not necessary to detail the articles of this schedule, as the treaty was never concluded; but it is of importance to notice those general causes, which led to the defect of an arrangement, which was stipulated by prior engagements; and which was in every respect so essential to the real interests and security of the British Government and it's Allies.

At the period when this proposition was first made to the Court of Hyderabad, a reference had been made by it to the British Government, relative to a dispute, which had occurred between the Nizam and Tippoo, about some claims advanced by the latter on the Nabob of Kernoul; and the Government of Hyderabad, with that puerility and petulance which too often characterize a native Court, demanded as the condition of it's consent to the proposition of Lord Cornwallis, the interference and support of the English Government in it's dispute with Tippoo Sultaun. The Nizam was, however, soon made sensible of the folly and unreasonableness of such a demand; and he made every reparation in his power for the errour, which he had committed, by a full and unqualified assent to the guarantee treaty proposed by the Marquis Cornwallis.

The conduct of the Court of Poonah was very different: it treated the guarantee proposed by the English Government with a delay and evasion, which clearly proved a desire of being relieved altogether from engagements, which might have the future effect of limiting or counteracting the designs, which it cherished against Tippoo and the Nizam. Acting upon these principles, a counter proposition for a guarantee treaty was given in by Nanah Furnavese, the Minister of the Poonah State, to the British Resident; which was, after some discussion, deemed altogether inadmissible, and rejected. This engagement included, among other articles, a recognition, on the part of the Allies, of claims of the Poonah Government on Tippoo for Chout, which was not authorized by the stipulations of the treaty of Seringapatam: and the Nizam, while he declared his perfect readiness to consent to the proposition made by Lord Cornwallis, was positive in the refusal of his acquiescence to the engagement proposed by the Paishwah.

After a vexatious and procrastinated negotiation, of considerably more than a year, this point was altogether abandoned; and the British Government contented itself with a declaration, that it was satisfied with the verbal acquiescence of the Nizam; and a vague promise, which had been made during the negotiation by the Poonah State, which conveyed no more than that it would always be ready to act agreeably to existing treaties. The Nizam, throughout the latter part of this negotiation, showed great anxiety for the conclusion of a separate treaty of guarantee. He argued, with much apparent justice, that the failure of one of three parties in the fulfilment of it's engagements, was no reason why the other two should neglect their faith; or sacrifice those advantages, which had been proposed in the union of their interests. It was also urged, that the conclusion of the treaty of guarantee, proposed by Lord Cornwallis, with the Nizam, would be the most certain mode of bringing the Court of Poonah to give it's consent to that necessary measure.

These arguments, however, had no weight with Sir John Shore; who thought it more prudent to lose the benefits of an arrangement, which had appeared to his predecessor essential to the security and tranquillity of the possessions of the Allies, than to incur any hazard of giving offence to the Mahrattas, whose jealousy he conceived would be further excited by the formation of any new engagement, which improved or consolidated the alliance between the English Government and the Nizam.

Before I proceed to state those causes, which produced a war between the Nizam and Mahrattas, it will be necessary to take a short view of the temper of those States, towards the British Government, previous to it's commencement. That of the Nizam's Court is fully described in a despatch under date the 1st of January 1794, which Sir John Kennaway, Resident at Hyderabad, addressed to the Governor

General. In this the Resident states his conviction, that the circumstances in which the Court of Hyderabad was then placed, and the character of those by whom it was ruled, were such, as gave us an opportunity, which it was wise and politic to use, to establish an influence and power in it's councils, which would enable us to command it's future exertions, and benefit from it's resources under any events that could occur.

"Should, however," Sir John Kennaway observes in this despatch, "such an alliance, and "the kind of interference above alluded to, be "deemed improper, and the limits to which "it is at present confined be considered as sufficient; the friendship and confidence in us, "which has been so happily established in his "Government, and the reliance which the "Nizam must ultimately place on the Company, for checking any hostile league, which "the Mahrattas may form against the rights or "dignity of his Government, will, I imagine, "prevent his engaging in any measures to our "prejudice, and induce him even to be "guarded in adopting any, of which our very "marked and pointed disapprobation may be "expressed."

The whole of the last political despatch of this distinguished public Officer is conclusive, as to the temper of the Nizam towards the British Government at this period; and shows in the clearest manner the nature of those expectations of aid and support, which he had been led by the whole tenour of Lord Cornwallis's policy to expect from the British Government, in the event of his being exposed to the risk of destruction from an attack of the Mahratta States.

The temper of the Court of Poonah towards the British Government, was not more strongly marked by it's refusal to conclude the guarantee treaty, than by the extreme jealousy, which it showed, of the connexion between the English Government and the Nizam; and the resentment, which it in consequence openly entertained against the latter. The councils of the Paishwah were at this period much swayed by Madhajee Scindiah, who was known to cherish views hostile to the general peace of India, over which it was his avowed ambition to re-establish the Mahratta authority. In a conference, which that Chief had with the agent of the Nizam at Poonah, he did not hesitate to state, in the most public manner, his dislike to the guarantee treaty; and to advise the Nizam not to enter into any such engagement with the British Government; of whose intentions, he said, he entertained the greatest suspicions.

Sir Charles Mallet, in his despatch to the Governor General, under date the 24th of July 1794, states the endeavours which Madhajee Scindiah had made to defeat the negotiations respecting the guarantee engagements. In the same letter he represents Nanah Furnavese to be very averse to the violent councils and language of Scindiah; who (Sir Charles observes) the Minister thinks is desirous of subverting his authority, and establishing his own, as more equal to the task of counteracting the dangerous increase of our power.

Sir Charles states, in a despatch under date the 14th of October 1794, his conviction, that no possible opening should be given to the encroaching spirit of the Court of Poonah; "which," he observes, "notwithstanding our "uniform firmness and candour, throughout "my whole ministry, continues to contem-"plate the mightiness of our power with a "jealousy unwarrantable, but in the conscious-"ness of it's own principles, and it's inability "to give others the credit due to purer mo-"tives."

This opinion respecting the temper of the Court of Poonah, was fully corroborated by every measure adopted by that Government; as well as by the language of those, who influenced it's councils, which is described in several despatches from the Resident, written about this period, to have been of a nature very inimical to the British Government. Madhajee Scindiah is indeed particularly stated to have avowed openly his reliance on Tippoo, as a counterpoise to our increased power.

What I have stated fully proves, that immediately before the occurrence of the rupture between the Nizam and the Mahrattas, the former entertained the most friendly disposition towards the British Government, on the good faith and sincerity of which he was disposed to place every reliance; and that he consequently rejoiced at those events, which had established it's great ascendency in the political scale of the Peninsula of India. Whereas the latter had reviewed the success of the English with alarm; and contemplated the actual state of their power with a degree of jealousy which approximated to hostility.

Under the influence of such feelings, the Mahratta States were likely to seek every opportunity of diminishing our power; and there can be no doubt, that while they saw, in the reduction of the Nizam, an increase to their own power, they contemplated this, as one mode of injuring the British Government, by depriving it of the benefit and strength which it might derive from it's political connexion with that Prince.

It is not necessary to enter into any detail of those grounds in which the quarrel between the Nizam and the Mahrattas originated. The seeds of rupture existed in the nature of their political relations. An unsettled account was always pending between them: the Nizam owed arrears of choute, the amount of which was exaggerated by one party, and perhaps under-estimated by the other. But this was not the only claim to be adjusted. The artful policy of the Mahrattas had taught them to subdue the other Nations of India in the mode best suited to their habits and genius. They did not, like other conquerors, endeavour to establish their authority in an open manner; but commenced by obtaining a cession of a part of the annual revenue of particular provinces; which the indolent and distracted Mahomedan Governments of India were glad to grant to these active freebooters, in the hope of obtaining, by such a concession, an exemption to Countries exposed to their inroads, from their ruinous depredations. But these concessions only generated further demands, and the establishment of other claims, on the part of the Mahrattas. They proceeded to assert their right to collect, through their own Officers, an equal share of the produce of some Provinces, and a duty upon the revenue of others. This vexatious right of interference gave them an influence in the internal management of the Country, supported by the aid of a large and corrupt body of revenue officers.

The mixed nature of this connexion was particularly suited to the character of the Mahratta Nation, which subsisted, as a confederacy of military States, almost entirely by plunder; and as they were, from their constitution, constantly liable to changes of fortune, it became important that they should be able to abandon, at a period of weakness, without any resignation of right, those advantages, which their predecessors had obtained. Hence they have often been known to unite, to enforce the payment of large arrears of claims, which their internal divisions had caused to lie dormant for years.

The Government of the Soubahdar of the Deckan had been a short time completely under their influence. The Nizam's former Minister, Rukeen ud Dowlah, had at one period acted more at their command, than at that of his master;* and the whole adminis-

* The subserviency of that Minister to the views of the Mahrattas, has generally been considered one of the chief causes that induced the Nizam to put him to death.

tration of his successor, Azeem ul Omrah, had been a struggle to emancipate his Government from this thraldom. Events had favoured his endeavours; and before the revival of the alliance with the English Government in 1788, he had succeeded to a considerable extent. But there can be no doubt, that the expectation of accomplishing this favourite object, was one of the principal motives, which led him to advise the Nizam to abandon all those alarms and prejudices, which that Prince had ever entertained of the designs of the British Government; and to seek in it's good faith, and friendship, that powerful aid and support, which, in the actual state of India, was necessary to the security, tranquillity, and independence, of his Government.

Directed by the same principles, which had led him to form the alliance with Marquis Cornwallis, the Nizam most earnestly solicited the interference of the English Government, to prevent those extremities, which he apprehended from the conduct and military preparations of the Mahrattas; and though the chief Officers of his Court acted, upon this occasion, in that weak and undecided manner, which is natural to almost all the natives, there cannot exist a doubt, from the evidence of all that passed upon this subject, that the Nizam would readily have pledged himself to have abided by the decision of the British Government on the dispute between him and the Paishwah; provided he had been assured that State would have adopted measures to make it's decision respected.

The Mahrattas, on the other hand, received the proffered mediation of the English Government, from the first, with evasion and inattention; and from the moment they were fully satisfied that we had no intention of aiding the Nizam, further than by the interposition of our friendly offices, and the expression of our earnest solicitude for an amicable accommodation between the two parties, they treated our interference with a neglect that approached insult.

The Governor General was fully sensible of the serious injury which the interests of the British Government were likely to sustain from a rupture, which might be said to commence in the annihilation of the most important of the political relations, which his predecessor had established, for the security of the British interests in India. He was also aware, that the disputes, which were made the pretext of this rupture, were easy of settlement; and were only a cover to the actual designs of the Mahrattas, which went to the annihilation of the power of the Nizam. "If" (Sir John Shore observed, in a letter under date the 1st of October 1794, to the Resident at Hyderabad) "the Mahrattas should proceed to extremities "against the Nizam, it can only be, I think, "with a resolution to annihilate the independ-"ency of his authority; for, notwithstanding "the sense which they may entertain of their "superiority in the field, I see nothing in the "articles disputed between the two States, as "far as they have appeared, that does not ad-"mit of adjustment; or of sufficient magnitude "to induce them to maintain the rumours of a "war. The preparations of the Nizam are "necessary for his own safety, and may contri-"bute to suspend the Paishwah's resolution."

The death of Madhajee Scindiah, which occurred during this negotiation, was an event most favourable to the effectual interference of the British Government; and the Resident at Poonah expressed his opinion, that advantage might be taken with success of an occasion so propitious to the accomplishment of the object in view. The Governor General was not, however, of opinion, that the smallest risk should be incurred of offending the Poonah State, by any alteration in the course of policy, which had been pursued; and Doulut Row Scindiah, who succeeded his uncle, hastened to assemble his army from the remotest quarters of Hindoostan; equally with a view of strengthening his personal authority, and of giving him an ascendency in the confederacy forming against the Nizam.

Immediately before the occurrence of hostilities between the Mahrattas and the Nizam, an alarm of a very serious nature attracted the attention of the British Government. Tippoo Sultaun, (whose active spirit of hostility against that State had led him to commence intrigues with the French Government, the Court of Hyderabad, and the Court of Poonah, almost at the same moment that the peace of Seringapatam was concluded,) had assembled an army, and threatened to come forward, as an Ally of the Mahrattas, against the Nizam, in the quarrel between those States.

It became, under such circumstances, a question, What part the British Government was to act, in the event of this extraordinary occurrence? and the subject was fully considered by the Governor General, who resolved, on the occurrence of such event, not to aid the Nizam. The leading arguments, which influenced Sir John Shore's mind upon this occasion, merit notice; as they elucidate very fully those principles, by which he judged it his duty to regulate his conduct, in the administration of the political affairs of the great Empire committed to his charge.

It had been before decided, that we should take no part in the existing quarrel between the Nizam and the Mahrattas; as the act of the Legislature prohibited an interference, which would necessarily involve us in hostilities: but, when it appeared probable that Tippoo would act against the Nizam, another question arose; in considering which, the Governor General not only took a view of our engagements, but of the peculiar claims which the Nizam appeared to have on our friendship and protection.

That Prince might urge, he thought, that he was by treaty entitled to the aid of the Company, as well as the Mahrattas, if Tippoo attacked him without just cause or provocation; that the defection of one party could not exonerate the other; and that, so far from being justified in refusing him aid against Tippoo, it was incumbent on us to stand forth, to compel the third party to perform it's stipulations.

The Nizam would, the Governor General knew, assert, that the obligation of assistance, as stated in the treaty, was clear, and admitted of no evasion; that his reliance, in making the treaty, was upon our good faith, not upon that of the Mahrattas, whose treachery he well knew, and of whom he had intimated his suspicions during the preliminary negotiations; that at the period we sought his alliance the connexion was so essential to our interests, that we must, if he had insisted upon it, have entered into an offensive and defensive engagement in general terms; and that if we considered ourselves at liberty to renounce the performance of our stipulations, because the Mahrattas had violated their engagements, or for other reasons of convenience or policy; there was an end to that faith, which is the basis of treaties, as such pretext could never be wanting, to authorize a departure from the most solemn obligations.

Tippoo's aggression, the Nizam would state, must be with or without the concurrence of the Mahrattas; and in either case we ought to oppose it; but more particularly if that Prince took the field as the Ally of the Paishwah; as that would be a direct and insulting violation of the treaty, which we were bound by every consideration of duty and honour to resent.

The Governor General, on the other hand, conceived that the treaty, on which the Nizam's claims to aid were grounded, was a tripartite engagement, which supposed a continued union between the three allied Powers: that such union was essential to it's continuance in any shape, because it was essential to the performance of the obligations imposed by it; and a war between two of the parties, therefore, totally changed the relations of all.

A junction between Tippoo and one of the two parties to the treaty, was, Sir John Shore thought, to be judged with reference to the causes of hostilities between the two parties; and supposing that the injustice of the war between the Mahrattas and the Nizam was decidedly on one side, and that the other was compelled by unprovoked aggression, self-preservation would justify an alliance between the aggrieved party and Tippoo; but a confederacy between him and one of the parties to the triple alliance, grounded on ambitious motives against another party, would no doubt be a gross infraction of the treaty by that State confederating with Tippoo. The inference from this reasoning, the Governor General thought, was rather against the Nizam, whose advance to Beder was, if not an aggression, certainly with a view of interfering in the internal affairs of the Mahratta Government; all the bad consequences of which had been repeatedly, though ineffectually, stated by the British Resident to the Minister at the Court of Hyderabad.

Should the English Government support the Nizam against Tippoo, if the latter seized the opportunity of a war between the former and the Mahrattas, to attack his Country without provocation, that Nation would necessarily be involved in a war with the Mahrattas; a predicament never supposed in the triple alliance. The stipulations of that alliance, which bound the English Government not to aid the enemies of either State, seemed to impose a strict neutrality on that Government, when these Powers were at war with each other; as such war was in fact a temporary subversion of the principles of the alliance. The arguments, which represented the treaty of Paungul as a separate treaty; or that the secession of one party did not release the other, because it is not so expressed in that treaty; were, Sir John Shore thought, quite inadmissible. The alliance was, he conceived, one formed by three parties, not two, and to be maintained by their joint efforts: and not to admit, that the secession of one party released the whole, required, in his opinion, more than ever the treaty intended, as it involved the necessity, or, at all events, the risk of a war with one of the parties to it; a case, which the treaty never supposed; and which is, indeed, contrary to that presumption upon which all it's stipulations are founded.

Though the occurrence of war had suspended the operation of this alliance; the return of peace would, in the Governor General's opinion, restore it to it's former footing: and it was his intention, if Tippoo attacked either the Nizam or the Mahrattas, while at war with each other, to call upon the third party to perform his stipulations. Such a call might, he conceived, induce the two parties at war to make peace; or, at all events, would show whether Tippoo's attack was in concert with one of the Allies, and establish a direct breach of the treaty against that Ally, who refused his aid in defence of the party attacked, and leave the English Government at liberty to act as it thought proper. But the Governor General did not conceive that State bound to assist either party, unless peace was previously concluded between the Mahrattas and the Nizam.

The Governor General did not expect the Nizam would ever yield his conviction to those arguments, which had satisfied his own mind upon this question. That Prince would, on the contrary, he thought, be inclined to view our neutrality as a desertion of his cause, which ill repayed his co-operation with us, and his anxiety to unite with us by the closest ties: and he concluded, from the above impression being made upon the mind of the Nizam, and from his political character, that, on the occurrence of the event alluded to, he would be likely to become in future an enemy to the British Government.

It was obvious to the Governor General, at this period, that the Nizam, unsupported by the English Government, must sink under the combined attack of the Mahrattas and Tippoo, who would become more dangerous than ever to that State by this change. But when he contemplated the difficulties, which presented themselves, from the vices of the Nizam's Administration; the impossibility of directing his politics, without usurping his Government; the difficulty of making any impression upon the Mahrattas; the comparative facility with which they could injure the British Government; the magnitude of the resources and number of troops necessary to oppose the Mahrattas and Tippoo; and the inevitable ruin of a long protracted war; he thought the inducement to support the Nizam, at the hazard of such impending consequences, ought to be much stronger, than the apprehension of future evils, from the subversion of his power.

In the event, however, of the Nizam's power being annihilated, by a combination of Tippoo and the Mahrattas, the Governor General thought there was as great a probability of their attacking each other, as of their uniting in an invasion of the frontiers of the Company. Our political consequence might, he conceived, lose something of it's importance in the estimate of the native Powers, by leaving the Nizam to his fate; but, although fully aware of the great value of opinion to the British Government in India, he did not think it was on this occasion to be put in competition with the greater evils attending a war with Tippoo and the Mahrattas, which he believed would be the certain consequence of supporting singly the Nizam against Tippoo, if that Prince should attack him whilst engaged in hostility with the Paishwah.

The Governor General appears to have been very sensible to the loss of reputation at this moment; as he justly conceived that the conduct of the British Government, in resenting the attack upon it's Ally, the Rajah of Travancore, and the character of the negotiation by which the war with Tippoo was terminated, had gained us the confidence of our Allies, and established the British reputation throughout India, for good faith, firmness, and moderation. But while Sir John Shore acknowledged the advantage of such impression, he conceived it more necessary to attend to considerations of self-preservation.

Such is a short statement of that reasoning, on which the Governor General concluded, that the British Government was neither bound by obligations of faith, nor considerations of political expediency, to support and defend it's Ally, the Soubahdar of the Deckan, in the event of his being attacked by Tippoo during the period when he was engaged in a war with the Mahrattas. Fortunately for the English Government, the speedy termination of the war between the Mahrattas and the Nizam, and the occupation of the Sultaun in his own Country, prevented the occurrence of the event, which was dreaded; and saved the British Nation from that great loss of reputation, and the many alarming evils, to which the Governor General foresaw it would be exposed; but which he deemed it better to incur, than to encounter the numerous difficulties, which he thought would attend a different line of action. Among these he considered a war, as one that was inevitable. But it may be doubted whether a war would have been the inevitable result of a more spirited and manly course of policy. There indeed appears every ground to conclude, that while those impressions, which had been made on all the native Powers of India, by the wise councils and military success of the Marquis Cornwallis, were yet in full force, the decided interference of the British Government would have deterred either the Mahrattas, or the Sultaun, from an attack upon the Nizam.

The Governor General thought, at this period, that whether the disputes between the

Nizam and Mahrattas were terminated by war or negotiation, they would end in the subjection of the power of the former to the latter; and, consequently, bring a great accession of strength to the Mahrattas, whose power he thought even then exorbitant. The Nizam must, he conceived, when he despaired of the support of the British Government, court the alliance of Tippoo; but their union he deemed impracticable: and he thought, that if the Sultaun attacked the Nizam without previous concert with the Mahrattas, that the latter would make their own terms with the Court of Hyderabad, and then unite with the English Government, to defend it's territories from the attack of Tippoo.

Though the weakness of the Nizam might offer a temptation to Tippoo, the subversion of the British Power, the Governor General concluded, was the great object of that Prince: and as he conceived the aid of the Nizam would not enable us to hold the balance of India, he thought the confirmation of our alliance with the Mahrattas was an object of the first importance; as, with their aid, we might always oppose Tippoo, or any European Power.

Sir John Shore expressed, at this period, his full conviction, that the only means of maintaining tranquillity, was to have our military establishment on so respectable a footing, as to impose peace upon our neighbours. This was, he thought, the wisest as well as most economical system. He appears also to have strongly felt (as Lord Cornwallis had done before) the injury and danger to which our interests might eventually be exposed, from the operation of the restrictions of the act of 1793, with regard to our alliances with the native States of India.

The clause of that act, which forbids us from declaring war, or commencing hostilities; except where hostilities have actually been commenced, or preparations made for their commencement, against the British Government; was, the Governor General conceived, in it's literal construction, decisive against any interference on our part, in favour of the Nizam, if attacked by Tippoo without the co-operation of the Mahrattas; and the circumstances of the case confirmed, he thought, this construction, in point of expediency. But he considered it very possible, without any view to the extension of our dominions, that a case might arise, in which the security of our possessions might be best consulted, at the risk and even certainty of hostilities, by taking part with one State against another: and the question was, Whether we should be justified in such a determination, where we are not bound by treaty to defend or guarantee a State, which it might, under such circumstances, be expedient to assist?

From the above short abstract of Sir John Shore's recorded sentiments upon this important question, it appears, that he had resolved to abandon the Nizam to the resentment of Tippoo Sultaun, on the ground of such a measure being, in his opinion, defensible in point of faith; expedient in point of policy; and conformable to the letter of the Act of the Legislature, for the better government of our possessions in India. He conceived, that the English Government would be fully justified in their abandonment of the cause of that Prince, as long as he was involved in a war with the Mahrattas; because the latter State was one of the parties to the triple alliance: or, in other words, that if Tippoo succeeded in the hostile design, which the Governor General believed him to entertain, of fomenting a disunion among the Allies, and entered into a league with the Mahrattas, (which formed, on their part, a complete breach of the triple alliance,) the English Government was thereby emancipated from all obligation to fulfil it's treaty with the Nizam, who had faithfully performed the conditions of an alliance, which had been negotiated (as stated by the Governor General) upon the admitted principle of his entire reliance on the good faith of the British Nation, and of his expressed conviction of the treachery of the Mahrattas.

The Governor General appears also to have been contented to sacrifice, upon this occasion, part of that high reputation and character, which the conduct of his immediate predecessor had obtained to the British Government in India; provided he could, by such sacrifice, secure immediate exemption from the difficulties and dangers to which, he thought, the State might be exposed by a more spirited and decided course of action.

One of the chief causes, which made the Governor General determine not to aid the Nizam, was the existence of that weakness in his Administration, and need of support, which three years before had been considered as the just and legitimate motive, which induced that Prince to seek and cultivate the connexion with the British Government.

The Governor General appears also to have been swayed by a hope, that he should in some degree disarm the hostile jealousy of the Mahrattas, by not supporting the Nizam, against whom it was obvious their resentment had been particularly excited, by the relations of friendship which that Prince had recently contracted with the English Government; and under the great and alarming political changes, which he foresaw would result from the destruction of the Nizam's power, he found a consolation in the possibility of a subsequent rupture between Tippoo and the Mahrattas, and in the hope that the latter (whose power he states to be already exorbitant) would find an occupation more immediately inviting, than an attack upon the British territories, in the consolidation of their vast power by the final subjection and reduction of the few petty States, which continued to resist their authority in Hindoostan.

He conceived that the literal construction of the Act of Parliament was, under his interpretation of the guarantee treaty, decidedly against the British Government aiding the Nizam, if attacked by Tippoo, while at war with the Mahrattas; and that the circumstances of the case were such, as to confirm the construction in point of expediency.

This conclusion, it is to be observed, was formed, after assuming that defection of one party from a triple offensive and defensive alliance, and it's actual union with that very Power against whom the alliance was originally formed, for the purpose of attacking one of the other parties of the alliance, cancelled the obligation of the remaining party, and gave it a right to remain neuter. But allowing this general position to be correct, it was hardly applicable to the particular case under discussion. For the Nizam, the party with whom it was argued, that the engagements of the English Government had become invalid, or rather dormant, by the secession of the Mahrattas, had (as I have before mentioned) concluded the treaty, which bound him to the triple alliance, on the declared principle of placing his sole dependence upon the faith of the British Government. He both entertained and expressed fears, at the very moment of signing the treaty, of the hostile and treacherous designs of the Mahrattas: and these fears were only removed by repeated and solemn assurances of the permanent friendship of the British Government.

Marquis Cornwallis declared, in his letter under date the 28th of February 1790, to the Resident at Poonah, that the Mahratta State, by acting against Tippoo in concert with the British Government, became entitled, in reason and equity, to a defensive alliance against that Prince, even though no previous engagement existed. This declaration sufficiently showed the sense, which that nobleman entertained of the obligations, which the mere act of aid, during hostilities, (independent of formal engagement,) imposed upon the British Government. He was fully sensible, that we owed our power in India to that reputation, which led the most perfidious Nations to rely with confidence upon the verbal assurances of our Representatives; and to consider, that in espousing our cause in any war in which we were engaged, they established a right, that nothing but their own misconduct could ever forfeit, to our future friendship, and to our protection against any Power whom they had offended by their exertions in our favour.

Sir John Shore, however, was fully aware of the reproaches which the line of conduct, that he proposed to pursue, might draw upon the British Government; and the loss of reputation and political consequence, which that State would sustain, by abandoning the Nizam. But though he declared himself fully sensible of the value of opinion in India, he did not "think it "could be placed" (on this occasion) "in com-"petition with the greater evils, which he "thought likely to attend a war with the "Mahrattas and Tippoo Sultaun." It may appear difficult to fix the nature or extent of the exertions, which a State would be warranted in making upon any occasion, to maintain it's reputation and character; because those are qualities, of which the precise value can never be ascertained: but the history of every Nation in the Universe sufficiently proves that they have been always most cherished by States, which were rising, or in the zenith of their power; and only neglected by those which were on their decline, or on the eve of dissolution. If this rule be just, with regard to States in general, how much more must it apply to that extraordinary Empire, which the British Nation has founded in the East! For there can be no doubt that Empire is held solely by opinion; or, in other words, by that respect and awe with which the comparative superiority of our knowledge, justice, and system of rule, have inspired the inhabitants of our own territories; and that confidence in our truth, reliance on our faith, and dread of our arms, which is impressed on every Nation in India.

These feelings are in the first place to be ascribed to that wretched and oppressive rule, from which the introduction of our power relieved our present subjects; and to the comparative tranquillity and happiness, which they enjoy under our dominion: and, in the second, to those principles of falsehood and treachery, which mark the intercourse of the native States of India with each other, and which make each of these, in their turn, anxious to cultivate the friendship of a Nation, which, though different in religion, in usages and in language, has maintained a character for faith and courage, which gives the highest value to it's friendship.

Assuredly, if this view of our situation be just, we can contemplate no danger so great, as that, which hazards the smallest diminution of that reputation, upon which the British Empire in the East is grounded.

The best criterion, however, of every system of policy, is it's result: and I shall now proceed to examine those events, which were produced by the course that the British Government on this occasion adopted towards the Government of Hyderabad.

In February 1795, a war between the Mahrattas and the Nizam became certain; and the advanced corps of the army of the former, under the command of Dowlut Row Scindiah, marched towards the Nizam; and on the 11th of March attacked that Prince, who had advanced from Beder (where he had been long encamped) to meet him. After a general action, in which both parties were thrown into some confusion, and neither obtained any decided advantage; the Nizam, carried away by the fears of his women, who attended him in the action, retreated during the night of the 11th, and took shelter in the small fort of Kurdlah. This fort is completely surrounded with hills, except on one part, which the Mahrattas immediately occupied; and by that means completely hemmed in his army, and cut it off from all supplies.

After remaining for some weeks in this situation, the Nizam was obliged to conclude a peace, the exact particulars of which were not known; but, independently of the full admission of all the former claims of the Mahrattas, as established by the treaty of Edghire, it was understood, that the Nizam agreed, by the convention of Kurdlah, to cede to his enemies a Country of about thirty-five lacks of rupees in annual revenue, including the fort and district of Doulutabad, and to pay them three crores of rupees, one-third paid immediately, and the remainder of this amount in annual instalments of twenty-five lacks. To these conditions were added one still more disgraceful, the delivery of his Prime Minister, Azeem ul Omrah, into the hands of the Mahrattas, as a hostage for the faithful performance of his engagements.

After the convention of Kurdlah was settled, the Nizam returned to Hyderabad; and the Mahratta confederates marched toward their respective countries; which they had hardly reached, when two unexpected events occurred—the sudden death of the young Paishwah, Madhoo Row, and the rebellion of Ally Jah, the eldest son of the Nizam. These two events conspired, in their effects, to revive the lost influence of the British Government at the Court of Hyderabad, and to restore the Nizam to his former consequence among the Powers of the Peninsula.

It is only necessary to my object to take a very cursory and general view of these events. I shall commence with that, which was of most consequence to the British Government, as it prevented the entire dissolution of the connexion established between that State and the Court of the Soubahdar of the Deckan.

The Nizam, when encamped at Beder, had shown great anxiety, that the two battalions, which he subsidized from the English Government, should join his camp. But a compliance with this wish was evaded, as it was thought their junction would give offence to the Mahrattas. It was, however, afterwards so arranged, that while the Nizam continued at war with the Mahrattas, the English battalions should be employed in preserving the tranquillity of his dominions.

After the Nizam returned to Hyderabad, he intimated his desire to dispense with the service of the two English battalions; and that corps, in consequence, marched to the territories of the Company.

The same feeling of resentment towards the British Nation, which dictated this measure, also led him to pay the greatest attention at this period to the increase and improvement of the large body of regular infantry in his service, which was commanded by French Officers. Their representations (it is stated in several of the despatches from the Resident) were at this time artfully directed to impress the Nizam with an exaggerated belief of the successes, which had attended the French arms in Europe. This corps, commanded by Monsieur Raymond, which had only consisted of two battalions in 1792, was augmented after the conclusion of the peace of Seringapatam; and no less a body, than twenty-three battalions, with twelve field-pieces, is stated by the Resident to have accompanied the Nizam in the campaign against the Mahrattas. After the return of that Prince to his capital, he not only ordered considerable new levies for this corps, but gave great power into the hands of it's Commander, by a large grant of territory for it's regular payment.

The British Resident endeavoured to make the Court of Hyderabad sensible of the dangers, which might eventually result from this measure; but little attention was given to him: and his remonstrances against the measure of sending a considerable part of this force to occupy the districts of Kurpah and Cummum, which were immediately upon the frontier of the Company's possessions, were equally disregarded.

This last measure appears to have occasioned much uneasiness to the Governor General, whose apprehensions of it's possible consequences were strongly stated in his minute upon the subject, under date the 15th of June 1795.

"The determination of the Nizam," he observes, "to depute a part of Monsieur Raymond's corps towards Kurpah, near the frontiers of the British possessions, requires, in my opinion, more serious opposition, than has been made to it by the Resident at Hyderabad. The measure itself has a suspicious, not to say criminal appearance: and although we may acquit the Nizam of any hostile designs against the Company, and should certainly avoid imputing them to him, I can entertain little doubt of the disposition of Monsieur Raymond and the Officers of his corps, to co-operate with the French in any attempts upon the Northern Sircars. Such an attempt may not be pro-

" bable; but as it would, if carried into execu-
" tion, be attended with very serious conse-
" quences to the British possessions in India,
" the strongest representations ought to be
" made, to induce the Nizam to recall the
" detachment of Monsieur Raymond."

In a letter to the Nizam upon this subject, Sir John Shore adverted in a general manner to the consequences, which might result from placing a force in such a position, under the command of men, who were the declared enemies of the British Government, and requested him to withdraw them. But, in the instructions to the Resident, he directed a more decided language to be used to that Prince. After stating the arguments, which the Resident was to use, to endeavour to prevail upon the Nizam to recall the detachment of Raymond's corps, he concluded by the following instructions:

" These arguments, urged in firm, but mode-
" rate and conciliatory language, will, I hope,
" prevail on the Nizam to comply with my
" wishes and request, in the recall of the
" detachment. I deem this a point of the
" first importance; but, if he should still per-
" sist in his determination to continue it at
" Kurpah, you will adopt the language of re-
" monstrance; and ultimately acquaint him,

" that I shall, in this event, be compelled, with " whatever reluctance, to advance a body of " troops towards our frontier."

A correspondence appears at this time to have been established between Raymond and several of the French Officers (prisoners of war) at Pondicherry; and nothing but the great vigilance of Lord Hobart, who then presided over the Madras Government, prevented his being joined by a number of them, who were apprehended at the moment when they meant to effect their escape.

The dismissal of the English subsidiary force; the increase of Raymond's corps; the detachment of a part of that corps to the frontier of the Company, in opposition to the remonstrance of the British Representative; combined to prove, that the influence, which had been established in the Nizam's councils by the wise and spirited policy of Lord Cornwallis, was entirely lost; and that the English Government not only could place no dependence upon the aid of that Prince; but had just reason to apprehend, that his resources might be early directed against the Company's possessions, either from the prevailing power of a French faction, the complete subjection of his Country to the Mahrattas, or his throwing himself, to escape that extreme, into the hands of the irreconcileable enemy of the English, Tippoo Sultaun, who was most active at this period in his intrigues to effect this object, which too well combined with the obvious views of the rising French interest in the Deckan.

These consequences, which threatened to be the inevitable result of the policy, which had been pursued, were fortunately averted by one of the events to which I have before alluded, the rebellion of Ally Jah. The flight of that Prince, which took place on the 28th of June, may be truly said to have saved the British Government from the serious evils to which it was on this occasion exposed.

The Nizam, alarmed by the flight and rebellion of his son, pressed the instant return of the English subsidiary force to Hyderabad; agreed to the recall of the detachment of Raymond's corps from Kurpah; and took every step, which could obtain him, at so critical a moment, the aid and support of a Nation, whose friendship he had so recently slighted.

The English Government had become, from a very short experience, fully sensible of the importance of this accident to it's interests. The battalions were directed to march to the Nizam's territory with every possible expedition; and they were already advancing to join the army acting against Ally Jah, when accounts were received of the defeat and capture of that Prince; whose death, soon after he was made prisoner, relieved the Nizam from those fears, which this rebellion had excited.

The advantage derived on this occasion from the countenance and support of the British Government, was fully recognised by the Nizam; and that Prince must have become more convinced of the value of the aid of the subsidiary force, from the activity and gallantry which it displayed, in March 1796, under it's able Commander, Captain James Dalrymple, in the reduction of the fort of Rachore; and the defeat of a large body of troops, who had, under the banners of the son of Darah Jah (the nephew of the Nizam), rebelled against the authority of that Prince.

But, however satisfied the Nizam might have been of the utility of the English force, in preserving the internal tranquillity of his Country, he had learnt from experience, that he could not hope for their support, in the case of any attack being made upon his dominions by those enemies, whose aggressions and rapacity he most dreaded; and his chief attention was in consequence bestowed on a rival corps, on whom he thought he could, on such an occurrence, depend. The battalions under Monsieur Raymond had acquired increased reputation by the active part, which they took in the reduction of Ally Jah. Their numbers and appointments were increased: additional lands were given over to their Commander, to insure their regular payment; arsenals and founderies were formed for their equipment; and, in short, every effort was made, which could add to the strength and stability of this favourite body of troops.

The ability of M. Raymond took advantage of this favourable disposition in the Prince whom he served. He made every effort to improve the discipline of his corps, and to strengthen himself by connexions with the chief Officers of the Court. This hostile spirit, and that of all his Officers, against the English Government, was displayed on every occasion. His battalions carried the colours of the French republic (then at war with England); and the cap of liberty was engraven on the buttons of their clothing: he encouraged desertion from the native corps in the English service; and, through the intrigues of his Officers, who commanded the detachment of his corps, which was stationed for a period on the British frontier, a partial mutiny was excited in a battalion of Sepoys on the Madras Establishment; and two native commissioned Officers, accompanied by a number of men, went over to the French party.

From this statement it is evident, even after the return of the English battalions, and the apparent re-establishment of confidence between the Company's Government and the Nizam, that the English corps was only retained for a period in the Deckan, from considerations of convenience; while the actual power and resources of the Nizam's Government were passing rapidly into the hands of a French faction, whose views (which it took no pains to conceal) were decidedly hostile to the British Government.

The Nizam was not insensible to the danger, which might result from the power, that necessity had forced him to place in the hands of this French party; and he continued to solicit that the British Government would enter into such engagements with him, as would prevent the necessity of his having recourse to such dangerous means of defence. To obtain this object, he offered to dismiss the French corps as soon as the British detachment in his service was increased. But the conditions on which he wished to make this arrangement, were thought by Sir John Shore to be incompatible with our engagements with the Mahrattas; and no decisive steps were taken.

The expedient of introducing English adventurers into the service of the Nizam, was tried at this period: but these, though indirectly supported by the British Resident, made little progress; and their corps never obtained a footing which afforded the least prospect of their rivalling that of Raymond; whose activity, and spirit of hostility, were naturally excited, by these inefficient attempts, on the part of the English Government, to reduce his power and influence.

The death of the young Paishwah, Madhoo Row, which I have before mentioned, contributed to restore to the Nizam, beyond every hope that could have been indulged, a part of that power and rank among the States of India, which he had lost by the disgraceful convention of Kurdlah.

This event, which occurred on the 27th of October 1795, occasioned the most serious divisions among the Mahratta Chiefs, whose interests were deeply involved in the succession. Nanah Furnavese, the principal Minister at Poonah, desired to place an infant, remotely connected with the family of the Paishwah, upon the Musnud, to the exclusion of the legitimate heir, Badjerow, the son of Ragobah, who was the paternal uncle of the deceased Paishwah. This plan was opposed by the agent of Doulut Row Scindiah: and that Chief, on receiving the account of the death of the Paishwah, prepared to march to Poonah, to support the cause of Badjerow, which he had determined to espouse. Under such circumstances, Nanah Furnavese endeavoured to add to his strength, by gaining the support of the Government of the Nizam; and for this purpose he released Azeem ul Omrah, and entered into a negotiation with that Minister, which terminated in a treaty, by which Nanah Furnavese resigned, on the part of the Poonah State, all those great cessions, which had been obtained from the Nizam by the convention of Kurdlah.

Azeem ul Omrah had artfully managed, at different periods during the course of this negotiation, to draw large bodies of troops from the Nizam's territories, to support the influence which he had established at Poonah; and to enable him to return to Hyderabad. But his views were in some degree frustrated by the arrival of Doulut Row Scindiah with a force, which gave him a decided ascendency; and enabled him to place Badjerow, whose just claim he supported, upon the vacant throne.

This change occasioned a new negotiation with Azeem ul Omrah, which terminated in his agreeing, on the part of the Nizam, to cede one-fourth of the territory, and to pay one-fourth part of the amount, fixed by the convention of Kurdlah. After this settlement was concluded, which, though much less favourable than that made with Nanah, was still highly advantageous to the Nizam, he obtained permission to return to Hyderabad; where he reassumed, upon his arrival, his office of Prime Minister.

The success, which attended Doulut Row Scindiah upon this occasion, established his ascendency in the Mahratta Empire. He soon afterwards made Nanah Furnavese prisoner; and the Minister only regained his liberty by the payment of a large sum, and an acquiescence in every measure which Scindiah thought necessary to establish his power. This was greatly augmented at this period by the death of the rival of his family, Tuckojee Holkar, most of whose possessions he usurped, after putting to death his eldest son, and making prisoners the other members of his family.

In addition to these usurpations, Doulut Row forced the Paishwah to cede to him the important fortress of Ahmednuggur and it's surrounding district; by which cession he not only obtained the command of the city of Poonah, but the best entrance into either the territories of the Paishwah, or the Soubahdar of the Deckan.

The extraordinary power, which Doulut Row Scindiah had obtained at this period, was rendered more alarming to the British Government, from the nature and constitution of that force of regular infantry by which it had been raised and established.

The command of that large corps, which General Deboigne had originally formed for Madhajee Scindiah, had devolved upon General Perron. The youthful ambition of Doulut Row Scindiah led him to take every step to render more efficient a force, which gave him so decided a superiority over the other native Powers of India. The principal European Officers were stimulated to exertion by every motive which could awaken avarice or excite ambition. The Officers of subordinate rank had adequate allowances regularly paid: and the men were not only well paid, but, by an arrangement, which had been effected by the influence and power of their European Commanders, they became entitled, when disabled by wounds or length of service, to retire on a pension establishment, formed on principles every way congenial to their habits.

Almost the whole of that part of Hindoostan, which had been subdued by Scindiah, as well as the realization of his claims upon the Rajpoot States, was intrusted by that Chief to the management of the French General, who commanded his infantry.

This corps, independently of several separate bodies of infantry, that acted with it, already amounted to several regular brigades. It was chiefly recruited from the Company's Provinces; clothed and armed like English Sepoys; had a numerous train of artillery, admirably equipped, and a considerable body of cavalry attached to them.

They were, from their strength, discipline and union, decidedly superior to all the rest of Scindiah's army; and their leader had become, in a great degree, independent of the authority of that Chief. There was therefore just reason to apprehend that Scindiah might be obliged (even if his avowed jealousy of the English should not incline him) to adopt, at a future period, any hostile projects, which this French party might cherish against the prosperity of the British Government.

There was, during the Administration of Sir John Shore, but little intercourse with Tippoo Sultaun. The two sons of that Prince, who had been given as hostages for the faithful performance of the treaty of Seringapatam, were conducted to Mysore, when that engagement was fulfilled. Tippoo received the Officer by whom they were conducted, with cold and constrained civility; and gave him no encouragement to make those overtures towards a more cordial union, which he had been authorized to do, if he found that Prince disposed to cultivate the friendship of the British Nation.

Tippoo Sultaun acted, upon this occasion, (as on every other,) in a manner, which showed that he entertained the most hostile sentiments towards the English Government; and that he only waited for a favourable opportunity of attacking it's power, which he thought he should be best able to do, by previously possessing himself, either by negotiation or war, of the resources of the Deckan.

To this object, his readiness to unite with the Mahrattas; his threatened attack of Karnoul; his assembling of a large force at Gooty in 1796; his intrigues with the nephew of the Nizam, Imteaz u Dowlah, when Azeem ul Omrah was confined at Poonah; and his active correspondence with Monsieur Raymond at the same period; may be all ascribed. Fortunately the revolution at Poonah, and the rebellion of Ally Jah, by restoring Azeem ul Omrah to power, and reviving the English connexion at Hyderabad, frustrated his designs.

Before I conclude this Sketch of the Political Administration of Sir John Shore, it will be necessary to refer to the principal events, which took place, during the period of his Government, at the Courts of the Nabob of the Carnatic and the Vizier of Oude; at both of which, changes of some importance occurred.

The unhappy operation of the treaty concluded by Lord Cornwallis with the Nabob of the Carnatic, has been already stated. No attempt was made, during the life of his Highness Mahomed Ally Khan, with whom it had been concluded, to modify this treaty. Upon his death, however, which happened on the 13th of October 1795, Lord Hobart, Governor of Fort St. George, thought it his duty to endeavour to effect a modification of the treaty of 1792, with his successor Omdut ul Omrah. His Lordship states, in his letter of the 25th of October to the Governor General in Council, that he had opened a negotiation for that purpose, in consequence of several communications, which he had with Lord Cornwallis and Mr. Dundas, previously to his leaving England, upon the subject of the advantages, which must arise from an alteration of the treaty of 1792: and he states, in the same despatch, as his reason for not delaying this negotiation till he heard from the Supreme Government, the active intrigues of those, who, from motives of personal interest, endeavoured to persuade Omdut ul Omrah to make no change whatever in the treaty. His Lordship concludes this letter by stating his concern, that his efforts have been unsuccessful; but he expresses his hope, that the representations, which he has made to England, will produce instructions, to put an end to a system (which he considers) "destructive to the resources of the Carnatic, and "which" (he thinks) "in some degree reflects "disgrace upon the British Government."

The modifications of the treaty of 1792, which Lord Hobart wished to effect with Omdut ul Omrah, were the entire cession to the Company of the Countries mortgaged for the regular payment of the pecuniary instalments: the cession of the right of sovereignty over the Poligars, which the Nabob retained, though the collection of the tribute from these Poligars had been made over to the Company: and the cession of some of the forts in the Carnatic.

The first of those conditions, his Lordship conceived, would be attended with equal benefit to the Nabob and the Company, as it would effectually release the former from the necessity of applying to those usurers, by whom his Country had been ruined. It was also likely to prevent every future subject of irritation between the two States; and, finally, to save the Countries ceded from a system of oppression and extortion, which had already greatly diminished their population; and which threatened to make them at a very early period inadequate, from their decrease of value, to that security for which they had been originally pledged.

The second condition required the cession of little more than a nominal power on the part of the Nabob; but it was essential to the Company, the exercise of whose authority over the turbulent Poligars had been much thwarted and obstructed by the name of sovereignty ever remaining with the Nabob. The third condition required the cession to the Company of some forts, the possession of which was at that period judged essential, to place the Carnatic in a proper state of defence; and the suspicious conduct of Tippoo Sultaun rendered this requisition, at the moment it was made, an object of some importance.

Lord Hobart offered considerable sacrifices to the Nabob, with a view to prevail upon him to acquiesce in this arrangement; but in vain: Omdut ul Omrah gave an unqualified refusal to all his propositions; and, in answer to the numerous arguments by which they were recommended to his attention, he only stated his immovable determination to abide by Lord Cornwallis's treaty, which he declared he had been directed to do by the most sacred of all commands, " the dying injunctions of his father."

Lord Hobart, in his minute under date the 4th of December 1795, conveys in very strong language his opinion of the total failure of the treaty of 1792. " If we look back," his Lordship observes, " to the origin of the treaty of " 1792, we shall find that it arose from the " representations of the Nabob Wallajah; that " without imposing burthens upon his people, " which they were not able to bear, he could " not make the payments to the Company sti- " pulated for in the treaty of 1787; but he had " no sooner prevailed upon the Government to " acquiesce in a reduction of those payments, " which he effected by the treaty of 1792, " than, by the manner in which he carried the " provisions of it into execution, he increased " the miseries of his people tenfold, and de- " feated every humane and salutary object it " was intended to attain.

" Under existing circumstances, the Com- " pany sustain no loss, except in the extinction " of the inhabitants of the Carnatic; but in the " arduous season of war they must experience " the most fatal defalcations.

" It has been," his Lordship adds, " with the

" deepest regret, that I have found the Nabob " unmoved by my entreaties and remonstrances " upon this subject: not that he has been insen- " sible to the justice and expediency of what I " have proposed, but, as he has candidly con- " fessed at several interviews with me, that he " has not the resolution to comply; informing " me, that his native Ministers, and European " advisers, so perplexed, plagued, and intimi- " dated him, that he could not venture upon " this measure, notwithstanding his conviction " that he ought to do so."

The Supreme Government, as soon as they received accounts of the death of the Nabob Mahomed Ally Khan, and before the receipt of Lord Hobart's letter, had sent instructions to the Government of Fort St. George, under date the 28th of October 1795, to endeavour to obtain the acquiescence of Omdut ul Omrah to the complete cession of all his territories to the Company.

They state in this despatch, that their sentiments entirely correspond with those, which had been expressed by Lord Cornwallis in his letter to the Court of Directors of the 9th of July 1793, in which his Lordship declares his conviction, that the disadvantage and danger arising from the separation of the internal

Government and management of the revenue of the Country, from the responsibility for it's defence, was so obvious, that, could he have indulged the slightest hope of the Nabob's consent, he would have proposed to him an arrangement, which would have vested the Company with the entire management of the Carnatic; under a condition to pay to the Nabob a liberal portion of it's revenues: and this plan, Lord Cornwallis had stated his full belief, was the one best calculated to promote the real interests of the Nabob, and the comfort and happiness of the inhabitants of the Carnatic.

The Supreme Government concluded this despatch by an expression of their own opinion of the great importance of this object. "Whe-" ther the difficulties stated by Lord Cornwal-" lis," they observe, "still exist in a degree to" preclude any negotiation for accomplishing" the arrangement pointed out, your Lordship" in Council must determine; but if there can" be any probability of obtaining the Nabob's" acquiescence to it, we have only to express" our wishes, that it may be attempted; and" our fullest conviction of the acknowledg-" ments, which will be due to your Lordship's" ability and address, in effecting an arrange-" ment of so much importance to the prospe-

"rity of the Country, the interests of the "Company, and the real happiness of the "Nabob."

When the Supreme Government received information of the steps taken by Lord Hobart, they approved fully of the modifications of the treaty of 1792, which that nobleman had proposed to Omdut ul Omrah, which were indeed of a much more limited nature, than the arrangement which they had recommended; and they directed, in their letter to Fort St. George, under date the 30th of November 1795, that the modifications should be again offered to his Highness's consideration, as they thought it possible he might be more inclined to comply with them, from observing so complete a concurrence of sentiment upon this subject between the two Governments.

The Supreme Government, in a subsequent part of this despatch, state their opinion, that the assumption of the district of Tinnevelly for the liquidation of a debt (termed the *cavalry loan*) due by the Nabob to the Company, and the requisition of the forts in the Carnatic, both of which measures had been suggested by the Government of Fort St. George, would be considered by the Nabob as an indirect mode of compelling his consent to the modifications of the treaty of 1792, and consequently an infraction of that engagement: and as they did not consider the English Government had any right, under the treaty of 1792, to assume any of the Nabob's territory on account of the above loan, which was not mentioned in that treaty; and as the case had not occurred, in which the forts in question, as specified in Lord Cornwallis's letter, were to be garrisoned by the Company's troops; it was their opinion, that neither of these measures should be attempted.

Sir John Shore addressed Omdut ul Omrah upon this occasion; and pointed out to that Prince how much he would promote his own interests, and those of the Company, by a compliance with the propositions, which had been made to him by Lord Hobart.

The exertions of the Governor General upon this occasion were, however, altogether unsuccessful. The Nabob persisted in refusing his consent to any modification whatever of the treaty of 1792; and he continued, under that treaty, to deliver over one district after another of his unhappy Country, into the hands of those usurers and extortioners, who excited him to this opposition to the wishes of the English Government, while they supplied him, at an enormous interest, with those sums which were necessary to fulfil punctually his pecuniary engagements with that State.

The tranquillity of the possessions of the Nabob Vizier Asuph u Dowlah was disturbed, in the year 1794, by a very serious rebellion of the turbulent tribe of Affghans settled in Rohilcund. This was occasioned by the death of Fyzullah Khan, the Chief of the Rohillas and Jagheerdar of Rampoorah. The sons of the deceased disputed the succession: and Mahomed Ally Khan, the eldest, was killed by his brother, Gholam Mahomed Khan, who usurped the Jagheer, and made every endeavour to obtain the sanction of the Vizier to his usurpation. That Prince appeared at first to listen to his overtures; but after some communication with the English Government, whose interests were to a certain degree involved in this question, from it's having guaranteed Rampoorah to the Affghan family, by whom it was held under the Vizier, it was determined to punish the rebels: and the Governor General, after the army had marched, under the command of General Sir Robert Abercromby, for that purpose, resolved to carry this punishment to the extent of depriving the family of Fyzullah Khan of their Jagheer.

Previously, however, to the arrival of these instructions, an action had been fought, in which the Rohillas, after making a partial impression upon the British line, had been defeated; and their complete submission, after this action, had induced the Commander-in-Chief, with the acquiescence of the Nabob Vizier, to restore the inheritance of the family, under the guarantee of the Company, to Ahmed Ally Khan, the infant son of Mahomed Ally Khan, who had been slain by Gholam Mahomed. The latter Chief, with several others, who had aided him, were pardoned on their coming into the British camp. This settlement restored complete tranquillity; and the Supreme Government subsequently expressed their acquiescence in the arrangement; which considerations of policy and of humanity had induced Sir R. Abercromby to adopt.

The death of Hyder Beg appears to have put an end to those prospects of reform, which, Lord Cornwallis had indulged a hope, the energy and ability of that Minister might have effected in the Administration of the Vizier. A nominal successor was appointed to Hyder Beg; but the real power of the State passed into the hands of a few personal favourites of the Vizier, who were most abandoned characters, and some of them known to entertain sentiments hostile to the connexion with the British Government.

Sir John Shore was fully sensible of the injury and danger to which the interests of the Company were upon this occasion exposed. He had, indeed, expressed a decided opinion, when speaking of the Vizier's dominions, that, whilst his Administration continued on it's present footing, we should derive no effective assistance from his troops, and that we must rather expect to find enemies, than friends, in his dominions.

This view of the actual state of the affairs of the Vizier does not, however, appear to have satisfied Sir John Shore of the necessity of taking any decisive measures to remedy those abuses; or to save the State from that great danger, to which he saw it might be eventually exposed, from the affairs of that Prince remaining in the condition which he described: nor does it appear that any effectual remedy whatever was applied to this evil, before the death of Asuph u Dowlah. Asuph u Dowlah was succeeded by his presumptive heir, Vizier Ally, who had been acknowledged as his son by the deceased Prince; though generally known to have been of spurious birth, and consequently to have no claim to the vacant Musnud. He was, however, supported by several persons of rank and influence at Lucknow; and his right was formally acknowledged by the British Government; to whose justice, Saadut Ally, the eldest surviving brother of Asuph u Dowlah, had on this occasion appealed.

Sir John Shore, in a minute of the 3d of January 1798, states, that he had decided against the claim of Saadut Ally, after great hesitation; and that he found it impossible to divest himself of the impression excited by universal belief and assertion, of the spurious origin of Vizier Ally; and of the apprehension, connected with it, that the justice and the reputation of the Company might suffer an imputation by a decision in his favour.

With such sentiments upon his mind, Sir John Shore proceeded to Lucknow: but he declares in the same minute, that the arrangements he had in view at that moment, had no reference whatever to the alteration of the succession; though he conceived it possible, that the repugnance of the people to the new Vizier might force him to a further consideration of the subject.

On the approach of Sir John Shore to Lucknow he was met by the Minister (Tuffiezel Hussein Khan), who informed him, that there was not a shadow of doubt but that Vizier Ally, as well as the other reputed sons of Asuph u Dowlah, were spurious; and that the right of succession belonged to Saadut Ally Khan. The Minister added to this communication, that though no objection was made at the moment to the elevation of Vizier Ally, it had since become a subject of astonishment and disappointment: that it was the general opinion, that the act of raising him to the Musnud had been hasty, and inconsiderate; but that few were disposed to declare their real sentiments, in opposition to the acknowledgment of his title by the English Government.

These accounts appear to have excited still stronger doubts in the Governor General's mind, with respect to the propriety of the steps which he had taken; and led him to make further, and more minute, inquiries respecting the legitimacy of Vizier Ally: the result of which, was a full conviction of his spurious origin.

The Governor General, in his minute upon this subject, enters into an examination of the conduct of Vizier Ally, since his elevation; and draws an inference from this examination, that he is a violent, unsteady, and sanguinary character, and already cherishes the most hostile designs against the interests of the Company; from an open opposition to whom, he considers him only to be restrained by a want of power.

Sir John Shore, after stating the general sentiments which prevailed respecting the conduct of Vizier Ally, adverts to the opinion which the natives of Oude entertain respecting the nature of the political relations between the Vizier and the Company; and also to that which foreign States have formed of the right of the latter to decide upon the question of succession to the dominions of Oude.

"The Government of Oude," he observes, "both in the opinions of the natives, as well as "externally, is considered a dependency upon "the English, whatever it's relations under "treaties may be. Scindiah refers the inves-"titure of Vizier Ally Khan by his Majesty "(Shah Allum) to the Governor General; and "there are many respectable families in Luck-"now, who live under the protection of the "British influence. In the estimate of the "natives of India, the Kingdom of Oude is "held as a gift from the Company to Shujah "u Dowlah; and as a dependent Chief. By "these remarks, I mean only to contrast the "behaviour of Vizier Ally Khan with the "popular sentiments and the conduct of his "predecessor, and to point out the political "discredit attending the subversion of our "influence in Oude."

He next states, "that he had the mortifica-"tion to find, that the reputation of the Com-"pany had suffered by an act, which, in the "opinion of all reputable people, had been "no less disgraceful than unjust. It was "impossible," he continues, "to silence these "impressions by arguing, that the Government "had not directly interfered in deciding upon "the succession; since, in the opinion of all, "Vizier Ally's elevation was considered an act "of the English Government; and it is cer- "tain, that, without their acknowledgment and "support, he could not have maintained his "situation."

Sir John Shore observes, that he was aware that the case had been materially altered by the formal acknowledgment of Vizier Ally in the first instance, and by the amicable correspondence and personal communication which he had subsequently maintained with him: but he considered that the first objection was answered by the precedent of the Tanjore succession, which, he affirms, though the sovereignty had been possessed eleven years by Omer Sing, was at that moment, by the sanction of the Directors, open to investigation and decision; and, with respect to the second, he thought, however unpleasant it might be, that he was bound to prefer justice, and the public interests, to a consideration of his own feelings.

Sir John Shore, after expressing, in very strong language, the great difficulties by which he had been embarrassed, and the agitation of his mind upon the question, adds, that, on a full view of the case, he had come to the following conclusion. "First: That Vizier Ally is "undoubtedly the son of a Furraush; has no "title to the Musnud; and, from his character, "is unworthy of it. This decision is supported "by evidence, as to his real birth, by the "sanction of the public opinion, by facts, and "information. Secondly: That to support "him on the Musnud, would not only be an "indelible disgrace to the reputation of the "Company, but, in all probability, would prove "the ruin of the Country, and the destruction "of the British interests in Oude. Thirdly: "That the justice and reputation of the Com-"pany, as well as their political interests, "require the establishment of the rightful "successor. Fourthly: That as all the reputed "sons of Asuph u Dowlah are undoubtedly "spurious, the line of succession should be "transferred to that of Shujah u Dowlah. "Fifthly: That Vizier Ally ought to be de-"posed, and Saadut Ally be placed on the "Musnud."

Acting upon these conclusions, the Governor General immediately adopted measures for eventually placing Saadut Ally Khan upon the Musnud, and for deposing Vizier Ally: and from the strength of the British force which was collected, and the unpopularity of the latter Prince, this measure was likely to be easily effected.

Sir John Shore transmitted a treaty to Mr. Cherry, at Benares, with instructions to offer it to the acceptance of Saadut Ally Khan, who resided at that city. But from these instructions, which were dated the 4th of January 1798, he does not appear at that period even to have finally resolved upon the line which he would pursue; as he states, that measures may still occur to frustrate his present intentions in favour of Saadut Ally Khan, whose acquiescence in, or refusal of, the treaty proposed, he requested to be immediately given, without qualification or reserve. With this view, he directed the Nabob to be informed, that the engagement had been transmitted in the form in which it was, for execution, because the actual state of affairs would not admit of either delay or discussion.

Saadut Ally Khan did not hesitate to give a ready assent to the treaty dictated by the Governor General; and expressed to Mr. Cherry his determination (if raised to the Musnud) to fulfil all it's stipulations in the most faithful manner.

This treaty consisted of twenty-three articles. It vested the Company with the defence of the Vizier's dominions; and the annual subsidy, to be paid by Saadut Ally Khan, was increased to the amount of seventy-six lacks of rupees;

and, in the event of the failure of any of the instalments, the Company were to be put in possession of Country in Oude of the annual value of ten lacks of rupees, which they were to retain till the amount due was fully liquidated.

By one of it's articles, Saadut Ally Khan stipulated to pay the amount of any expense which the Company might incur in placing him upon the throne. He also agreed to cede the important fortress of Allahabad to the Company, and to pay the amount of eight lacks of rupees to put it into a state of repair; and to give three lacks of rupees to repair the fort of Futty Ghur. It was agreed by this treaty, that as the Country of Oude was henceforward to be considered entirely under the protection of the Company, and the Nabob relied upon them for it's defence, he was not to maintain a larger force for the internal police of the Country, than 35,000 men, ten thousand of whom were to be cavalry. The Company was vested with a right to change the stations of their troops in the Vizier's dominions, if such measure was deemed necessary for the better protection of the Country; and, in the event of such change of cantonments, all expense attending it was to be defrayed by the Nabob. It was also stipulated, that the force of British troops to be stationed in the Vizier's dominions should be afterwards specified; but that if at any time the troops, employed for the defence of the Country, should exceed the number of 12,000 men, including infantry, cavalry, and artillery, Europeans and natives, the Nabob was to pay the amount of the actual expense month by month.

These were the principal conditions of this treaty, which altered in some very essential points the political relations between the Vizier and the Company. The latter State became, by this engagement, exclusively charged with the defence of the territories of the former; the number of whose troops was limited, and, by the expression of the treaty, only to be employed in maintaining the internal police. The increase of subsidy, it is to be concluded, was judged sufficient to defray the charge of the force stationed in Oude in ordinary times; and, when necessity required an addition to this force, for the defence of the Country, the Nabob was bound, by a specific article of the treaty, to defray any actual increase of expense with which such measure might be attended.

This article, though indefinite, was evidently meant to provide against the Company suffering a loss by the general engagement which they had contracted, of defending in future, with their own troops, the Nabob's dominions. The conditions of this article were absolute: and, by the principle of the treaty, the English Government was left the sole judge of the necessity that existed for an increase of the troops requisite to the protection of the Nabob's territories from external enemies. This principle was virtually confirmed by those stipulations, which restricted the Nabob from all negotiations with foreign States; and, indeed, from having communications of any nature with such, except with the previous knowledge and consent of the British Government; as this restriction must obviously deprive the Vizier of the means of forming a judgment upon such affairs.

Before the Governor General received accounts of Saadut Ally Khan's accession to the treaty which he had proposed, he wrote to Mr. Cherry, to desire that he would inform the Nabob, if he had acquiesced in the arrangement, that he must proceed to Cawnpore instantly, where measures would be taken to place him on the Musnud; and, in the event of his having withheld his acquiescence, he was to be informed, that although the Governor General admitted his right to the Musnud of Oude, he did not think himself bound to run the risk of hostilities, in supporting it, but under conditions, which equally provided for the political interests of the Company.

Mr. Cherry communicated the wishes of the Governor General to Saadut Ally Khan, who immediately went to Cawnpore, and from that was escorted by a large body of European troops to Lucknow, where he was proclaimed Vizier upon the 21st of January 1798.

After the elevation of Saadut Ally Khan, another treaty was concluded between him and the British Government, which differed in few material points from the preliminary engagement which that Prince had been required to sign before he left Benares. The most essential of the articles, which related to the future defence of the Country by the Company, and the subsidy to be paid by the Nabob, remained the same in both principle and substance, though they differed somewhat in the terms. It was by the last treaty stipulated, that the force to be maintained by the Company in Oude was never to be less than ten thousand men, including cavalry, infantry, artillery, &c.

If at any time it became necessary to augment this force beyond thirteen thousand, the Nabob agreed to pay the actual difference occasioned by the excess above that number;

and if the troops of the Company should, from any necessity, be less than eight thousand men, the Nabob Saadut Ally Khan became entitled to a deduction from the annual stipend of seventy-six lacks of rupees, (which he had agreed to pay the Company,) equal to the actual difference of men below the specified number.

By this treaty, the Nabob agreed to pay the sum of twelve lacks of rupees to the Company, as a reimbursement for the expenses incurred in placing him upon the throne; and, instead of the article in the preliminary engagement, which gave the Company a right to take possession of part of his Country on his failure in the regular payment of any of the instalments, and that which limited to a specific number the troops which he was to maintain by the treaty concluded at Lucknow, it was generally stipulated, that, on a failure in the regular discharge of any instalment, the Vizier was to give such security for the payment of existing arrears, and future regularity, as should be deemed satisfactory by the English Government; and that he should, on a consideration of the increased subsidy, and other permanent charges upon his revenue, make such reductions in superfluous charges of his public establishments, servants, &c. as were necessary to prevent his disbursements exceeding his assets. It was further agreed, by the same article, that he was on this point to consult the Company's Government; and to devise, in concert with them, the proper objects of reductions, and the best means of effecting them.

The meaning of these alterations is obvious. The Vizier himself had probably no strong objections, either to the stipulations for the eventual cessions of districts, to make good any failure of his instalments, or to the numbers of the troops, which he was to maintain, being limited; but the insertion of such articles in a specific form, was likely to hurt and degrade him with his subjects; and it was therefore an object of policy to have the terms, if not the spirit, of this article altered.

By this treaty Saadut Ally Khan agreed to make an annual allowance of one lack and a half of rupees, for the support of Vizier Ally, who, overawed by the force which the Governor General had collected, and deserted by all parties, had not ventured to make any opposition to the arrangement; and who, after it was concluded, was conducted to Benares, where Sir John Shore had determined that he should reside, in the enjoyment of the stipend allotted for his personal support, which was secured to him by the guarantee of the Company, through whom it was to be paid.

It appears here necessary to advert to a danger of some magnitude, which threatened to disturb, during the Administration of Sir John Shore, the tranquillity of Hindoostan, particularly the dominions of the Vizier; and which may be supposed to have considerably influenced those arrangements, which the Governor General made with that Prince.

Zemaun Shah, King of Kabul, the son of Timour Shah, and the grandson of the celebrated Abdallee, advanced in 1796 to Lahore, and threatened to visit Dehly, from which Lahore is not more than twenty marches to a light army. The accounts of his approach appear to have excited the greatest hope among the more turbulent Mahomedans of Hindoostan. The supposed design of the Shah to restore the fallen dignity of the imperial house of Timour, to which he was nearly allied by blood, gave popularity to his cause with almost all that tribe; while it created great consternation to the Mahrattas, who were at that period ill prepared to resist so formidable an invasion.

The movements of the Affghan Monarch, and the local weakness of the Mahrattas, induced the English Government to make some preparations against a danger, which, though uncertain, was of too serious a nature to be altogether neglected. The troops at the cantonments of Cawnpore and Futty Ghur, were ordered to encamp; and every arrangement was made, to enable them to move to any quarter where their services might be required.

The alarm, which had been excited upon this occasion, was dispelled by the retreat of Zemaun Shah to his own dominions, the tranquillity of which had been disturbed by the rebellion of one of his brothers: but the facility with which he had advanced to Lahore, showed that no confidence could be placed upon the union or resistance of the Seikhs. From every account, indeed, as well as from actual occurrences, it appeared that this Nation was so much distracted by the violence of it's own internal divisions, as to be incapable of acting with concert; and, of course, that it was no longer to be considered as a barrier against the Affghans; whose invasion of India became, from this circumstance, more probable than it ever was before.

Sir John Shore, in a minute under date the 4th of July 1797, enters into a full consideration of this subject. In this document he states the force, which the Shah brought to Lahore, not to have exceeded thirty-three thousand men, which were almost all cavalry: and from this fact he appears inclined to conclude, that the Affghan Monarch did not at that period contemplate the invasion of Hindoostan; but that his expedition to Lahore was experimental, with an ultimate view to that object.

The Governor General, however, observes; that there was no doubt, if Zemaun Shah had advanced, he must have reached Dehly, as the Mahrattas were not prepared to oppose him, and were greatly alarmed. They afterwards, he states, assembled a respectable army, and made overtures to the Company to unite in repelling him: but, though these preparations might have enabled them to dispute the possession of Dehly, or to molest his retreat, he is convinced they would not have been able to have prevented his advance. Under this impression, he proceeded to consider the probable consequences of his advance, and particularly as those would have affected the tranquillity of the territories of the Nabob Vizier.

"In this case," he observes, "the numerous "adventurers in Hindoostan, always ready to "enlist for plunder, would either have joined "his army, or have availed themselves of the "protection afforded by it's advance, to com-"mit depredations. Bumbhoo Khan, the bro-"ther of Gholam Kader Khan, had assembled "a considerable force, near Broreea Ghaut, "and pretended, that he had received orders "from Zemaun Shah for this purpose; and "wrote letters of invitation to several of the "Rohillah Chiefs at Rampore to join him; "which, with a single exception, were con-"cealed from Nusser Ulla Khan.

"Without dwelling on the presumption," Sir John Shore continues, "arising from this "circumstance, we are sufficiently apprised of "the disposition of the Rohillas, to be assured "that they would seize the first favourable op-"portunity for rebellion; and that they would "have considered the arrival of Zemaun Shah "at Dehly, as furnishing it. The Patans in the "district of Furruckabad, though less independ-"ent, are equally disposed to disaffection and "plunder; and nothing but the protection of "the Company's arms would have prevented "the greatest disorders in the Vizier's domi-"nions, if Zemaun Shah had approached them. "My opinion is, that they would have been "overrun with marauders; that a total tempo-"rary stoppage of the collections would have "ensued; and that these disorders, if not "speedily quelled, would have ended in ge-"neral insurrection.

"On this occasion," he adds, "we had "fresh experience of the imbecility of the

" Vizier's Government, and of the insufficiency
" of his military establishment. The troops
" under Almas were respectable. The other
" troops of the Vizier, with little exception,
" would rather have proved an encumbrance,
" than an assistance, to the British forces; and
" nothing but the most urgent remonstrances
" would have ensured the exertions or supplies
" of the Vizier."

From these circumstances, Sir John Shore justly concluded, that the future designs of the Affghan Monarch must always be an object of great interest to the British Government: and, under this view of the subject, he entered into a consideration of the likelihood of his invasion of Hindoostan. It was not, he thought, very probable that Zemaun Shah would undertake such an expedition; but there were, he was aware, many motives, which might impel him to it's adoption. It was possible that an ambition, stimulated by the entreaties and misrepresentations of the Court of Dehly, might lead the Shah to aspire to the character of the deliverer of India from the dominion of infidels, in emulation of his grandfather the Aballee; and a desire of effacing the disgrace of his late ineffectual attempt, and of revenging the defeat of a body of his troops, which the Seikhs had attacked after his retreat, might lead him again to carry his arms eastward. The Governor General stated in this minute, that, by all the accounts which he had received, a general opinion prevailed, that Zemaun Shah would advance at once to Hindoostan, without previously establishing his authority in the Punjaub; and this opinion, however contrary to probability, was of a nature that should not, in his judgment, be altogether neglected.

Sir John Shore professed himself averse from the adoption of any expensive measures of preparation against Zemaun Shah's designs. The Mahrattas had, he states, from a dread of his power, made proposals to the British Government for uniting their forces to oppose it: but he was not decided in his own mind upon the policy of that measure; nor, indeed, whether it was most for the interests of the Company, and their Ally the Vizier, to support the Mahrattas, or to leave them to their fate. That the power of that Nation in Hindoostan should be diminished, the Governor General thought highly desirable; but he doubted, whether the substitution of that of Zemaun Shah would not be more dangerous: and it was his opinion, that, if that Monarch should ever advance to Dehly, the danger would be very alarming to the Vizier; and that it would require the greatest vigour and exertion to preserve peace in his dominions, even though the Affghans should not invade them. The Rohillas appear to have been, upon this occasion, one of the chief objects of the Governor General's apprehensions; and he stated it as his opinion, that it might be found prudent to require or compel the principal persons of that tribe to deliver themselves up as hostages for the good behaviour of the rest.

That there were just grounds for these apprehensions cannot be denied. The invasion of India had always been too favourite a project among the northern tribes of Kabul and Candahar, to leave a hope that it would be relinquished from any cause but from their want of power, arising from internal dissension, to carry it into execution. The state of the whole country, from the Attock to the Jumnah, was such, as opposed no obstacle whatever to their advance: and these barbarians, impressed with an exaggerated opinion of their own valour, and with a hereditary contempt for the natives of India, were not likely to be deterred from it's invasion, by a contemplation of difficulties, which their forefathers had so often encountered and overcome: nor was it more probable, that they would be guided by a consideration of the actual strength of the Power which possessed Hindoostan. It was indeed unlikely, that they should possess correct intelligence upon that point; or, if they did, that their rude understandings, and savage pride, would permit them to estimate justly the efficiency of armies, which were constituted on different principles from their own.

The occurrence of such an invasion was likely, as Sir John Shore observed, to excite many of the chief Mahomedans to rebellion; and their junction with the Affghans would have made it difficult for the Mahrattas to have repelled them; particularly as that Nation must, on such an occasion, have placed it's chief reliance upon it's regular brigades, of which all the men were natives of Hindoostan, and most of the Officers French. They had consequently no tie or attachment to the Mahratta State, but that of temporary interest: and there was, perhaps, good ground to believe, that under the establishment of a Mahomedan Empire in Hindoostan, which must have been the object of Zemaun Shah's policy, there would have been little difficulty in corrupting the fidelity of this corps, as the men, of whom it was composed, would have lost nothing by a change of masters; and the Officers might, under such circumstances, not only expect to improve their condition, but to obtain better means of accomplishing their ambitious designs; and above all, those which were directed against the prosperity of the British Government.

Upon the whole, it was obvious, on this occasion, that no dependence could be placed upon the Mahrattas, as an efficient barrier to the territories of the English Government and it's Allies, against those dangers to which they might be eventually exposed, from any future invasion of the Affghan Monarch: and it appeared not improbable, that the schemes of the invader might have ultimately coalesced with the views and interests of the French corps in the service of Doulut Row Scindiah, to whom the defence of Hindoostan must have been intrusted; and if they had not, and the French Commander had, by his ability and courage, and the skilful application of the great military resources which he had accumulated, defeated Zemaun Shah, he and his party would have acquired an increase of fame, influence, and power, which would have rendered them much more dangerous neighbours than either the Mahrattas or Affghans.

Several expeditions against the Eastern Settlements of the European enemies of Great Britain took place during the period in which Sir John Shore was Governor General of India; but these were all fitted out from Madras: and to the eminent ability and energy of Lord Hobart, the Governor of that Presidency, aided by the cordial and zealous co-operation of his Majesty's naval Commander, Admiral Rainier, the British Government was indebted for the complete reduction of the Dutch Settlements upon the Island of Ceylon and of Malacca, and the valuable Islands of Banda and Amboyna. More important expeditions were prepared against the French Settlement of the Mauritius, and the Spanish possessions of Manilla; neither of which, however, were carried into execution. The first division of the armament for the latter, which took place in 1797, had actually sailed to Penang, the port of rendezvous: but the complexion of the accounts received from Europe, combined with the conduct of Tippoo Sultaun, and the general state of the native Powers in India, obliged the Government of Fort St. George to abandon this expedition; which, from the nature of the equipment, there can be no doubt, would, if it had proceeded, have been crowned with complete success.

Sir John Shore, who had been raised to the peerage by the title of Lord Teignmouth, sailed for England in the beginning of the year 1798. The situation of the different native Powers, at the period of his taking charge of the administration of the affairs of British India, has been already described. It may be useful to take a short view of their condition at the period of his departure; and to examine the causes of those great changes, which had occurred during his Government.

Tippoo Sultaun, whose spirit of hostility continued always the same, had greatly recruited his resources, and continued most active in his intrigues with the French, the Mahrattas, and with the discontented party at the Court of Hyderabad. The Nizam, greatly reduced in reputation, as well as in real strength, no longer placed that confidence, which he had done, in the British Government, whose friendship he had before sought, as has been shown in the preceding chapter, not more with a view of immediate benefit, than of securing, by the improvement of those relations upon which his connexion with the English Government was established, the permanent welfare and prosperity of his dominions. This great object he had been led to expect by the assurances of Lord Cornwallis; but his hopes were completely frustrated; and he had, in despair, thrown himself into the hands of a French faction, of a nature the most dangerous, that could be imagined, to the British Government.

The power of Doulut Row Scindiah had arrived, at this period, at a most alarming eminence; and was indeed acknowledged paramount over almost the whole of the Mahratta Empire. It had completely annihilated the independence of the Paishwah's Government; and that Prince only exercised a nominal rule in the city of Poonah, under the immediate control and direction of a subordinate Officer of Scindiah's Court. By this revolution in the Deckan, the triple alliance, and that balance of power, which had existed at the departure of Lord Cornwallis from India, were destroyed. The strength and resources of the Poonah State were at the disposal of a Chief, who was known to be unfriendly to the English Government; and it appeared almost certain, from the ambition of Scindiah, the local position of his territories, the constitution of his regular brigades, and the principles of those by whom they were commanded, that this Nation must become the ultimate object of his attack.

Several opportunities had occurred, of which the British Government might have taken advantage, (probably without any danger of hostilities,) of checking the growth of the enormous power of the House of Scindiah; or, if it had been preferred, of securing an alliance with that family, which would have prevented it's resources being ever directed against the British possessions in India.

Nanah Furnavese was very jealous of the rising power of Scindiah, long before the influence of that Chief was established over the Poonah Government; and this jealousy had led to that indirect overture, which was made to Lord Cornwallis, through Hurry Punt, to induce that nobleman to form a subsidiary alliance with the Paishwah: but the approach of Doulut Row Scindiah to Poonah, after the death of the Paishwah, Madhoo Row, changed this feeling into that of alarm; and Nanah would, at that moment, have most willingly entered into any improved alliance with the English Government, which secured the independence of the Poonah branch of the Mahratta Empire. Nor can there be a doubt, that the interposition of the British Nation, at this remarkable crisis, would have effected that object: and the exertion of our power and influence, on that occasion, would, in all human probability, have enabled us to dictate to the contending parties an amicable adjustment of the disputes regarding the succession to the office of Paishwah; and not only have secured our interests from the dangers to which they were exposed by our neutrality, but have added in the greatest degree to our reputation.

Madhajee Scindiah had repeatedly solicited the aid of the English Government; and had been desirous, at one period, of subsidizing a force from that State. His successor, Doulut Row, had evinced on several occasions a similar disposition; and it would probably have been easy, either at his elevation, or when he returned to Poonah to support Badjerow, or at the period he was under so great an alarm of an intended attack on his possessions in Hindoostan by the Affghans, to have negotiated an alliance, which might have effected the removal of the French party, which was daily gaining strength.

But that system of neutral policy, which had been prescribed by the authorities in England, and which was closely followed by the Governor General, prevented any attempt being made to avert, or influence, the changes at Poonah, or to improve our alliance with the family of Scindiah, although it was conjectured at the moment, that our noninterference might be pregnant with the worst consequences to the interests of the British Government.

Those who support this system have constantly asserted, that it is the only one consistent with the intention of the Act of Parliament relative to the administration of the affairs of India. But it appears difficult, if not impossible, to imagine, that the wisdom of the British Legislature, when it imposed restrictions upon ambition, and prohibited a policy which had for it's object conquest and extension of territory, could ever mean (whatever may be the literal construction of the legal terms by which it's intentions are expressed) to deprive the local Government of India of the power of adopting preventive measures, against dangers, which it saw in progress; and to prescribe, as a positive maxim of policy to a great State, a disregard to the concerns of it's neighbours: or, in other words, to deny to a Nation the exercise of that influence and power, which it's former wisdom and courage had acquired; and which is, in fact, one of the principal and most legitimate means, which it can possess, of maintaining peace and tranquillity.

This system, however, while it might have in some degree the effect of promoting wars among other States, did not seem likely to secure the exemption of the Nation, by which it was followed, from that evil. It was, in fact, one State withdrawing, as much as circumstances would permit, from any concern in the interests of that Commonwealth of Nations among whom it was placed: and that secession not only deprived it of the exercise of all those means by which Governments preserve their security, but exposed it to all the dangers of the aggrandizement of a rival State, or the confederacy among numbers against it's power; events, which became more probable, from that decrease of fame and estimation, which was the obvious and inevitable result of the policy pursued.

The merits of this system, however, were fully tried during the Administration of Sir John Shore, who appears to have been uniformly actuated by a sincere and conscientious desire to govern India agreeably to the strict and literal sense of the Act of the Legislature, and to the wishes of his superiors in England; to the implicit execution of whose orders, his great ability and experience were on all occasions most zealously applied. The result of this experiment offers an important lesson to those, who are intrusted with the Administration of British India. It was proved, from the events of this Administration, that no ground of political advantage could be abandoned, without being instantly occupied by an enemy; and that to resign influence, was not merely to resign power, but to allow that to pass into hands hostile to the British Government. The consequence of political inaction was equally obvious. No one measure of importance was taken, except the elevation of Saadut Ally to the Musnud of Oude; which the Governor General states, in express terms, was forced upon his adoption. But this inactive system of policy, so far from attaining it's object, which was to preserve affairs upon the footing in which it had found them, had only the effect of making the British Government stationary, while all around it advanced; and of exposing it to those dangers, which resulted from the revolutions of it's neighbours, while it was even denied the power of adapting it's policy to the change of circumstances. The ultimate consequences were such as might have been expected. A period of six years' peace, so far from having added to the strength, or improved the security, of the British dominions in India, had placed them in a situation of comparative danger. Though the British strength was not lessened, the power and resources of the other States of India had increased. The confidence and attachment of our Allies were much shaken, if not destroyed; and the presumption and hostile disposition of the principal native Powers in India too clearly showed, that it was to a principle of weakness, or of selfish policy, and not of moderation, that they ascribed the course which had been pursued by the British Government.

The extent of the danger to which our possessions in India had been exposed by this neutral system of policy, and the encouragement which the enemies of that Nation had derived from our inaction, were not fully known, till some time had elapsed; but the period at which Sir John Shore left India, though a season of peace, was regarded by no person in India, who had the slightest knowledge of the subject, as one of security: and the authorities in England had felt, and expressed, considerable alarm at the numerous dangers which they saw collected; and which threatened early to disturb the tranquillity of the British possessions in that quarter of the globe.

CHAPTER IV.

ADMINISTRATION

OF

MARQUIS WELLESLEY.

CONTENTS.

View of the State of India at the Commencement of this Administration.—Maturity of Tippoo's Plans.—French Party at Hyderabad and Poonah very strong.—Vigorous Course of Policy adopted by Lord Wellesley.—Negotiations at Hyderabad and Poonah.—Treaty with the Nizam.—French Corps in his Service disbanded.—View of the Causes of the War with Tippoo.—Overthrow of his Power.—Establishment of the Government of the Mysore.—Policy of the Governor General respecting the conquered Provinces.—Partition Treaty.—Subsidiary Treaty with the Rajah of Mysore.—Treaty with the Nizam.—Negotiations at the Court of Poonah.—War between Scindiah and Holkar.—Treaty of Bassein.—British Army marches to Poonah.—Mahratta War.—Treaty of Peace with the Rajah of Berar—with Scindiah.—War with Holkar.—Embassy to Persia.—Treaty with the Vizier of Oude. View of the Transactions in the Carnatic.—Treaty with the Nabob, vesting the civil and military Government of the Carnatic in the Company. —Lord Wellesley leaves India.—Observations upon the principal Measures of Policy adopted during his Administration.

Lord Teignmouth was succeeded in the Government of British India by the Marquis Wellesley; a nobleman, whose rank and talents enabled him to enter upon the great duties committed to his charge with every advantage. The period at which Lord Wellesley reached India, (26th April, 1798,) was one of a most critical nature for the British interests in that quarter of the globe. The hostile designs of Tippoo Sultaun were ripe for execution. A French party was paramount at the Courts both of the Nizam and of Scindiah. The Court of Poonah was at the mercy of the latter Chief; and that of Berar was known to be adverse to the English, on whose progress to power it had long looked with peculiar jealousy.

The Country of Oude, still agitated by the recent change which had been made in it's Government, was not likely to be kept in a state of tranquillity by it's new ruler Saadut Ally, who continued openly to proclaim his alarms, and to call upon the British Government to protect him in the exercise of that power, to which he had, by their interference, been raised.

The state of the Carnatic was little better. Omdut ul Omrah, who had been only irritated by the ineffectual attempts made to induce him to a modification of Lord Cornwallis's treaty, continued to deliver over his Country to the gripe of usurers, in order to anticipate his revenue; and it's resources were rapidly declining, at a period when it was obvious they must soon be urgently required to aid in the general defence of the Empire.

To add to these difficulties, the finances were much exhausted, by the equipment of large, but necessary armaments, which had been sent to reduce the Settlements of the Dutch to the eastward, and the Island of Ceylon; and a considerable part of the army of the coast of Coromandel was also sent on those expeditions.

Lord Wellesley had hardly arrived in Bengal, when the occurrence of an overt act of hostility on the part of Tippoo Sultaun, and the active intrigues of the French party at Hyderabad, demanded all his exertion. But the suddenness with which these circumstances were forced upon his decision, did not lead him to resort to any of those delusive political expedients, by which a momentary and partial exemption from danger is so dearly purchased at the price of future security. His mind embraced the whole scheme; and at the time he deliberated upon the measures, which the emergencies of the moment required him to adopt, he took an extended view of the general condition of the British dominions in India; and having fixed in his mind those principles of policy which appeared to him best calculated to lead to a state of permanent peace and prosperity, he proceeded to combine the introduction of those principles into every branch of his Administration, with the adoption of the means requisite for the defeat of immediate danger.

Before I enter upon the narrative of Lord Wellesley's Government, it appears of importance to notice in a cursory manner those general considerations, which induced him to resolve upon that system which he pursued. This is the more essential, as all political measures must be judged with constant reference to the actual circumstances of the period under which they were first adopted. Their wisdom, moderation, or justice, can be decided by no other criterion; for, when in progress, they become subject to the influence of an infinity of events, some of which may be of a nature that could neither be foreseen nor controlled, and against the effects of which no human wisdom could have guarded.

The designs of Tippoo Sultaun against the English Government had been fully developed. Those of the French were known at this period to be directed with more than usual activity to the object of subverting the British power in India; and the means which they possessed for the accomplishment of such views, though irregular and difficult of combination, were far from contemptible. Tippoo Sultaun, from a similarity of sentiments, was disposed to join with zeal in every effort that had for it's object the attack of the British power: and the influence, which individuals of the French Nation had established at the Courts of the Nizam and Scindiah, by obtaining the command of the principal military resources of both these Princes, afforded a just ground of belief, that any plan, which was formed, might eventually receive the greatest aid from their efforts. Of the dispositions of these individuals to promote the success of their Country, there could be no doubt; and their power and influence were of a nature, which gave every reason to conclude, that they might possess ample means of acting agreeably to the dictates of that disposition.

Other circumstances were favourable to the

designs of Tippoo Sultaun and the French. The triple alliance, which had been formed by Lord Cornwallis, as a defence against the future ambition of the former, had, from the neutral policy of the British Government, been annihilated; and the Courts of Hyderabad and Poonah seemed more likely, from causes before stated, to act against, than with the British Government, in the event of a rupture with Tippoo Sultaun.

The absence of Doulut Row Scindiah from Hindoostan was, at this period, as injurious to the British interests, as his presence at Poonah. For while he staid in the Deckan, the power of the Paishwah was dormant, if not extinct; and a large corps of infantry, commanded by French Officers, was kept in a situation, where it was likely that it might, either from the operation of the national spirit of it's Officers, or the ambition of Scindiah, be led by events to act against the British Government. On the other hand, the absence of Scindiah from Hindoostan threw almost the whole defence of that quarter of India, against the expected invasion of Zemaun Shah, upon the British Government; and that invasion was rendered more probable from the defenceless state in which the possessions of this Chief were left.

Under these circumstances, Lord Wellesley

resolved upon the adoption of those political measures, which appeared calculated, in the first instance, to check and frustrate the designs of Tippoo Sultaun and the French; and, in the second, to promote the permanent security of the British Government in India. The means which he took to effect these purposes, while they afforded a reasonable hope of obtaining security against the designs of the Sultaun and the French, without the extremity of a war with the former, gave the surest promise of war being successful, in the event of it's proving inevitable.

The disposition of Azeem ul Omrah, the Prime Minister at Hyderabad, who had returned from Poonah, was favourable to the English Government; but that Minister, however secretly adverse to the French party in the army of the Nizam, had not the power of dismissing it, without the active aid of the British Government; nor could he, with common attention to the security of his master, advise him to disband that corps, until assured of the aid of a large body of English troops, and of eventual protection against any unjust aggression of the Mahrattas.

The young Paishwah, Badjerow, was at this moment anxious to be released from the thraldom in which he was kept by Doulut Row

Scindiah; and earnestly solicited the interference of the British Government. The Resident* at his Court, in a letter under date the 1st of June, states, that "the authority of that "Prince would be restored by the appearance "of a strong British force at Poonah; and "that Scindiah, under the circumstance of "Tippoo's recent aggression, could on no just "pretence object to such a movement of our "troops; nor, in his present condition, be able "to oppose it."

This was the actual state of affairs when the Marquis Wellesley resolved to endeavour, through the means of improved defensive engagements, to reobtain the efficient aid of the Government of Hyderabad and Poonah; or, rather, to prevent the power and resources of those States being employed against the British Government. While endeavouring, through the means of negotiation, to effect these objects, he resolved to adopt the most moderate course towards Tippoo Sultaun, which attention to the security and dignity of the Government under his charge would admit. Nor was he without a sanguine hope, that the complete success of the negotiations, which he had commenced at the Courts of Poonah and Hydera-

* Colonel Palmer.

bad, would place the English Government upon such a footing, as would satisfy even that Prince of the inutility of any farther attempt against it's power; and ultimately induce him to change his principles; to abandon his French Allies; to rest satisfied with his own dominions; and to cultivate (as his true interests dictated) a good understanding with the British Nation and it's Allies.

From what has been stated it will appear, that the views, which led to the adoption of this system of policy, were as moderate and just, as they were wise and enlarged; that it's end was altogether defensive; and that it was dictated by a desire of security and peace, not a spirit of ambition or aggrandizement. This will be more clearly shown in the course of the narrative of the leading political events that occurred during Lord Wellesley's Administration, to the relation of which I now proceed.

The state of the Court of Hyderabad, at the period of that nobleman's arrival in India, has been described in the preceding chapter. Though that was, in the actual condition in which affairs stood, very unfavourable to the British interests, some circumstances had occurred, which promised success to measures of so decided a nature, as those which Lord Wellesley had resolved to pursue. The chief Minister, Azeem ul Omrah, enjoyed a plenitude of power; and was prepared (as has been before stated) to agree to any treaty which secured the Government of the Nizam against the future aggression and excesses of the Mahrattas, by whom his power had been so recently reduced. This Minister was led, about this period, to entertain the greatest jealousy and alarm at the designs of the Sultaun, with whom his enemies at Hyderabad had, during his absence, carried on the most active intrigues. He was sensible, from experience, that however the corps under French Officers might add to the military strength of the Nizam, it was not, in it's actual state, equal to the protection of his dominions from the attack with which these were threatened; and he could not be ignorant, that any addition to it's numbers, or improvement of it's equipment, would be likely to excite a jealousy in the British Government, which might terminate in an open separation of interests, and perhaps in a war between the Court of Hyderabad and the only State in India which could efficiently protect and support it's tottering power.

Under these impressions, Azeem ul Omrah was fully disposed to receive the overtures of the English Government for an improved connexion; and was solicitous to engage that

State to enter into engagements of a more intimate nature, as the best means of preserving the Government of Hyderabad from the ruin with which it was threatened. He had, however, no easy task to conquer the prejudices of his Sovereign, the Nizam, against such an alliance; which, that Monarch argued, would, from the inequality of the parties, early terminate in rendering his dominions virtually dependent, for their future security, upon the British Government. This the Minister admitted: but he contended, that it was better to be dependent upon a State, whose regard to good faith was acknowledged, and whose power to protect was evident, than to continue exposed to the treacherous intrigues and unlimited demands of the Mahrattas, or the more daring and ambitious projects of the Sultaun: that, as it was clear that the situation of the State of Hyderabad was such as to make it impossible for it to remain without the alliance of some one of those Powers, it was assuredly wise to prefer a connexion with a Government, which brought with it's protection the substantial blessings of security and peace, to the nominal friendship of Powers, whose professed objects were plunder and conquest, and who had repeatedly shown that they held in contempt even the forms of public faith. The

Nizam's prejudices and fears were at last subdued by this reasoning; and he gave his assent to the negotiation for the dismissal of the French corps, and the increase of the English subsidiary force, provided these objects could be connected with a pledge on the part of the British Government, to protect his dominions from any future unjust demands on the part of the Mahrattas.

The causes which had led the Governor General to seek an improved alliance with the Court of Hyderabad, were of too urgent a nature, and too much connected with the immediate security of the British territories, to admit of his being influenced by a consideration of the effect which the line of policy that he pursued might have upon the Court of Poonah. That consideration, indeed, could not, in the actual condition of affairs, be for one moment put in competition with the advantages to be gained by the dismissal of the French corps, and the complete introduction of the English influence at the Court of the Nizam. These points were of the highest importance; as they not only removed, at a period of actual danger, every apprehension for the safety of the Company's territories, but placed the power of that State upon so commanding a ground, as to make it probable, that the hostile designs of Tippoo Sultaun would be abandoned, and that he would purchase, by early concessions, an exemption from that punishment, which his conduct had provoked.

When mutual interests so strongly recommended an alliance, serious difficulties were not to be expected in it's negotiation. A treaty was accordingly concluded on the 1st of September 1798, by which the subsidiary detachment of British troops with the Nizam was made permanent; and an addition of four battalions was made to the two fixed by the former treaty. The subsidy to be paid by the Nizam, for the support of the whole, was increased from 57,713 rupees per month, to 201,425 rupees per month, or 2,417,100 rupees per annum. The Nizam also engaged by this treaty to disband the French corps in his service, and to deliver over it's Officers to the British Government, whenever the whole of the English force, to be stationed in his dominions, reached his capital. The British Government became, on it's part, pledged to arbitrate, on principles of impartiality and justice, the points in dispute between him and the Poonah Government, and to obtain the consent of the Poonah State to that arbitration; or, in the event of that being withheld, to protect the Nizam from any unjust or unreasonable demands of the Mahrattas.

The strength of the French corps, which was about fourteen thousand men, with a large train of artillery, rendered the execution of that part of the treaty, which stipulated for it's dismissal, a more arduous undertaking than it's negotiation; but the internal state of the corps at the moment, was favourable to the accomplishment of this difficult object. Raymond, by whom it was originally formed, and who was an able man, and possessed of much influence, had died some months previous to the conclusion of the treaty; and disputes, respecting the succession to the command, had introduced much disunion into the corps; and though these were apparently settled, and General Perron had succeeded to that station, his character and influence were not such, as to enable him to take, with any prospect of success, those decided steps, which, under other circumstances, a Commander of this corps might have adopted, to have prevented it's destruction.

The measures, however, directed by the Governor General for the full execution of the treaty, were, from their celerity and vigour, calculated to ensure success. A corps of four battalions, with their guns, which had been collected on the frontier of the Nizam's dominions pending the negotiation, immediately marched to Hyderabad, where it joined the two battalions formerly stationed there, on the 10th of October. The moment this detachment arrived, the full execution of the treaty, as far as it related to the French corps, was demanded by the British Resident (Major James Achilles Kirkpatrick): but the Nizam, either from the influence of intrigue, or alarm, appeared at one time to hesitate how he should act; and even Azeem ul Omrah, whose character was very timid, shrunk from the fulfilment of his own plans, and expressed a desire to avoid, or at least to delay, extremities. The Nizam and his Minister were, however, soon brought to a just sense of the attention due to public faith, by the representations of the British Resident, who informed them in the most express terms, that, under the orders of the Governor General, he could, at that advanced stage of affairs, admit of nothing short of the complete execution of the engagements into which the Court of Hyderabad had entered with the British Government; whose interests would, he stated, be exposed to the most serious danger, by allowing the French party to exist, for any period however short, after the resolution to disband it had been made public. It was therefore, he added, his determination, if the Nizam should persevere in his wavering conduct, to authorize an attack upon the French camp by the British forces; and the Hyderabad Court would become responsible for all the consequences of an event, which must ever be deemed the result of it's weakness and want of faith. To this communication, which was made on the 21st of October, was added a movement of the British troops to the ground that commanded the French lines, which sufficiently evinced the resolution to attack them, in the event of further delay: but the impression made by this determined course of proceeding put an end to all evasion. A proclamation was issued, a few hours after the message from the Resident was received, and sent to the French camp, by which the troops were informed, that the Nizam had dismissed their European Officers from his service; that they were released from their obedience to these Officers; and that, if they supported them, they should be considered and punished as traitors. This proclamation, aided by the menacing position of the British troops and the internal divisions in the French party, produced a violent mutiny in their lines, of which immediate advantage was taken. A strong body of horse belonging to the Nizam, and the whole of the British detachment, surrounded the cantonments at daylight, on the 22d of October. The men of the French corps, who continued in a state of mutiny, were promised a liquidation of their pay, and future service, if they laid down their arms; to which, after some discussion, they consented: and in a few hours, a corps, whose numbers were nearly fourteen thousand men, and who had in their possession a train of artillery, and an arsenal filled with every description of military stores, was completely disarmed, without one life having been lost.

Such is the short history of this great political measure. The wisdom with which it was planned, and the promptness and vigour displayed in the execution, gave alarm to the enemies of the British Government, and diffused joy and confidence among the subjects and Allies of that State: and these impressions, no doubt, greatly promoted it's future success.

Negotiations for an improved defensive alliance were carried on at Poonah at the same time, and with the same activity, as at Hyderabad; but with very different success. The measures taken at Hyderabad were regularly communicated to the Paishwah: but that Prince, either influenced by his weak Counsellors, or acting under the control of Doulut Row Scindiah, obstinately continued to withhold his formal consent to any acknowledgment of the right of the British Government to arbitrate in his disputes with the Court of Hyderabad.

The double injury which the interests of the British Government sustained from the absence of Scindiah from his northern possessions, and his presence in the Deckan, gave that Government the justest grounds to use every endeavour to oblige him to leave Poonah: and as it was evident, from the state of the English army in Hindoostan, and the weakness of Scindiah in that quarter, that we had the power, if ever actuated by ambition, of seizing his most valuable possessions; the urgent solicitude which we showed upon this occasion could not be misinterpreted, or ascribed to any cause but that by which it was really produced.

A change occurred in the Councils of Doulut Row Scindiah in the month of August 1799, which, from it's nature, gave, at one period, cause to hope a successful termination to the discussions at Poonah. That, however, was disappointed; and, after a negotiation, marked by weakness and evasion on the part of the Paishwah, and by intrigue and duplicity on that of Scindiah, the British Government was forced to procced in it's operations against the Sultaun, without any satisfactory settlement with either of these Chiefs, who were strongly suspected (particularly the latter) to be at this period much more inclined to take part with our enemy.

I shall now proceed to an examination of those causes, which led to the war with Tippoo Sultaun; and the conduct pursued by the Marquis Wellesley, previously to that event, and on it's occurrence.

The whole tenour of Tippoo Sultaun's proceedings, subsequent to the peace concluded by Lord Cornwallis, had shown the implacable spirit of revenge which that Prince cherished towards the British Government. This appeared to have been more inflamed, than mitigated, by those unremitting endeavours, which we made to conciliate his friendship. His intrigues at Hyderabad, his embassies to Poonah, to the Mauritius, to Kabul, Persia, and Turkey, were all the result of the same spirit of hostility: and the destruction of the British power in India continued to be the sole and constant object of his contemplation. Though this disposition of the Sultaun had been long evident, and had produced more than once considerable danger to our interests, it had not (previously to the arrival of Lord Wellesley) shown itself in any direct act of hostility. Immediately after that period a communication had taken place respecting a boundary dispute in Wynaud: on which occasion, that nobleman, overlooking the impropriety of Tippoo's moving a body of troops towards the districts in dispute, had made a proposition, for an amicable adjustment of the difference, in the most mild and conciliatory terms. The Sultaun, therefore, had not the slightest pretext to complain of the English Government: he had, indeed, never alleged any; and his letters had uniformly expressed his satisfaction with it's conduct, and the firmest reliance upon it's continued friendship.

Under such circumstances, it was with some astonishment that the Governor General received, upon the 18th of June 1798, accounts of the arrival of the Ambassadours of the Sultaun at the Isle of France; and of the proclamation issued at that Island, with their participation and sanction, inviting volunteers to enter into the service of Tippoo, who was represented in this document to be on the eve of commencing an attack upon the English, in concert with the French Government.

This public avowal of hostility appeared so imprudent and precipitate, that the account of it was at first received with great caution; and the Governor General deemed it his duty to substantiate it's authenticity, by the most patient inquiry, before he made it the ground of any measures of even defensive precaution.

The result of these inquiries are fully stated by Lord Wellesley in his minute under date the 12th of August 1798; in which his Lordship gives an account of the arrival of the Ambassadours of the Sultaun at the Isle of France, and their proceedings there, in the following words:

" Tippoo despatched two Ambassadours, who
" embarked at Mangalore for the Isle of France,
" and arrived there at the close of the month
" of January 1798. They hoisted Tippoo's
" colours, upon entering the harbour of Port
" Nordouest; were received publicly and for-
" mally by the French Government, with every
" circumstance of distinction and respect; and
" were entertained during their continuance in
" the Island at the public expense. Previously
" to their arrival, no idea, or rumour, existed in
" the Island of any aid to be furnished by the
" French, or of any prospect of a war between
" him and the Company.

" The second day after the arrival of the Am-
" bassadours an advertisement was published,
" of the same purport as the proclamation; and
" immediately afterwards the proclamation was

" fixed up in the most public places, and circu-
" lated through the town. One of the Ambas-
" sadours was said to be conversant with the
" French language. A person accompanied the
" Embassy from Mangalore, who was habited
" in the Turkish dress, who spoke French and
" English with uncommon correctness and
" fluency, and who appeared to possess consi-
" derable knowledge and talents, and to be well
" acquainted with most of the country lan-
" guages of India. This person had been
" known at Bussorah by the name of Abdool-
" lah; at Surat, by that of Dervish; and in the
" Isle of France passed under that of Talomash;
" under which last name he had also passed in
" Bengal, where he resided for some years.
" The Ambassadours, far from protesting against
" the matter or style of the proclamation, held
" without reserve, in the most open and public
" manner, the same language which it contains,
" with respect to the offensive war to be com-
" menced against the British possessions in India:
" they even suffered the proclamation to be pub-
" licly distributed at their own house. Talo-
" mash's conversation, though with more caution
" and mystery, corresponded in substance with
" theirs. In consequence of these circumstances,
" an universal belief prevailed in the Island,
" that Tippoo would make an immediate attack

" on the British possessions in India: which opi-" nion had gained so much force, that the per-" sons who gave this evidence, and all those who " arrived at that period in India from the Isle " of France, expected to find us at war with " Tippoo: but they all concurred in declaring, " that the temerity of Tippoo's designs had ex-" cited general ridicule in that Island. The " Ambassadours were present in the Island " when the French Government proceeded to " act under the proclamation in question; and " they aided and assisted the execution of it, " by making promises in the name of Tippoo, " for the purpose of enticing recruits to enlist. " They proposed to levy men to any practi-" cable extent, stating their powers to be " unlimited with respect to the number of the " force to be raised.

" The Ambassadours aided and assisted in a " levy of an hundred Officers, and fifty privates, " for the service of Tippoo, under the terms, " and for the purposes, stated in the proclama-" tion. Few of the Officers are of any experi-" ence or skill; and the privates are the refuse " of the lowest class of the democratic rabble " of the Island: some of them are volunteers: " others were taken from the prisons, and com-" pelled to embark: several of them are Cafrées, " and people of half cast. With such of these

" troops as were volunteers, the Ambassadours
" entered into several stipulations and engage-
" ments in the name of Tippoo.

" On the 7th of March, 1798, the Ambassa-
" dours embarked on board the French frigate
" Preneuse, together with the force thus raised;
" and they publicly declared an intention of
" proceeding to the Isle of Bourbon, with
" the hope of obtaining more recruits for the
" same service.

" The proclamation therefore originated," his Lordship adds, " in the arrival of the Ambassa-
" dours at the Isle of France, and was distri-
" buted by their agents; was avowed in every
" part by their own public declaration; and,
" finally, was executed, according to it's te-
" nour, by their personal assistance and co-
" operation.

" The proclamation itself furnishes the most
" powerful internal evidence of the concurrence
" of the Ambassadours in all it's essential parts.
" The principal facts stated therein are:

" That Tippoo Sultaun, through two Ambas-
" sadours, despatched for the purpose to the
" Isle of France, had addressed letters to the
" Colonial Assembly of the Isle of France; to
" all the Generals employed there; and to the
" Executive Directory of France; and had made
" the following propositions:

"1st, That he desired to form an alliance, offensive and defensive, with France; and offered to maintain at his expense, during the continuance of the war in India, whatever troops should be furnished by the French; and to supply (with the exception of certain stores) every necessary for carrying on the war.

"2dly, That he had given assurances, that all his preparations were already completed; and that the Generals and Officers would find every thing necessary for carrying on a species of war to which Europeans have not been accustomed in their contests with the native Powers in India.

"3dly, That he only waited for the succour of France, to declare war against the English; and that it was his ardent desire to expel the English from India.

"Upon the ground of these facts, the proclamation recommends a general levy of men for the service of Tippoo; and it concludes, by assuring all the citizens, who shall enlist, that Tippoo will give them an advantageous rate of pay and allowances, which will be fixed by his Ambassadours, who will also engage, in the name of their Sovereign, that the Frenchmen, who shall have enlisted in his army, shall never be detained there after they

" shall have expressed a desire of returning to " their native country."

Lord Wellesley, after some comments upon the avowed purpose of this proclamation, draws such a series of conclusions from the facts adduced and the arguments used, as established, on the most incontrovertible grounds, the hostile nature of Tippoo's proceedings, throughout the whole of this negotiation with the French Government of the Isle of France; the character of which was, he justly observes, strongly corroborated by the conduct of that Prince in his communications with other Powers: and the Governor General concludes these observations by recording his opinion, that the motive of Tippoo Sultaun, in sending an Embassy to the Isle of France, " was no other, than that avowed " in his correspondence with the enemy, and " published under the eyes of his own Ambassa- " dours: *An ardent desire to expel the British* " *Nation from India.*"

From a conviction of such being his intentions, the Governor General was fully satisfied, (as he stated in a letter to the Court of Directors under date the 13th of September 1799,) " that an immediate attack upon Tippoo Sul- " taun, for the purpose of frustrating the exe- " cution of his unprovoked and unwarrantable

" projects of ambition and revenge, appeared to " be demanded by the soundest maxims of jus- " tice and policy.

" The act" (his Lordship adds in the same despatch) " of Tippoo Sultaun's Ambassadours, " ratified by himself, and followed by the ad- " mission of a French force into his army, was " equivalent to a public, unqualified, and un- " ambiguous declaration of war: but, while his " hostile purpose had been clearly manifested, " the immediate means of accomplishing it " had happily disappointed the ardour of his " hopes."

The immaturity, however, of the Sultaun's plans, formed, in Lord Wellesley's opinion, the strongest reason for an immediate attack upon his possessions; and such was his Lordship's original intention: but the delay which was likely to occur in assembling the army on the coast of Coromandel, which had been reduced to a very low establishment, and was in a very divided and unequipped state, obliged him to alter it; and he made no communication whatever to Tippoo Sultaun on the subject of his proceedings, till the military preparations, both at Madras and Bombay, were complete: and the alliance with the Nizam had, by the course of the events which I have described, not merely been restored, but rendered so efficient, as to secure the full application of the resources of that Prince in aid of the common cause.

When these essential measures of precautionary policy were accomplished, Lord Wellesley addressed a letter to the Sultaun, under date the 8th of November 1798; in which, after replying in a most moderate and conciliatory manner to a letter from that Prince, respecting some villages in the possession of the Rajah of Coorg, to the revenues of which Tippoo laid claim, his Lordship proceeded to expostulate with him upon the nature of the connexion which he had recently formed with the French Government; and pointed out, in the most explicit and strongest terms, the consequences which were likely to result from it. "This connexion" (Lord Wellesley observes) "not only "threatens to subvert the foundations of friend-"ship between you and the Company, but to "introduce into the heart of your kingdom the "principles of anarchy and confusion; to shake "your own authority; to weaken the obedience "of your subjects; and to destroy the religion "which you revere."

His Lordship, in this letter, after adverting to the amicable professions of Tippoo, and the proofs which the Company's Government had given of it's sincere disposition to maintain the relations of peace and friendship with that Prince, states the causes which had obliged that Government and it's Allies to adopt measures of precaution and defence: but those, his Lordship added, were not connected with any views incompatible with their respective engagements, and were directed to no object, but that of maintaining the permanent security and tranquillity of the dominions and subjects of the British Government and it's Allies. He earnestly recommended this letter to the serious consideration of the Sultaun; whom he informed, that it was his intention to depute Major Doveton, (an Officer well known to him,) to explain, in a full manner, those means which appeared most likely to banish all distrust and suspicion, and to establish peace and good understanding on durable foundations.

"I shall expect your answer," said Lord Wellesley, "to this letter, with an earnest "hope that it may correspond with the pacific "views and wishes of the Allies; and that you "may be convinced, that you cannot in any "manner better consult your true interests, "than by meeting, with cordiality, the present "friendly and moderate advance to a satisfac- "tory and amicable settlement of all points on

" which any doubt or anxiety may have arisen " in the minds either of yourself or of the " Allies."

The accounts, which had been received of the landing of the French army in Egypt; and the immediate or remote connexion, which it was concluded that expedition had with an attempt upon India, had confirmed Lord Wellesley in the absolute necessity of either compelling Tippoo Sultaun to detach himself from the interests of France, or of depriving him of the means of co-operating with that Nation in any project hostile to the British Government. The great victory gained over the French fleet by Lord Nelson, intelligence of which had reached Bengal on the 21st of October; the extraordinary success, which had attended the measures adopted at Hyderabad; and the complete state of the preparation of the armies at Madras and Bombay; made Lord Wellesley, when he wrote to the Sultaun under date the 8th of November, expect that Prince would accede to the proposal, which he had made for a pacific negotiation, and that the terror of the British arms would render their actual employment unnecessary. But, notwithstanding this hope, he resolved to be prepared for every event; and, with this view, he proceeded in person to Madras, that he might, by being near the scene of negotiation or military operations, avoid the incalculable evils of delay; and give to the public service the advantage of a prompt decision upon every question, military or political, which could arise. He informed Tippoo Sultaun of his having taken this resolution, in a letter under date the 10th of December; and at the same time urged that Prince to give the earliest and most serious consideration to the communication which he had made to him under date the 8th of November.

Lord Wellesley reached Madras on the 31st of December, and found, on his arrival there, a reply had been received from the Sultaun to the letter which he had written to that Prince before he left Calcutta.

In this reply, Tippoo repeated his former professions of unalterable friendship to the English; expressed his bad opinion of the French; and asserted, that the reputed embassy to the Mauritius was merely a mercantile speculation of some of his subjects, and it's destination to the French Islands altogether accidental. Forty persons, he stated, among whom were twelve artificers, had returned in the vessel sent there; and to some of these he had given service, and others had departed from his dominions. "But "the French," he observes in this letter, "who "are full of vice and deceit, have perhaps taken

" advantage of the departure of the ship, to " put about reports, with a view to ruffle the " minds of both Governments."

Tippoo expressed, in this communication, great surprise at the allusion to war in the Governor General's letter; and, on this ground, he evaded an assent to the proposition made of deputing Major Doveton, as he conceived no further means, than those already taken, could be necessary to give strength and stability to a friendship, which rested upon such firm foundations, as that which then existed between him, the British Government, and it's Allies.

In his answer to this evasive letter, Lord Wellesley stated in the fullest manner the grounds of the measures which he had adopted. All the proceedings of the embassy to the Mauritius were recapitulated; and the Sultaun was further informed, that he had, by his conduct, compelled the Allies to seek relief from the ambiguous and anxious state in which they had been placed for years past; and that they could no longer suffer those constant preparations for war, and hostile negotiations with their enemies, which exposed them, during a period of supposed peace, to all the solicitude, and hazard, and much of the expense, of war. In reply to that part of Tippoo's letter in which he evaded our negotiation, Lord Wellesley observed,

" That a new arrangement had become indis-" pensable, in consequence of that Prince's " new engagements with the common enemy " of the Allies;" and, after repeating his entreaties to the Sultaun to meet with cordiality this moderate and sincere advance to an amicable explanation, he plainly informed him, that no further delays could be admitted; and required an answer to the letter then sent, a day after it's receipt.

This letter was dated the 9th of January, and it reached the Sultaun about the 15th of that month. No reply, however, was received to it until the 13th of February, when a short letter was received, which took a very cursory notice of Lord Wellesley's proposition in the following terms: " Being frequently disposed " to make excursions, and hunt, I am accord-" ingly proceeding upon a hunting excursion. " You will be pleased to despatch Major Dove-" ton, (about whose coming your friendly pen " has repeatedly written,) slightly attended."

The delay, which the Sultaun had made in his reply to the letter of the 9th of January, had been considered as a rejection of the proposition for an amicable settlement, combined with a design on the part of that Prince to procrastinate, till the favourable season for the attack of his capital was past. Under such impressions, which were greatly strengthened by his having at this period deputed another embassy to the Isle of France, the British army under General Harris, and the Nizam's army under Meer Allum, had been directed, on the 3d of February, to advance against his dominions.

Lord Wellesley, however, in a letter under date the 22d of February, acknowledged the receipt of the Sultaun's last short letter; and informed that Prince, that his long silence on so important and pressing an occasion, had compelled him to the measures which he had adopted. The deputation of Major Doveton, his Lordship stated, under actual circumstances, could be productive of no advantage; but that as the Allies still retained a desire to effect a settlement, General Harris had been instructed to receive any embassy which Tippoo might send; and he was empowered to enter into a new treaty of friendship with him, founded upon such conditions as should appear to the Allies to be indispensably necessary to the establishment of a secure and permanent peace.

It will be useful, before I touch on the events of the war with Tippoo Sultaun, to advert to the nature of those terms, on which the Governor General was disposed, at different periods, to come to an amicable settlement with that Prince; as a reference to them will best show those principles of policy, by which Lord Wellesley's conduct was governed throughout the whole of this arduous and difficult proceeding.

From his Lordship's letter to the Court of Directors, under date the 3d of August 1799, it appears, that when he discovered the inadequacy of the requisite means to reduce the Sultaun's power and resources by a sudden and unexpected attack, that his views were limited to the object of detaching that Prince from his friendship with the French Nation; and that he would have been contented with any adjustment, which offered a reasonable prospect of securing that object. This he judged might be effected by the establishment of a permanent Resident at Seringapatam; the dismission of all the French in the Sultaun's service; and the perpetual exclusion of the French from his armies and dominions.

The invasion of Egypt by the French, which, if it had not been originally planned with a view to the assistance of Tippoo, might, the Governor General thought, be converted to that purpose, rendered the reduction of that Prince's power more urgent than before; while the success at Hyderabad, and the forward state of the military preparations at Madras and Bombay, made the accomplishment of that object less difficult. These combined considerations caused Lord Wellesley to extend his views; and, at the period when he addressed the letter under date the 8th of November to the Sultaun, he was resolved, in addition to the terms before specified, to insist upon Tippoo's agreeing to exchange the Province of Canara (the only line of sea-coast in his possession) for an equal extent of territory in some other quarter: for he conceived such an adjustment was then requisite, to afford complete security against any designs which the Sultaun might have in combination with the French, whose intercourse with Mysore would by this arrangement have been completely cut off. No opportunity, however, was offered of discussing these terms; and the perseverance of the Sultaun in the cultivation of a connexion with the French, and his neglect of every advance to an amicable settlement, combined with the concentrated state of the forces of the British Government and the Nizam, made the Governor General, after his arrival at Madras, resolve to add to the other demands, the payment of a considerable sum of money, as an indemnification for the expense to which the hostile and treacherous conduct of Tippoo had exposed the Allies.

It was not till the month of February 1799, that the Governor General found himself compelled to abandon all hopes of effecting any amicable settlement with Tippoo; and he then directed the British armies to advance against that Prince; empowering, however, the Commander-in-Chief, General Harris, to treat with the Sultaun, if he showed a sincere desire for peace. The terms upon which this was to be concluded, were, of course, to depend upon the stage of the war at which negotiations commenced; but in the event of any decided victory, or of the batteries against his capital having been opened, the demands were to be extended to the cession (by the Sultaun) of one half of his dominions, and the payment to the Allies of two crore of rupees; and he was to be required to give four of his sons, and four of his principal Officers, as hostages, for the faithful performance of these conditions.

The army under General Harris, after having been joined by that of the Nizam, had entered the territories of Mysore on the 3d of March, unopposed by the Sultaun; who had, when he saw the advanced state of the preparations of the Allies, hastened to attack the Bombay army under General Stuart, which was posted in Coorgah, and ready to co-operate in the reduction of his capital. When repulsed in this attack, which was with great loss, his next object was to obstruct the march of General Harris's army, which he met between Sultanpet and Malavelly on the 27th of March, where a partial action took place, which terminated in the Sultaun's defeat, and instant retreat to Seringapatam; and that fortress was, a few days afterwards, regularly invested by the combined armies of the British Government and the Nizam.

The Sultaun, who had hitherto made no communication whatever to General Harris, addressed a short note to that Officer on the 9th of April, in which he required to know the cause of the hostile advance of the British army. In reply to this demand, he was referred to the letters which he had before received from the Governor General; which, he was informed, were fully explanatory upon that subject. The Sultaun returned no answer to this letter till the 20th of April, when the operations of the siege were far advanced. On that date he again addressed General Harris, desiring that he would appoint a person to conduct a conference for the purpose of restoring peace. To this communication the General replied by sending him the draft of the treaty, which he had been instructed, under such circumstances of advantage, to conclude.

To this communication he made no reply; and the siege continued till the 4th of May, when the fort was taken by assault, Tippoo

Sultaun slain, and the Empire of the House of Hyder subverted.

Such was the termination of a war, which, whether we consider the temper and wisdom that marked the negotiations by which it was preceded, the ability and courage with which it was prosecuted, or the important political consequences by which it was attended, will be found unparalleled in the annals of British India. In the short period of a few months a rival Power was destroyed; which, from the first day of it's existence, till that of it's dissolution, (a period of thirty-eight years,) might be said to have directed all it's efforts against the English power in India.

Important as the conquest of Mysore was to the British interests in India, the solid and permanent advantages to be derived from that great event, depended chiefly upon the settlement of the territories which had been subdued. The justice and success of the war had given to the Company, and the Nizam, an undoubted right to dispose of these territories as they judged proper; but on the manner in which they exercised this right, not only the reputation of those States, but the future tranquillity of the southern part of the Peninsula of India, in a great degree depended.

The Nizam, who had given the Governor

General, at the commencement of the war, full powers to negotiate a peace, directed, after the fall of Seringapatam, the Commander of his forces to acquiesce in any plan of settlement upon which Lord Wellesley should decide, respecting the disposal of the territories of the Sultaun. From this act of honourable confidence, the Governor General was left free to make such a settlement of the conquered kingdom of Mysore, as should, in his opinion, be consistent with those principles of moderation and justice upon which the war was undertaken.

It will only be necessary to take a short general view of the character of the arrangement which Lord Wellesley made, and of the leading considerations which governed his conduct upon this important occasion. But, in doing this, it is impossible to refrain from giving occasional extracts from those clear and luminous despatches, in which that nobleman reported to his superiors in England the motives of his proceedings. "In regulating "the exercise of our right of conquest," Lord Wellesley observes in his letter to the Directors, under date the 3d of August 1799, "it appeared to me, that no principle could "more justly be assumed, than that the original objects of the war should constitute the

" basis of the peace, and of the general settle-
" ment of our territorial acquisitions. These
" objects had been repeatedly declared by the
" Allies to be a reasonable indemnification of
" our expense in the war, and an adequate
" security against the return of that danger,
" which originally provoked us to arms.

" With a view," he continues, " to each of
" these just and necessary objects, it was re-
" quisite that the Company, and the Nizam,
" should retain a large portion of the con-
" quered territory; but it required much con-
" sideration to determine the precise extent of
" that portion, as well as the just rule of par-
" tition. The war had not been undertaken in
" pursuit of schemes of conquest, aggrandize-
" ment of territory, or augmentation of revenue.
" In proportion to the magnitude and lustre of
" our success, it became a more urgent duty to
" remember, that a peace, founded in the grati-
" fication of any ambitious or inordinate view,
" could neither be advantageous, honourable,
" nor secure.

" The approved policy, interests and honour,
" of the British Nation, required that the settle-
" ment of the extensive Kingdom subjected to
" our disposal, should be formed on principles
" acceptable to the inhabitants of the con-
" quered territories; just and conciliatory

" towards the contiguous native States; and " indulgent to every party, in any degree " affected by the consequences of our suc- " cess.

" To have divided the whole territory " equally between the Company and the Ni- " zam, to the exclusion of any other State, " would have afforded strong grounds of jea- " lousy to the Mahrattas, and aggrandized " Nizam Ally's power beyond all bounds of " discretion. Under whatever form such a " partition could have been made, it must " have placed in the hands of the Nizam many " of the strong fortresses on the northern fron- " tiers of Mysore, and exposed our frontier, in " that quarter, to every predatory incursion. " Such a partition would have laid the " foundation of perpetual differences, not " only between the Mahrattas and the Ni- " zam, but between the Company and both " those Powers.

" To have divided the Country into three " equal portions; allowing the Mahrattas " (who had borne no part in the expense or " hazard of the war) an equal share with the " other two branches of the triple alliance, in " the advantages of the peace, would have " been unjust towards the Nizam, and towards " the Company impolitic, as furnishing an

" evil example to our other Allies in India; " and dangerous, as effecting a considerable " aggrandizement of the Mahratta Empire, at " the expense of the Company and the Nizam. " This mode of partition also must have " placed Chittledroog, and some of the most " important northern fortresses, in the hands " of the Mahrattas; while the remainder of " the fortresses, in the same line, would have " been occupied by the Nizam; and our unfor- " tified and open frontier in Mysore would " have been exposed to the excesses of the " undisciplined troops of both Powers.

" The Mahrattas, unquestionably, had no " claim to any portion of the conquered ter- " ritory; and any considerable extension of " their Empire was objectionable, especially " when accompanied by the possession of " strong fortresses bordering on the line of " our frontier. It was, however, desirable to " conciliate their good will, and to offer to " them such a portion of territory as might " give them an interest in the new settlement, " without offence or injury to the Nizam, and " without danger to the frontier of the Com- " pany's possessions. On the other hand, it " was prudent to limit the territory retained in " the hands of the Company and of the Ni- " zam within such bounds of moderation as

" should bear a due proportion to their respec-
" tive expenses in the contest, and to the ne-
" cessary means of securing the future safety
" of their respective dominions."

After these observations, his Lordship concludes this part of the subject by stating, that an attentive investigation of every comparative view of these important questions had terminated in his deciding; " that the establishment
" of a central and separate Government in My-
" sore, under the protection of the Company,
" and the admission of the Mahrattas to a
" certain participation in the division of the
" conquered territory, were the expedients
" best calculated to reconcile the interests of
" all parties; to secure to the Company a less
" invidious and more efficient share of reve-
" nue, resource, commerce, advantage, and mi-
" litary strength, than could be obtained under
" any other distribution of territory or power;
" and to afford the most favourable prospect
" of general and permanent tranquillity in
" India."

His Lordship next explains, in this despatch, the considerations which had regulated the partition of the Country. The districts of Canara, including all the sea-coast of Mysore, and the Provinces immediately contiguous to the possessions of the Company on the coast of

Malabar, and the Carnatic, were of course assigned to the English Government; to which were added the forts and posts at the heads of the different passes into Mysore, and the fortress and island of Seringapatam, which was deemed essential, to secure the communication between the possessions of the Company on the coast of Coromandel and that of Malabar, and to connect the different lines of defence.

The districts of Goorum Condah, Gooty, and others contiguous to his dominions, were assigned to the Nizam: and though that Prince had no claim, from the letter of his engagements, which could entitle him to a share in the advantages of the settlement, beyond his relative proportion in the expenses and exertions of the allied forces during the war, Lord Wellesley thought it desirable that the territorial revenue retained in sovereignty by the Company, after deducting whatever charges might be annexed to tenure, should not exceed that assigned to the Nizam; "reserving, however," (as his Lordship states in his letter to the Directors,) "to the "Company, as a just indemnification for their "superior share in the expenses and exertions "of the war, the principal benefit of whatever "advantages might flow from any engagements "to be contracted with the new Government of "Mysore."

The share of territory reserved, as an eventual cession to the Poonah Government, Lord Wellesley resolved should be of an amount which did not exceed in value two thirds, or was not below one half, of the portion allotted to the Company and Nizam Ally Khan; and this share composed the Harponelly, Soondah, Annagoondy, and other districts contiguous to the possessions of the Paishwah. But as this cession could only be considered as a favour, the Government of Poonah having taken no share in the war, Lord Wellesley determined it should not be made unconditionally; but should form the basis of a new treaty with the Mahratta Empire.

This cession amounted in annual revenue to upwards of two lacks and sixty-three thousand Canterai pagodas; while that, reserved for the establishment of the Government of Mysore, was in value upwards of thirteen lacks of pagodas; and comprised more than the ancient possessions of Mysore, previously to the usurpation of Hyder Ally Khan.

The reasons which led Lord Wellesley to determine upon restoring the ancient Hindoo family of Mysore, are very fully stated in his letter, to which I have before referred. The strongest considerations of policy forbade the re-elevation of the family of Tippoo. They had been brought up in hereditary hatred of the English Government; and could not, under any arrangement which it was possible to make, be expected to forget the great power and independence from which they had fallen. The sentiments of Lord Wellesley upon this subject are forcibly expressed in the following passage:

" The heir of Tippoo Sultaun must have " been educated in the same principles, encou" raged to indulge the same prejudices and " passions, and instructed to form the same " views of the interests and honour of the " throne of Mysore. These sentiments would " necessarily acquire additional force in his " mind, from the issue of the late war. But un" exampled success had subverted the founda" tions of his father's Empire, and transferred " to our possession every source of the civil or " military power of Mysore; and placed on the " throne by our favour, and limited by our " control, he must have felt himself degraded " to a state of humiliation and weakness so " abject, as no Prince of spirit will brook. " Under such an arrangement, our safety " would have required us to retain at least all " the territory which we now hold by the par" tition treaty of Mysore. Whatever we re" tained must have been considered by this

" Prince as a new usurpation upon his royal " inheritance, and an additional pledge of his " degradation and disgrace. In proportion to " the reduction of his territory and resources, " he would have had less to lose, and more to " regain, in any struggle for the recovery of " his father's Empire; nor does it seem unrea- " sonable to suppose, that the heir of Hyder " Ally and Tippoo Sultaun, animated by the " implacable spirit and bold example of his " parents, and accustomed to the commanding " prospect of independent sovereignty, and to " the splendour of military glory, might deli- " berately hazard the remnant of his hereditary " possessions in pursuit of so proud an object, " as the recovery of that vast and powerful " Empire, which for many years had rendered " his ancestors the scourge of the Carnatic, " and the terror of this quarter of India.

" In the most narrow view," his Lordship adds, " of the subject, it must be admitted, " that the son of Tippoo Sultaun must have " felt a perpetual interest in the subversion of " any settlement of Mysore, founded on a par- " tition of his father's dominions, and a limita- " tion of his own independence. If, therefore, " a Prince of this race had been placed on the " throne of Mysore, the foundation of the new " settlement would have been laid in the very

" principle of it's own dissolution. With such " a Prince, no sincere alliance, no concord of " sentiment nor union of views, could ever have " been established: the appearance of amity or " attachment must have been delusive; even " his submission must have been reluctant, if " not treacherous; while all his interests, his " habits, prejudices and passions, his views, " and even his virtues, must have concurred " to cherish an irreconcileable aversion to our " name and power, and an eager desire to abet " the cause, to exasperate the animosity, and " to receive the aid, of every enemy of the " British Nation. Whatever degree of influ- " ence or strength might have been left to the " native Government of Mysore, in such hands " would always have been thrown into the scale " opposed to their interests. The hostile Power " of Mysore would have been weakened, but " not destroyed: an enemy would have still " remained in the centre of your possessions, " watching every occasion to repair the mis- " fortunes of his family at their expense, and " forming a point of union for the machina- " tions of every discontented faction in India, " and for the intrigues of every emissary of the " French."

Under these impressions, he resolved to exclude this family from all power, and to raise the ancient House of Mysore to the Government of that Country: a measure, which was recommended by every consideration of policy, humanity, and justice.

"The indignities" (Lord Wellesley states in his letter to the Directors upon this subject) "which the family of Mysore had suffered, "especially during the cruel and tyrannical "reign of Tippoo Sultaun, and the state of "degradation and misery to which they had "been reduced, must naturally excite a senti- "ment of gratitude and attachment in their "minds towards that Power, which should not "only deliver them from oppression, but raise "them to a state of considerable affluence and "distinction. Between the British Govern- "ment and this family an intercourse of "friendship and kindness had subsisted: in "the most desperate crisis of their adverse for- "tune they had formed no connexion with your "enemies: their elevation would be the spon- "taneous act of your generosity; and from "your support alone could they ever hope to "be maintained upon the throne, either against "the family of Tippoo Sultaun, or against any "other claimant. They must naturally view "with an eye of jealousy all the friends of the "usurping family, and consequently be adverse "to the French, or to any State connected

" with that family in it's hereditary hatred of " the British Government. The heir of the " Rajah of Mysore, if placed on the throne, " must feel that his continuance in that sta- " tion depended on the stability of the new " settlement in all it's parts; it must therefore " be his interest to unite, with cordiality and " zeal, in every effort necessary to it's har- " mony, efficiency and vigour. The effect of " such an arrangement of the affairs of Mysore " would not be limited to the mere destruction " of the hostile Power, which menaced our " safety; in the place of that Power would " be substituted one, whose interest and re- " sources might be absolutely identified with " our own: and the kingdom of Mysore, so " long the source of calamity or alarm to the " Carnatic, might become a new barrier of our " defence, and might supply fresh means of " wealth and strength to the Company, their " subjects, and Allies."

Having resolved upon these measures, orders were given for their immediate execution. The descendants of the Sultaun were removed to Vellore; where excellent accommodations were prepared for their reception; liberal pensions assigned for their support; and every attention and indulgence shown, which were due to their rank and situation, and could be rendered compatible with the object of preventing their escape from that fortress. The chief Mahomedan Sirdars of the Sultaun were also provided for by liberal pensions: and every step was taken, which could tend to reconcile the family, adherents and servants, of the late Sultaun, to the arrangement which was intended.

Immediately after the departure of the sons of Tippoo Sultaun from Seringapatam, Kistna Raji Oudawer, a child of three years of age, the lineal descendant of the ancient family of Mysore, whose power Hyder Ally Khan had usurped in the year 1761, was raised to the throne of his ancestors; and Purneah, a Bramin of great ability and reputation, who had been the chief finançial Minister of Tippoo, was appointed Dewan or Minister to the young Prince. Two treaties were formed with this Prince; one termed the partition treaty, under date the 22d of June 1799; and the latter, the subsidiary treaty of Seringapatam, under date the 8th of July 1799.

The first of these treaties was contracted between the English Government, that of the Soubah of the Deckan, and the new State of Mysore. The exact amount of the territories to be kept by the British Government, and that of Hyderabad, was settled in this treaty;

and the amount and mode of payment of the pensions allotted for the support of the family and chief Officers of the Sultaun, was also fixed. The territory, which it had been resolved to secure for the State of Poonah, was, by the conditions of this treaty, to be given to the Paishwah; provided that Prince acceded to it within a month from the day on which it was communicated to him; and provided he gave satisfaction to the English Government, and that of Hyderabad, respecting some points which were pending between these Courts and that of Poonah. In the event of the Paishwah not acceding to the treaty which it was meant to offer to his acceptance, the territories reserved for the Paishwah were to be divided between the Nizam and the Company; but a proportion of two thirds was to be given to the former.

To the subsidiary treaty of Mysore the Soubahdar of the Deckan was not a party. It was an engagement, formed to settle the relations between the new State of Mysore and the British Government; and, from it's stipulations, the former became in a great degree dependent upon the latter for it's political existence.

By this treaty it was stipulated, that the Company should maintain a military force for the defence of the kingdom of Mysore against all external enemies; and that the Rajah should pay an annual subsidy of seven lacks of pagodas for the support of this force. It was further agreed, that in the event of extraordinary expenses being incurred for the defence of the territories of the contracting parties, or in preparations for hostilities against any enemy of the two States, the Rajah of Mysore was to contribute towards such expenditure in such a proportion, as should appear to the Governor General of India, after an attentive consideration of his means, just and reasonable.

Under the declared resolution of providing against the possibility of the Company's Government suffering by any future failure of the funds appropriated for the support of the forces which it was bound to maintain for the defence of Mysore, it was stipulated, that, on such event appearing probable, the English Government possessed a right, either to introduce such regulations and ordinances in the internal management of the revenues, or to assume, and bring under it's direct management, such part or parts of the Country of Mysore, as appeared necessary to render the funds fixed for the maintenance of the troops, efficient and available. The British Government agreed, on it's part, to render the Rajah a true and faithful account of the revenues so assumed; and it was stipulated, that the actual receipts of the Rajah, under no possible circumstances or arrangement, were to be less than one lack of pagodas territorial revenue, and one fifth of the produce of the Countries ceded to him by the treaty of Mysore.

The Rajah of Mysore agreed, in this treaty, to refrain from all communication or correspondence with any foreign State, and to admit no European foreigners into his Country or service. He also agreed to permit the British Government to garrison with it's own troops such fortresses in the Country of Mysore, as it might think necessary to enable it to fulfil it's engagements, of protecting and defending that kingdom.

These were the principal conditions of the treaty, which fixed the relations between the new State of Mysore and the British Government. I shall hereafter speak of the operation of this arrangement. It will now be necessary to treat of those important political events, by which the conquest of Mysore was immediately followed.

The jealous, and almost hostile, spirit with which the Mahrattas regarded our operations against Tippoo; and the conflicts with which the southern part of the Peninsula was threatened, from the weak and distracted condition of the Paishwah's Government; pointed out the urgent necessity of adding, by every practicable means, to the efficiency of the alliance with the Nizam; as that became the chief, and, after the defection of the Paishwah, the only means of protecting the British possessions, and those of it's Allies, in a state of peace and tranquillity.

For the attainment of this object, it was necessary to add to the strength of the subsidiary force with the Nizam; and to adopt measures, that would secure the English Government against those risks, to which it was probable this connexion would be early exposed, from the weak and fluctuating councils of that Prince.

To effect this important point, nothing seemed so desirable, as to commute the monthly pecuniary payment of subsidy for a cession of territory. The advantages of such an arrangement were manifold, and obvious. An end would undoubtedly be put, by it's adoption, to that constant recurrence of irritation, which must always be expected to attend large pecuniary payments from sordid or extravagant Courts. The resources upon which the support of a large English force must depend, would be placed in the hands of the British Government, instead of being in those of another State, whose imprudence, distress, or treachery, might, at any critical moment, endanger the general safety. And the wish, which, it was possible, a future weak or fickle Administration at Hyderabad might entertain, of freeing that State from a connexion, from which it might think it had derived all the benefit that it could expect, and the expense of which continued a burden upon it's finances, would cease to operate; when it had, by a cession of territory, paid in perpetuity, and by advance, for the services of the corps by which it's dominions were protected. These were among the leading considerations which induced Lord Wellesley to enter into the negotiation with the Nizam; which terminated in the conclusion of a new treaty with that Prince, bearing date the 12th of October 1800.

By this treaty, the British Government engaged to permit no Power nor State whatever to commit, with impunity, any act of unprovoked aggression or hostility upon the territories of the Nizam: and to enable the Company to fulfil this engagement in an efficient manner, two battalions of Sepoys, and a regiment of native cavalry, were permanently added to the subsidiary force to be maintained by the State of Hyderabad. To secure the constant and regular payment of this augmented force, the Nizam ceded in perpetuity to the Company all the territories, which he had acquired by the treaty of Seringapatam in 1792, and the treaty of Mysore in 1799. With a view of preserving a well-defined boundary, some changes were made in this cession; the Nizam retaining Kupoor, Gujunder, Ghur, &c. and giving Adone, &c. in their lieu, Countries situated to the south of the river Toombuddrah, which, by this settlement, formed the boundary between the two States.

In the event of war taking place between the contracting parties and a third State, the Nizam agreed, that the whole of the subsidiary force, except two battalions, which were to be kept near his person, were to be employed against the enemy; and that the force was, on such event, to be immediately joined by six thousand infantry and nine thousand horse of his own troops.

The Nizam also agreed to enter into no negotiation with other States, without informing and consulting the Company's Government: and the latter agreed, that it would in no instance interfere with the Nizam's children, relations, or subjects; with respect to whom it would always consider him absolute.

The Nizam engaged not to commit hostilities against any other State; and, in the event of differences arising between him and another Power, it was stipulated, that they were to be adjusted by the Company's Government, and that the Nizam was to acquiesce in the justice of it's decision.

It was stipulated, that in the event of either the Paishwah, Ragojee Bhonslah, or Doulut Row Scindiah, desiring to be a party in this treaty, they should be admitted to all it's advantages.

The revenue of the territories ceded to the Company by this treaty was about 1,758,000 of pagodas: but their importance, in a political and military point of view, was still greater than their pecuniary value: For this cession, while it terminated, as has been shown, those constant recurring causes of irritation, to which we were subject as long as this payment was made in monthly instalments, added, from the local situation of the districts, to the security of the former possessions of the Company on the coast of Coromandel, and to those of the new State of Mysore; to both of which they formed a defined and good military barrier.

It has been before stated, that the British Government had reserved a considerable portion of the conquered territories of Tippoo Sultaun, to be given to the Paishwah, on the condition of that Prince acceding to an alliance calculated to preserve the general tranquillity. Badjerow, however, acting under the control of Doulut Row Scindiah, who continued with a large army, and almost the whole of his French brigades, at Poonah, rejected this equitable proposal; and the reserved territory was shared agreeably to the stipulations of the partition treaty between the English Government and that of Hyderabad.

In the beginning of the year 1801, the occurrence of war between Jeswunt Row Holkar and Scindiah had forced the latter to move from Poonah; and the distraction, which this event had created among the Mahratta States, appeared to Lord Wellesley to constitute a most favourable crisis, for effecting the complete establishment of the British interests at the Court of Poonah. This he desired to do upon a basis, that, while it secured the stability and efficiency of the Paishwah's authority, interfered with none of the real rights or possessions of the great Feudatories in the Mahratta State; and, consequently, could only be opposed by them on the grounds of it's defeating their plans of encroachment and aggrandizement, which it had become the imperious policy of the British Government to check, as their prosecution was altogether incompatible with the maintenance of that system, which it had been compelled to adopt, for it's own safety, and that of it's Allies.

The Paishwah had himself made a general proposition for entering into a defensive alliance with the British Government: but the nature of the conditions of the treaty which he proposed, and the actual state of his power, made the Governor General deem it advisable to reject his proposition; which he thought was merely calculated to give the Paishwah the assistance of the British power, to re-establish and support his personal authority, without admitting it to the exercise of that influence, which it appeared necessary the English Government should possess, in order to maintain it's own security, and that of it's Allies.

Before June 1802, the date on which Lord Wellesley received the negotiations at Poonah, accounts had been received of the peace of Amiens. The scene was consequently open to French intrigue: and if Scindiah regained, by the defeat of Holkar, an event then probable, the complete ascendency over the Paishwah, and the entire control of the Mahratta Empire, from the banks of the Ganges to the sea of Malabar; there could not be a doubt in the mind of any man in the least degree acquainted with the constitution of the army of that Chief, and the influence and authority of the French Officers by whom it was then commanded, that the French Nation might, in a very few years, without violating one article of the treaty of peace, have aided him to the consolidation of a military power, which would have struck at the very existence of the British Government in India. It did not appear likely, that the execution of such a plan would meet with any serious obstacle in the jealousy of Scindiah, who had become familiar with the system, which it was the policy of the French to pursue. To it both his predecessor and himself had owed their power; and he was consequently disposed to pursue it.

The territories of the Paishwah had been the scene of continual conflict, from the death of Madhoo Row; and were not able, in their exhausted state, to support, even for a few months, the hordes of banditti, which were daily pouring in from Malwah and Hindoostan, to contend at Poonah for the Sovereignty of the Mahratta Empire.

This fact, which cannot be disputed, made it evident, that if the armies of Scindiah, Holkar, and Ragojee Bhonslah, were permitted to make the Provinces of the Poonah State their theatre of warfare, the armies of these Chiefs must be early forced by want, if not invited by policy, to invade the territories of the British Government, or it's Allies: and this circumstance formed in itself a strong proof, not merely of the expediency, but of the necessity, of the measures pursued on this occasion by Lord Wellesley.

In the contest, which took place in 1802, between Doulut Row Scindiah and Holkar, the

Paishwah joined with the former, whose force at Poonah sustained a signal defeat near that city on the 25th of October. Badjerow, who had moved out of his capital before the action commenced, immediately fled towards the sea-coast, having previously sent his Minister to the British Resident,* with a writing, sealed with his own seal, containing his consent to receive a subsidiary force, and to cede, for their subsistence, territory, either in Guzerat, or in his southern territories, producing an annual revenue of twenty-six lacks of rupees. The Minister, at the same time that he made this proposition, assured the Resident in the most positive manner, that it was the intention of his master to conclude a defensive alliance with the Honourable Company, on the basis of the treaty of Hyderabad.

The Governor General confirmed the preliminary engagement, which the Paishwah had offered to his acceptance, as soon as he received it; and desired that Prince should be informed, that all the resources of the British Government should be employed for the re-establishment of his authority. The Resident was also directed to give to the preliminaries the form of a defensive treaty, and to obtain the Paishwah's con-

* Colonel Close.

sent to such articles as were necessary to give the British Government all those advantages which it expected from this alliance.

The Paishwah, when near the sea-coast, demanded the aid of a vessel, and eventual protection, from the Government of Bombay, which was complied with; and, as Jeswunt Row Holkar continued at Poonah, he lost all hopes of being able to return to that city, and embarked on board the Herculean, an English vessel, sent for his accommodation, and proceeded to Bassein, where he arrived on the 16th of December. He was joined at that place by the British Resident; and, after a short negotiation, a definitive treaty of defensive alliance was concluded on the 31st of December, and ratified by the Governor General in Council on the 28th day of January 1803, the date on which it reached Calcutta.

By this treaty, the English Government bound itself to furnish to the Paishwah a subsidiary force of six battalions of native infantry, with a complement of field-pieces and European artillery-men: for the payment of which force, the Paishwah agreed to make over territory to an amount of twenty-six lacks of rupees. All claims of the Paishwah, and his family, on Surat, and the districts under the English Government in Guzerat, were finally adjusted; and that Prince agreed to abide by the arbitration of the Company in all his unsettled disputes with the Soubahdar of the Deckan; and in the adjustment of some unsettled accounts with the family of the Guickwar in Guzerat, whose previous engagements with the Company he fully recognised. The Paishwah also engaged to discharge any Europeans from his service, that belonged to Nations hostile to the English, or were discovered meditating injury, or carrying on intrigues injurious to the interests of that Nation.

Such were the principal conditions of this treaty. It will be next necessary to state the measures that were adopted to facilitate it's complete execution, and to secure to the British Government all those advantages that were expected from this important measure.

The army of Fort Saint George, under the command of General Stuart, had advanced to the bank of the Toombuddra, to support this treaty, which included the restoration of the Paishwah to his throne at Poonah. General Wellesley was detached in front, with a select corps, to effect this object: and advancing in co-operation with the subsidiary force in the Deckan, commanded by Colonel Stevenson, through the southern parts of the Paishwah's territories, he reached Poonah on the 20th of

April. The troops of Holkar fled at his approach; and Badjerow, who had left Bassein when he learnt that the British forces were coming to his aid, entered Poonah; and was reseated on his Musnud, in that capital, on the 13th of May.

This great measure was effected without any opposition: and all the principal southern Mahratta Jagheerdars (who are considered as the more immediate Feudatories and dependents of the Paishwah) gave, by their actions as well as expressions, a full assent to this connexion. Appah Saheb, the son of Purseram Bhow, his brother Chumajee Goklah Appah Depaye, and several others, joined their troops to those of General Wellesley, and advanced with him to the capital of the Mahratta Empire, where they paid their obeisance to the Paishwah, whose Court several of them had not visited for many years before.

The first fruits of the alliance, which were, the flight of Holkar, and the cheerful and dutiful obedience of some of his chief Feudatories, gave great satisfaction to the Paishwah, and afforded to the English Government a momentary hope, that this great measure of policy would be effected without a war. These hopes were, however, early disappointed, by the advance of Doulut Row Scindiah, and the Bhonslah, towards the frontier of our Ally the Nizam; and the delays and evasions with which these Chiefs treated the different propositions offered to their consideration by the British Resident* at the Court of Scindiah.

Doulut Row Scindiah had, after several communications with the Resident, acknowledged, that he could have no right, from his being guarantee to the treaty of Salbye, (the ground of objection he had first taken,) to oppose any treaty between the British Government and the Paishwah; and after admitting, that his interest had been advanced by the expulsion of Jeswunt Row Holkar from Poonah, and the re-establishment of Badjerow, he declared in explicit terms, " That he had no intention to " impede the performance of the arrangements " lately concluded between the Paishwah and " the British Government; but that he should, " on the contrary, desire to perfect the amity, " which then existed between the Paishwah, " the British Government, and his own States."

Five days after this declaration, Scindiah's Ministers remonstrated with the Resident against the advance of the British troops to Poonah; which, however, they were informed, could not be prevented, as it was a condition of

* Colonel Collins.

the engagement into which we had entered with the Paishwah; and of which, they were reminded, Scindiah had expressed his full approbation.

About the period at which the Resident reached Scindiah's camp at Boorhanpore (February 27th), he received secret information of a league between the principal Mahratta Chiefs, with objects hostile to the British Government, being in agitation; and the advance of the army of the Rajah of Berar to join Scindiah, combined with the active negotiations which the latter Chief carried on with Holkar, gave some credibility to this information. But there appeared, on the other hand, when the nature of their respective Governments was considered, every cause to doubt their power of combination; and it was quite evident, that if such a league was even formed, their rooted animosities, and clashing interests, would prevent it's being attended with any serious danger.

Scindiah had, in fact, no objection to the interference of the British Government for the restoration of the power of the Paishwah, as long as he saw a prospect of that being usurped by Jeswunt Row Holkar; and he thought, that, by acting in aid of this project, he should come into the chief direction of the affairs of the Empire, and be enabled to destroy his rival, who had, from his success at Poonah, obtained great power and reputation: but the moment he found that the British Government had, by it's energy, and the great celerity of it's operations, obliged Holkar to fly, and established the Paishwah at Poonah without his aid, his plans changed; and he resolved to oppose the treaty, to which he had given, at one period, the most unqualified assent.

To effect this, his first object was to reach Poonah. But as his presence at that capital could have no effect, but that of disturbing, if it did not altogether annul, the recent engagements concluded with the Paishwah, the Governor General determined on not permitting it; and he directed the Resident at his Court to insist upon Scindiah either retreating from the threatening position he then occupied upon the Nizam's frontier, across the Nerbuddah; or, that he should give some unequivocal proof of his intention, in nowise to seek to derange the engagements concluded between the British Government and the Paishwah.

As, however, there were grounds of apprehension, that Scindiah would not relinquish his schemes without a contest, orders were at the same time given to Major General Wellesley, to be prepared to act; and that Officer, with a view of eventually co-operating with the subsidiary force in the Nizam's territories, advanced a few marches to the northward of Poonah, where he established a constant, and almost daily, intercourse with the British Resident in Doulut Row Scindiah's camp.

The Resident, at an interview with that Chief on the 27th of May, communicated the treaty of Bassein; and, after a careful perusal of every article, Scindiah and his Minister declared, that it contained nothing in the slightest degree injurious to his legitimate authority. But, though he made this declaration, he would not explain to the Resident what were his intentions; and on being much pressed at this conference for an explanation, Scindiah broke it up with saying; "After my inter-"view with the Rajah of Berar, you shall "be informed whether we will have war "or peace."

This extraordinary menace, which placed the question of war or peace, between the English Government and Doulut Row Scindiah, upon the result of a conference with the Rajah of Berar; and which was, in itself, a direct insult to the former State; lessened those hopes, that had been entertained, of an amicable termination to this negotiation. The Bhonslah, on whose decision it was likely to turn, had never been on a cordial footing with the English Government; and there was reason to think, that he would view any measures which strengthened the power of the Paishwah with particular jealousy, as he was known to cherish hopes of obtaining for himself the first dignity in the Mahratta Empire, to which he had some claims, from birth. The Governor General, aware of these sentiments, had taken every means within his power to conciliate this Chief; and had addressed a letter to him explanatory of the scope and intention of his proceedings at Poonah. But the manner in which this communication was received, did not afford any sanguine hope of his being an advocate for peace: on the contrary, there was just ground to believe, that the Bhonslah would, upon this occasion, stimulate Scindiah, and every Chief over whom he had influence, to attack the British Government: and, though his character was the opposite of warlike, he, like almost all the Mahrattas, anticipated success in such a contest; as it was evident, both from their expressions and correspondence, that they drew all their conclusions from the events of the former war which they had carried on against the English. They seemed, indeed, at this moment to have forgotten the changes, which a period of twenty-two years had effected; and it was early obvious to all persons near the scene of negotiation, that the constant recurrence of the Mahrattas to the success, which had formerly attended the combination against us, and the obstacles which their ignorance and pride opposed to their taking a just view of the increase of our power subsequently to that date, would make them precipitate a war, in spite of every effort which could be used to prevent that extremity.

Lord Wellesley, as soon as he received an account of the unfavourable state of the negotiations with Scindiah, vested the Officers in command of the armies in Hindoostan and the Deckan with the completest civil, military, and political powers in those quarters. Major General Wellesley was specifically authorized, at this early stage, to negotiate arrangements or treaties, either by himself, or through Residents or Agents, with Scindiah, Holkar, or the Rajah of Berar; with a view of prevailing upon those Chiefs to retire with their armies within the boundaries of their own States, or to give some sufficient pledge of their pacific disposition towards the British Government and it's Allies.

General Wellesley was charged, in these instructions, to demand of Scindiah a peremptory declaration of his intentions, and to insist upon his giving that in a certain number of days, which were to be settled at the discretion of the Major General; but reasonably fixed with reference to the season, and to the possible opening of the campaign in an advantageous manner to the British Government. If the explanation given by Scindiah was not full, and satisfactory, the General was instructed to recall the Resident from his camp; and directed, if war became inevitable, to carry it on in the most active manner, and to follow up his success, without listening to any proposal for peace, until the power of the Chiefs, against whom the war was made, should be totally annihilated. If circumstances required it, General Wellesley had authority given him to conclude a peace with Scindiah, or the Rajah of Berar, conjointly, or separately, as might appear to him most advisable.

In the instructions to Lord Lake, who was at the head of a large army in Hindoostan, the objects to be accomplished, if a war occurred, were fully pointed out. These were, in the first place, the complete reduction of that independent and formidable French authority, which had been established in Hindoostan. His Lordship was directed to occupy the whole space of the Country, forming the Duab, between the Jumnah and the Ganges to the mountains of Cumaoun, and also to possess himself of Dehli, Agra, and a chain of posts on the right banks of the Jumnah, from the mountains of Cumaoun to the Province of Bundlecund. It was not, the Governor General informed Lord Lake in these instructions, his intention to extend the Company's possessions beyond the line of the Jumnah, Agra and Dehli included, and a chain of posts to protect the navigation of the river. All the connexions, which might be formed to the south and west of the Jumnah beyond this line, he desired to have upon the principles of defensive alliance, or tributary dependence, so as to leave existing between the British possessions and the Mahratta Empire a barrier formed by petty States freely exercising the rights of independent Government, each in their respective limits, in alliance with the Company, and under the protection of the British Government.

The Governor General, in these instructions, placed great importance in the early rescue of the person and titular authority of the Moghul from the French party. He also signified his intention of subduing Bundlecund, as the vicinity of that Province to Benares, and several of the richest and most valuable possessions of the Company, made it dangerous to leave it in the hands of the enemy.

The detailed opinion of the Governor General, respecting the best mode of carrying every part of his instructions into execution, was conveyed to Lord Lake; but that Officer was intrusted with the fullest power of altering or modifying every part of his orders, as circumstances might demand; and the commencement of his operations was of course to depend upon the result of the negotiation then pending between General Wellesley and Doulut Row Scindiah.

Major General Wellesley, in conformity with the instructions which he had received, addressed a letter to Doulut Row Scindiah, under date the 14th of July; wherein, after stating the amicable objects of the treaty of Bassein, and remarking upon the hostile spirit of the measures adopted by the confederate Chiefs, since the conclusion of that treaty, he demanded the separation of the army of Scindiah from that of the Rajah of Berar, and the retreat of the former across the Nerbuddah; and stated his intention, in this letter, of making the British troops resume their ordinary stations, as soon as the Mahratta Chiefs had complied with this requisition.

On the 18th of July, when General Wellesley received the instructions of the Governor General, dated the 26th of June, he addressed another letter to Scindiah, informing him of the full and extensive powers with which he was vested; and he directed the Resident with that Chief, to demand of Scindiah and the Rajah of Berar, their separation, and the return of their armies to their usual stations; and instructed him, if these demands were not complied with, to withdraw himself instantly from the Mahratta camp.

Doulut Row Scindiah seemed at first inclined to comply with General Wellesley's requisition; but, after a consultation with the Rajah of Berar, and a delay of several days, it was at last stated to the Resident, at a conference which he had with both Chiefs on the 25th of July, that their troops were within their own territories, that they would promise not to pass the Adjuntee hills, nor to march to Poonah; and that they had given written assurances to the Governor General, that they would never attempt to overthrow the treaty of Bassein.

In reply to these assurances, the Resident repeated Major General Wellesley's observation, that it was altogether impossible to confide in their professions while they continued to occupy a position which was not necessary for their security, and which threatened the frontier of our Ally the Nizam. After hearing these, and similar arguments, the Chiefs requested a further delay, till the 28th of July, when they promised a definitive answer; and the Resident was induced, by his knowledge of the anxious desire of the Governor General to avoid, if possible, the occurrence of war, to depart from the positive instructions of General Wellesley, and grant a further delay.

On the 28th the Resident sent to require the final answer, which he had been promised. He received a message, in reply, that Doulut Row Scindiah and the Rajah of Berar meant to have a conference that day, at which it would not be proper for him to assist; "but that he should "be informed of the time which should be "fixed to receive him."

The Resident replied to this communication, by accusing Doulut Row Scindiah of having violated his promise. He would, he informed that Chief, wait till next day at noon for an answer; and, if he did not then receive one that was satisfactory, he would send off his tents towards Aurungabad, and follow himself next day.

After several further evasions, the Resident agreed to meet Doulut Row Scindiah and the Rajah of Berar once more, on the 31st of July; and at this conference he received from those Chiefs several propositions for an amicable adjustment. They proposed to retire to Boorhanpore (a town upon the Taptie, a few marches from their position), provided General Wellesley would agree to march his troops to their ordinary stations: but, on being told this proposition was altogether inadmissible, as it would leave them in a situation to pursue any measures which they chose, while it deprived the Company's Government of the means which it then possessed of opposing their designs; they suggested, that the Resident should appoint a day for the march of the respective forces of these Chieftains from the place of their encampment, and that he should pledge the faith of the British Government for the retreat of the army under General Wellesley on the day on which the armies of the Confederates should return to their usual stations.

Though the acceptance of this proposition was in opposition to his instructions from General Wellesley, his ardent desire for an amicable result to the negotiation which he had so ably conducted, led Colonel Collins to consent to forward the letter, containing this offer of adjustment, to General Wellesley, and to remain in camp till he received an answer. But that spirit of evasion, deceit, and falsehood, which had marked every stage of this negotiation, was conspicuously shown at it's close. The letters of

Doulut Row Scindiah and the Rajah of Berar to General Wellesley, were sent to the Resident; but, instead of this proposition, which he had consented to forward, they contained no more than the offer to retreat with their combined armies to Boorhanpore, while they required General Wellesley to return with his troops to their ordinary stations. As the Resident had before given the most formal and positive refusal to this proposition, he could not but consider this conduct on the part of the Chiefs as equally insulting and faithless; and he was confirmed by it in a belief, which he had been reluctant to entertain, of their unalterable resolution to endeavour to reduce, if they could not destroy, the strength of the British Government, by an attack upon that State and it's Allies; which they were only delaying, till they had collected all their means, and increased, by their negotiations and intrigues, the strength of that combination, which they desired to form against it's power.

Colonel Collins left the camp of Doulut Row Scindiah on the 3d of August; and the war was commenced by Major General Wellesley, by an attack of the fortress of Ahmednughur, on the 8th of that month.

Such were the negotiations, which immediately preceded a war, the justice and actual necessity of which can only be denied by those who refuse their assent to the wisdom of the policy which ensured the destruction of that inveterate enemy to our name, Tippoo Sultaun. It was altogether impracticable for us to fulfil, without constant recourse to arms, those engagements, which we had been compelled to contract with the Nizam, to induce him to aid us in the accomplishment of that first object of Lord Wellesley's policy, unless we succeeded in establishing a commanding influence in the Councils of the Poonah State; and, after that had been effected, it would have been a base abandonment of those, whom we had become pledged to support, if we had been induced, by any circumstances, to hazard their interests or security, for the sake of obtaining to ourselves a short exemption from the evils of war.

It is foreign from the object of this Sketch to enter into any detail of the military operations of the war between the British Government and the Mahratta Chiefs, Doulut Row Scindiah and the Rajah of Berar, which only continued five months; but was marked by a series of the most brilliant and decisive victories. The battles of Dehli and Laswaree, of Assye and Arghaum, and the reduction of the strong forts of Allyghur, Agra, and Gwalier, of

Ahmednughur, Asseerghur, Gawilghur, and Cuttack, and a number of inferior conquests, were crowded into this short but eventful period. The confederate Chiefs were compelled to sue separately for peace, after the annihilation of their infantry and cannon, and the loss of their finest Provinces, and a number of fortresses, which they had deemed impregnable. The complete destruction of the regular brigades in the service of Scindiah, was certainly one of the most important events of this war. These brigades formed, all together, a body of nearly forty thousand well disciplined men, with a very large train of artillery, acting entirely under the control of a French Commander, and supported by the revenues of the finest Provinces in India, under his management; and having every military resource within itself. It was the early extinction of this force, which obliged Scindiah to abandon all thoughts of a further prosecution of hostilities, and to throw himself completely upon the generosity of the British Government.

He was anticipated, however, in this design by the Rajah of Berar; who, immediately after the fall of his principal fortress, Gawilghur, entered into a treaty with General Wellesley, by which he agreed to give up the Province of Cuttack (an acquisition of the greatest value to the Company), and all his share of the Provinces of Berar westward of the Wurdah, of which he had before collected the revenues in participation with the Soubahdar of the Deckan, to whom this cession was not of more importance, as it added to his revenue, than as it strengthened his frontier, and freed him from those continued contests, that naturally attended the existence of a double authority collecting the revenues of the same Country.

The Company engaged, by this treaty, to arbitrate all differences, which might henceforward arise between the Rajah of Berar, the Soubahdar of the Deckan, and the Paishwah; and the Rajah agreed, that he would never admit any Frenchman, or the subject of any other European or American Power, which might be at war with England, into his service. It was stipulated, that each of the contracting States should keep a resident Minister at the Court of the other.

These were the principal conditions of this treaty of peace, which was concluded on the 17th of December 1803. It was immediately followed by the treaty with Scindiah, of which the following were the leading articles:—Scindiah ceded to the Company all the territories he possessed in Hindoostan to the northward of those of the Rajahs of Jypore, Jodepore, and the Ranah of Gohud; and the fort and territory of Baroach. He ceded also all lands to the south of Adjuntee; and all claims of every description upon the British Government and it's Allies, the Soubahdar of the Deckan, the Paishwah, and the Guickwar family in Guzerat.

It was a condition of this treaty, that if Scindiah should hereafter enter into a defensive treaty with the British Government, the pay of any English corps, fixed in his service, should be defrayed from the revenues of the territories ceded in the treaty of peace.

The Company agreed by this treaty, in consideration of the great losses sustained by the principal Officers of Scindiah's court and army, from the cession of the Provinces of Hindoostan, to grant pensions to them, agreeably to a list given in by Scindiah, to an annual amount of fifteen lacks of rupees.

These were the leading articles of this treaty, which was negotiated by General Wellesley upon the admitted principle of Scindiah's being completely subdued; and which, under the circumstances in which he was then placed, was, as his Ministers acknowledged, more favourable than he could have expected. It contained many small recessions of Provinces and villages, which had been hereditary in his family; and the grant of which was intended, and had in a great degree the effect, to reconcile him to the great losses, which he had sustained.

By one article in this treaty, Scindiah agreed to resign, with some modifications, all claims upon Rajahs, and others of his former Feudatories, with whom the English Government had made treaties or alliances. This engagement gave rise to a dispute, concerning the fortress of Gwalier and the territories of Gohud, which had, for the moment, the effect of disturbing the harmony, that would otherwise have immediately followed the peace between the two States. In this dispute justice was, no doubt, on the side of the British Government; but that did not prevent Scindiah and his Ministers from endeavouring to obtain their object, by a constant and vexatious agitation of the subject; and, though they were compelled to admit, that strict justice was against them, they continued to entertain hopes of success, declaredly grounded on that liberal and conciliating spirit with which the English Government had used it's great victories. Even the formal renunciation of this claim did not prevent their reurging it, the moment an occasion appeared the least favourable to their wishes.

This treaty of peace was concluded on the

30th of December 1803; and the connexion with Scindiah was further cemented by a treaty of defensive alliance, concluded by the acting Resident* at his Court on the 27th of February 1804.

By this treaty, Scindiah became entitled to the assistance of a corps of six battalions of Sepoys, which were either to be stationed within his territories, or at a convenient frontier post in the Honourable Company's territories, (as Scindiah preferred); and this corps was to be paid out of the revenues of those Countries which Scindiah had ceded to the Company.

The other articles of this defensive alliance were nearly the same as those formerly concluded between the Company and the Courts of Hyderabad and Poonah.

The conduct pursued by Jeswunt Row Holkar, during the war between the British Government, Scindiah, and the Rajah of Berar, was in conformity to the most characteristic features of a Mahratta Chieftain. He had not only promised to join the confederacy against the British Government, but had concluded, through the medium of the Rajah of Berar, a treaty with Scindiah, in which great cessions were made by Doulut Row, to induce him to

* Lieut. Colonel Malcolm.

enter into their plans. But, though he promised every thing, he showed no inclination, after hostilities were commenced, to assist the Confederates. There is, indeed, ground to believe, that he rejoiced in the first reverses which his rival Scindiah sustained: and if this sentiment underwent a change, as has been supposed, when he saw the ruin of that Chief, the course of action was too rapid and too decisive to give him time for interference; though, before the treaties of peace were concluded, he had advanced towards Hindoostan, as far as the frontier of the Rajah of Jypore, who was then under the British protection.

Though Jeswunt Row Holkar continued to profess his friendship for the British Government, his conduct at this period indicated other designs; and the Governor General instructed Lord Lake to enter into a negotiation with that Chief, that would lead to an early and full explanation of his views, and relieve the Company's Government from the expense and alarm to which it's Provinces must be subject while such a horde of freebooters, as the army under Holkar's command, were assembled on it's frontier, or that of it's Allies.

Lord Lake addressed a letter to Jeswunt Row Holkar, dated the 29th of January 1804, stating generally the terms on which the British Government was disposed to leave him in the unmolested exercise of his authority; but requiring, as a proof of the sincerity of the amicable professions which he had made, that he should withdraw his army from the threatening position it then occupied, retire within his own territories, and abstain from the exaction of any tribute from the Allies of the British Government.

Holkar, after some delay, sent Vakeels (or Agents) to wait upon the Commander-in-Chief; to whom they made, on the part of their master, the following propositions:

1st. That Holkar should be permitted to collect the choute, agreeably to the custom of his ancestors.

2d. That the ancient possessions formerly held by his family (twelve of the finest districts in the Duab, and a district in Bundlecund), should be given to him.

3d. That the Country of Humanah, which was formerly in the possession of the Holkar family, should be ceded to him.

4th. That his Country should be guaranteed to him, and a treaty concluded with him on the same terms as we had done with Scindiah.

These extravagant demands were of course rejected; and their nature, as well as the manner in which they were made, satisfied Lord

Lake of the real designs of Jeswunt Row; which were soon afterwards more fully developed by the contents of several letters, which he wrote to the tributaries and dependents of the British Government in Hindoostan; whom he excited, by every argument which he could use, to revolt against that State; whose territories, he informed them, it was his immediate intention to ravage and destroy. Lord Lake also obtained about this period a copy of a letter from Jeswunt Row Holkar to General Wellesley (supposed to be written early in February), in which he had demanded the cession of several Provinces of the Deckan, which he affirmed were originally the property of the Holkar family. This letter concluded with this remarkable expression:

" Countries of many hundred coss shall be " overrun, and plundered. Lord Lake shall " not have leisure to breathe for a moment; " and calamities will fall on lacks of human " beings, in continual war, by the attacks of " my army, which overwhelms like the waves " of the sea."

These insulting menaces were followed by acts of more positive aggression: Holkar sent an Agent to Scindiah's camp, and solicited openly the aid of that Chief in an attack upon the British possessions; and at the same time commenced the plunder of the territories of the Rajah of Jypore. The Commander-in-Chief, who could not but consider these proceedings as the commencement of hostilities, advanced against Holkar, who retreated from the position which he had occupied, and was pursued to some distance by a British force.

Thus commenced a war; the great successes of which were checkered by some remarkable failures. But, though the circumstances which attended the retreat of Colonel Monson's corps, and the very severe loss of Officers and men at the siege of Bhurrutpore, must be deemed serious reverses, they did not prevent the destruction of Holkar's power being effected, before the close of Lord Wellesley's Administration. The battle of Deeg was fatal to his regular infantry and artillery; and the action at Futtyghur broke altogether the spirit of his cavalry. The fortresses of Chandore and Gaulnah, which were the strong holds of the family, were also taken; and in April 1805, this boasting freebooter retreated across the Chumbul with an army reduced from forty thousand cavalry, twenty thousand infantry, and upwards of a hundred pieces of cannon, to a wretched body of about eight or ten thousand horse, four or five thousand infantry, and between twenty and thirty guns: and, though peace with this Chief was not immediately concluded, all his future efforts served only to show how completely he had been subdued.

In the years 1799 and 1800, Hindoostan was threatened with an invasion by Zemaun Shah; and, among other means adopted by Lord Wellesley to avert this danger, was an Embassy to Persia, to which Country he had before sent a native agent, who had been received with honour, and had succeeded in the limited objects of his mission. The Embassy deputed to the Court of Teheraun was in a style of splendour corresponding to the character of the Monarch and the manners of the Nation to whom it was sent, and to the wealth and power of that State from whom it proceeded. It was completely successful in all it's objects. The King of Persia was not only induced by the British Envoy* to renew his attack upon Khorassan, which had the effect of withdrawing Zemaun Shah from his designs upon India; but entered into treaties† of political and commercial alliance with the British Government; which, while they completely excluded the French from Persia, gave the English every benefit which they could derive from this connexion: nor can there be a

* Lieut. Colonel Malcolm.

† See a copy of this treaty in the Appendix.

doubt, that, if this alliance had been cultivated with the same active spirit of foresight and penetration with which it was commenced, it would have secured the influence of the British Government in that quarter from many of those attacks to which it has subsequently been exposed.

Lord Wellesley, in the year 1800, equipped an Expedition to Egypt: and a considerable force from India, under the Command of Sir David Baird, marched from Suez to Alexandria: presenting the extraordinary spectacle of a British army, chiefly composed of the Natives of India, on the shores of the Mediterranean.

The political Administration of the Marquis Wellesley was marked by a number of lesser measures, undertaken and executed on the same principles, and with the same spirit and success, as those which I have described.* On these, however deserving of notice, it is impossible to dwell, without swelling this Sketch to a size beyond what is intended. I shall therefore

* The flight of Vizier Ally from Benares, after the atrocious murder of Mr. Cherry the Resident, when he was on a friendly visit to that gentleman, called forth all the vigour and resolution of Lord Wellesley's character; and he obliged the Rajah of Jypore, who had afforded him protection, to give up the just object of the vengeance of the British Government, who has ever since been kept a close prisoner at Fort-William.

proceed to give as concise a statement, as the subject will permit, of those radical changes, which he effected in the connexion between the British Government and the dependent States of Oude and the Carnatic.

When Lord Wellesley returned to Bengal from Madras, after the reduction of Tippoo Sultaun, one of the most important objects, which occupied his attention, was the reduction of a part of the mutinous and useless military establishment of the Nabob Vizier; and at the same time increasing the efficient force, which the Company maintained to defend that Prince's dominions. He was urged to the immediate adoption of this measure, as well as to the general improvement of the principles of our alliance with the Vizier, by a strong sense of the dangers to which the territories of that Prince were exposed from internal tumult, or foreign attack.

The Vizier at first concurred in the expediency of reducing his troops, and of increasing those subsidized from the English Government for the defence of his dominions; but, repenting of this assent, as he found the operation of such an arrangement tended to lessen his consequence with his immediate adherents, he endeavoured, by every evasion, to frustrate the execution of a measure, the necessity of which he had first admitted.

This Prince had, in the year 1799, proposed to abdicate his throne, and persisted for some time in this resolution, in spite of every argument which the British Resident could offer against it. The reasons which he gave for this extraordinary measure, were,—the state of the Country, his inefficiency to rule, and the rooted and reciprocal aversion that subsisted between him and his subjects, which had, he stated, on his part grown into absolute disgust. The notoriety of the truth of all he advanced led the Governor General to believe him perfectly sincere in his proposition; and Lord Wellesley was confirmed in this belief from Saadut Ally having intimated a desire to retire with the treasures which he had amassed, as this wish was quite consistent with his weak and avaricious character.

There was, subsequently, reason to believe, that this proposition of the Vizier was only illusory, and meant to delay the execution of the plan for reforming his military establishment. But the grounds for proceeding in that reform were too urgent, and too much connected with the general security of the interests of the British Empire in India, for Lord Wellesley to allow it's progress to be arrested by such weak and puerile evasions. He, indeed, considered the Vizier's conduct on this remarkable occasion, to furnish another ground for the necessity of that final arrangement, which it was his object to accomplish.

The Company were, agreeably to the 7th article of the treaty concluded by Sir John Shore with the Vizier at his accession, at liberty to increase the force serving in Oude, if they deemed such increase requisite for the security of the two States; and the most irrefragable proofs of that necessity had occurred within the last two years.

Lord Wellesley resolved, therefore, to send an additional force, the annual expense of which amounted to fifty lacks of rupees; which, with the former fixed subsidy* of seventy-six lacks,

* Besides the fixed subsidy paid by the Vizier of Oude, there had formerly been a charge for extraordinaries. The fixed subsidy of Asoph u Dowlah was fifty lacks; but Lord Cornwallis states, that that Prince had paid, previous to the year 1787, an average of thirty-four lacks per annum extraordinaries. By Lord Teignmouth's treaty, the increase of our force in Oude was to be at the discretion of the British Government. It has been argued, that the Vizier's consent was necessary to this increase, even under the construction of the treaty: but if this assertion had not been refuted by the evidence of the respectable nobleman who framed the treaty, it must have been by it's own absurdity; for the cause of the increase is stated to be the existence of external danger; of which one party, the English Government, can alone be the judge; as the other (the Vizier) is precluded by one of the articles of this treaty from all intercourse or communication whatever with foreign States.

made a total of one crore and twenty-six lacks of rupees.

The Governor General, when he directed this increase to the force of Oude, desired to combine it with reductions of the Vizier's useless, and indeed dangerous troops. This arrangement would have prevented that Prince from feeling any burthen upon his finances, by the execution of a measure which so greatly contributed to his security. But Saadut Ally was led, either from weakness, or the wicked designs of the interested rabble by whom he was surrounded, to offer the most serious obstacles to the accomplishment of this measure: his open opposition to which, combined with the whole of his former conduct, and the progressive ruin with which his mismanagement threatened his Country, led Lord Wellesley to resolve upon the conclusion of a final arrangement; which, while it placed those resources, that were to maintain the Company's troops on the frontier of Oude, beyond the reach of the Vizier, should free both the Company and that Prince from a constant and increasing source of irritation—the monthly payment of a heavy pecuniary subsidy.

Lord Wellesley conceived, that the whole conduct of the Vizier;—his proffered abdication, his professed inability to rule, the light in which he considered his own troops when an invasion of his Country was apprehended,* his consent to reduce them, his subsequent efforts to counteract, by the most unjustifiable means, an arrangement to which he had agreed, and the ruin which his system of mismanagement was bringing upon his Country;—fully warranted his insisting upon the Vizier entering into an engagement, that would at once settle every cause of contest; and provide, as completely as it was possible, for the security of his dominions; as well as for the regular and permanent support of those troops by whom they were protected. Acting upon these considerations, Lord Wellesley instructed his brother, Mr. Henry Wellesley, whom he deputed to Lucknow, to conclude a treaty, by which a territorial cession should be made to the British Government, equal to the payment of the increased subsidiary force stationed within the territories of Oude.

The Vizier entered into this engagement with

* The Vizier had declared that they would only be useful to the enemy, and required that a detachment of the British army should be sent to guard his person. His statements were fully confirmed by the letters of Sir A. Clarke and Sir James Craig, who described them as a rabble, who would, in the event of service, require part of the army to watch and keep them in awe, instead of affording any aid.

an extreme degree of reluctance; which, however, from his character, was perhaps in some measure assumed, to prevent that unpopularity,* which would have attached to an appearance of satisfaction with an arrangement, which deprived so many of his dependents of that annual plunder, which they had been accustomed to derive from the Provinces which he was required to cede.

The principal article of this treaty, which was settled by Mr. Henry Wellesley, and Colonel Scott, Resident at Lucknow, stipulated for the immediate cession of all the frontier Provinces of Oude to the Company. These were estimated at the gross revenue of one crore, thirty-five lacks, twenty-three thousand four hundred and seventy-four rupees, eight anas, and three pice; which was received for the payment of the troops (whatever were their number) maintained by the British Government for the defence of Oude.

By this cession, the territories of the Company were interposed, as a barrier, between the dominions of the Vizier and any foreign enemy. The actual nett receipts of that Prince's trea-

* This is a motive in every way consistent with the character of the Vizier, and is greatly confirmed by his subsequent conduct.

sury from these districts, was not more than the amount which he had before paid as a fixed subsidy, and far less than he had become liable to pay under the 7th article of the treaty concluded by Lord Teignmouth, as the Company's troops in Oude had been necessarily increased to a number exceeding thirteen thousand men, whose actual pay (which the Vizier would have been obliged to pay) exceeded the fixed subsidy by more than fifty lacks of rupees per annum.

The Company obtained an ample remuneration for this temporary pecuniary loss, in the happy settlement of it's continual and irritating disputes with the Court of Lucknow; in the prospect of an augmented revenue, under an ameliorated system of management, from Provinces which had been ruined by misrule and oppression; and in the substitution of it's own troops and resources for those of the Vizier, on a frontier from which the only danger that could affect the two States was to be apprehended.

The other articles of this treaty were of minor consideration. They stipulated, that the Vizier should dismiss all his troops, except a certain number; and that he should be entitled to the service of British troops, on all occasions and under all circumstances, without ever being subject to further charge or demand for such aid.*

The Vizier agreed to introduce (under his own Officers) into the territories which remained to him, such a system of Administration, as should be conducive to the prosperity of his subjects, and to the security of the lives and property of the inhabitants. He also agreed always to advise with, and act in conformity to the counsel of, the Officers of the Company's Government.

Several subordinate, and comparatively unimportant, arrangements were subsequently made with the Vizier, who became soon reconciled to a treaty, which, however much it's first proposal might have wounded his feelings, had so happy an operation on his own comfort and that of his subjects; and he took every future opportunity that offered, of proving, both by his professions and actions, his attachment to the British Government.

* The Vizier cannot be said to have shown any unconquerable aversion to the principles of this treaty, as he at one period offered to cede territory to the amount of one crore and twenty lacks of rupees per annum, provided an abatement was made, on account of arrears. This was rejected, and the cession of one crore and thirty-five lacks of rupees, gross revenue, insisted upon.

When the war with the Mahrattas commenced, Lord Wellesley had the satisfaction of receiving the cheerful and voluntary aid of this Prince towards it's prosecution. He not only sent a present of a number of fine horses from his stud, sufficient to mount a regiment of dragoons, but contributed, by large voluntary loans from his treasury, to the general success of the war. The manner, as well as substance, of the Vizier's conduct on this occasion, afforded to all, the least acquainted with his character, a convincing proof of the nature of those impressions, which the whole of the proceedings pursued by the Governor General had made upon his mind; and of that relief and happiness, which had been extended both to him and his Country, by an arrangement that was final; that closed all irritating questions between the two States; and provided, under every contingency, for the permanent support of the British troops employed in the defence of the territories of Oude.

Lord Wellesley received from the Secret Committee of the Court of Directors an early expression of their approbation of the measures which he had taken to reduce the military establishment of the Nabob Vizier. In their letter, which is dated the 4th of December 1800, the Secret Committee observe, that they entertain a due sense of the high services of the Governor General in effecting that reform, which, they state, was "a measure not less contributing to "the preservation of his Excellency's dominions, than to the relief of the Company's "finances, by furnishing a large additional subsidy to the amount of fifty-lacks per annum, "to reimburse the charges of the late augmentation of our troops in that quarter, so necessary to be made, with a view to the ultimate "security of our own possessions against the "invasion of Zemaun Shah, or of any other "Power hostile to the British interests."

The treaty with the Vizier, dated November 1801, received an equally full approbation from the same authority; which was not, however, given till two years after it's conclusion, and until the Court of Directors were in complete possession of all the circumstances connected with the negotiation which had preceded it. The commendation of this measure was conveyed to the Governor General in a letter, dated the 19th of November 1803, from the Secret Committee of the Directors, who gave a greater value to their approbation, by the just and clear view which they, upon this occasion, took of those grounds that gave importance to the arrangement.

"Having taken" (the Secret Committee

observe) " into our consideration the treaty " lately concluded between the Governor General and the Nabob Vizier, and ratified by " his Lordship on the 10th of November 1801, " we have now to signify our approbation of " the provisions of that treaty.

" We consider the stipulations therein contained, as calculated to improve and secure " the interests of the Vizier, as well as those of " the Company; and to provide more effectually hereafter for the good Government and " prosperity of Oude; and, consequently, for " the happiness of it's native inhabitants.

" Although the revenue of the territory " ceded, according to it's produce when in the " hands of the Vizier, does not exceed the subsidy payable by his Highness for the number " of troops which it appeared expedient permanently to station in Oude, together with a " reasonable charge for the civil Administration " of the same; we, nevertheless, do not disapprove of the Governor General, in consideration of the cession, having liberated his Highness from all extraordinary charges, which " may hereafter be incurred by the Company, " in providing for the internal as well as " the external security of Oude; to which " charges his Highness would have been liable " under the treaty of 1798: we are satisfied to "accept, as compensation for such extraordinary expenses, the increased revenue, which may reasonably be expected to arise from the superior Administration of the ceded districts under the Company's management. And we feel the more satisfaction in such an indemnity, as, whilst it can alone arise out of the improvement and prosperity of the Country, it will be unattended by any sacrifice on the part of the Vizier, under whose ruinous and oppressive system of collection the produce of those districts was likely annually to decline, as it had hitherto done.

"We also entertain a sanguine hope, that the Vizier,—relieved from the embarrassment, as well as the charge, of a licentious and worse than useless army; and rescued, by the dissolution of the great proportion of that force, from the most abject dependence on his own powerful subjects, at whose disposal those mutinous and disaffected troops chiefly were,—will now, supported and defended by a disciplined and orderly force, apply himself with energy to the internal Administration of his affairs."

In this letter, a just compliment was paid to the great merits of Mr. Henry Wellesley, the brother of the Governor General, who, after the conclusion of the treaty of Lucknow, had proceeded to take charge of the ceded Provinces, as Lieutenant Governor, in order to effect a settlement of their revenues: An arduous labour, which he performed in a manner as honourable to his own character, as it was advantageous to the public interests.

This account of the proceedings at Lucknow has been more prolix than was originally intended; but it was impossible to abridge it, without an omission of essential facts; and the same reasons oblige me to enter into some detail on the subject of the transactions which took place, during Lord Wellesley's Administration, with the Nabobs of the Carnatic; as my object is to explain, as clearly as I am able, the motives and principles by which that nobleman was governed, in the conduct which he pursued towards those dependent Princes.

Omdut-ul-Omrah, the late Nabob of the Carnatic, succeeded his father on the 16th of October, 1795. He took possession of the Musnud under the conditions of the treaty concluded between his father and the Marquis Cornwallis in 1792. This Prince was specifically named in the preamble to that treaty, as the successor and eldest son of the Nabob Mahomed Ally Khan; and, under that designation, he is made a party in the engagement.

The treaty of 1792 was soon found, both by

the Administration at home and by Government abroad, to have produced few of those salutary effects, which were anticipated. Mahomed Ally Khan, after it's conclusion,* pursued a conduct not more at variance with his own interests and with those of the Company, than destructive of the happiness of his subjects and the prosperity of his Country.

I have already stated, that when Lord Hobart was appointed Governor of Fort St. George, in 1794, he was instructed by the Court of Directors to endeavour to negotiate a modification of Lord Cornwallis's treaty, on principles which were calculated to secure the interests of the Company, to improve the condition of the inhabitants of the Carnatic, or, rather, to save that Country from ruin, and to put an end to those vexatious disputes, which, from the character of the Nabob and his principal servants, were found to attend the fulfilment of several of the most important stipulations of the treaty of 1792.

The obstinate and intemperate resistance which the Nabob Omdut-ul-Omrah (who succeeded his father soon after Lord Hobart's arrival) opposed to all his Lordship's endeavours

* The state of the Carnatic, and the operation of this treaty, are very fully shown in Lord Hobart's minutes, under date the 24th of November, 1795.

to negotiate a modification of Lord Cornwallis's treaty, appeared, at the moment, inexplicable: and the influence attributed to some low and interested counsellors seemed insufficient to account for his steady refusal to listen to any arrangement, which was so eagerly pressed upon his acceptance by his Majesty's Ministers, the Court of Directors, and the Government of Fort St. George; and which could not, under any construction, be judged injurious to his personal interests, or his power, as long as he stood in the relation he then bore to the Company.

When the Marquis Wellesley arrived at Madras in 1798, he employed the few days he remained at that Presidency (previously to embarking for Calcutta) in fruitless attempts to effect the same object. The impression made upon his Lordship's mind, by the mode in which the Nabob treated his proposal, was, that farther negotiation was useless; though he at the same time felt and expressed a conviction, that every moment tended more to prove the indispensable necessity of some arrangement, to save the Company from loss, the Nabob from ruin, and the inhabitants from misery; all which he considered the inevitable consequences of permitting affairs to remain in the state in which they were placed by the treaty of 1792.

When Lord Wellesley returned to Fort St.

George, to prosecute the war against Tippoo Sultaun, in 1799, he became still more sensible of the inconveniencies of the existing engagements with the Nabob, which were aggravated by the conduct of that Prince, who, on that critical occasion, acted more like an enemy than a friend.

The want of exertion of his Officers in every part of his Government, when supplies were collecting for the army, and the manner in which some of them obstructed that service, gave rise to suspicions in the mind of the Governor General, which were much confirmed by a personal act of the Nabob, that had nearly defeated every object of the war. His Highness agreed, on certain conditions, to advance three lacks of pagodas for the immediate use of the army, then on the eve of marching into Mysore. All the conditions which he proposed regarding this advance, were agreed to by the Governor General; and the Nabob succeeded so fully in establishing a belief of his sincerity respecting this important supply, (the promise of which he reiterated, in the most positive manner, the very day the army moved,) that the whole of the cash in the treasury was appropriated, in the confidence of it's receipt; and it is not easy to calculate the evils, which might have been the result of his failing in the fulfilment of his solemn promise on this critical occasion, had not treasure arrived from Bengal. Lord Clive concludes a paper on the Nabob's conduct, in this transaction, with the following remarkable words:—"I am unwilling to attribute systematic treachery to the Nabob; but "I have looked in vain for another motive to "account for his extraordinary conduct."

Soon after the capture of Seringapatam, documents were discovered among the secret records of the Sultaun, containing the most conclusive evidence of a secret intercourse having been carried on between the Nabobs, Wallajah and Omdut-ul-Omrah, and Tippoo Sultaun, which had objects hostile to the interests of the Company.

These documents were carefully examined, and reported upon, under the orders of the Governor General, by Mr. Edmonstone, the Persian translator; and the evidence drawn from them appeared to establish the following conclusions in the most satisfactory manner.

1. That, in violation of an express article of the treaty of 1792, the Nabob Mahomed Ally Khan, by the agency and with the concurrence of his eldest son, Omdut-ul-Omrah, maintained a secret intercourse with Tippoo Sultaun, through the medium of Gholaum Ally Khan and Ally Reza, Vakeels of that Prince; that

this secret intercourse was directed to objects hostile to the interests of the Company; and was, consequently, subversive of the fundamental principles of his alliance with the Company.

2d. That the Nabobs, Mahomed Ally Khan and Omdut-ul-Omrah, had made communications to Tippoo Sultaun, on political subjects, of a nature calculated to promote the interests of that Prince, and eventually to injure those of the Company.

3d. That the Nabob had, both by communication from himself personally, and through Omdut-ul-Omrah, to Gholaum Ally Khan and Ally Reza, manifested his marked disapprobation of the triple alliance (of the English, Nizam, and Mahrattas), which had reduced the power of the Sultaun; and that he had on such occasions stigmatized the Nizam, as having acted contrary to the dictates of religion, which required that all true believers should join in support of that cause, of which, he repeatedly stated, he considered Tippoo Sultaun as the chief pillar.

4th. That the evidence contained in the communications made to Tippoo Sultaun by his Vakeels, of the treacherous nature of the intercourse subsisting between the Nabobs, Wallajah and Omdut-ul-Omrah, and Tippoo Sultaun, was confirmed by the discovery of a cipher, the key to which was found among the Sultaun's secret records; and which was not only written in the same hand in which all the letters of the Nabobs, Wallajah and Omdut-ul-Omrah, to the English Government are written, but noted at the bottom by Tippoo's head Moonshy, as a paper from Omdut-ul-Omrah: and several of the fictitious designations in this cipher were found to have been used in the correspondence. If the very circumstance of Omdut-ul-Omrah's having transmitted a cipher to Tippoo Sultaun was not of itself sufficient to establish the treacherous nature of his views, the names which, it was discovered by the key to the cipher, were used to signify the English and their Allies, removed all doubts upon this subject. The English were designated by the name of *Taza Wareeds*, or *new comers;* the Nizam by that of *Fleech*, or *nothing;* and the Mahrattas, by that of *Pooch*, or *contemptible.*

5th. That Omdut-ul-Omrah continued this secret intercourse as late as the year 1796, as appears by a letter found in the Sultaun's records; which, though it has neither seal nor signature, is written by the person who wrote all the Nabob's letters to the British Government, and has the name of Gholaum Hoossain upon the cover; which, it is established by incontrovertible documents, was the fictitious name under which the Nabob corresponded in his own hand-writing with Gholaum Ally Khan in 1794. The authenticity of this letter is also proved by it's being found in the Sultaun's records, along with the other correspondence of the Nabob of the Carnatic, and it's evident connexion with those letters, in subject.

These were the principal points which appeared to be established by the documents found in Tippoo's palace. They were not only in violation of the spirit of the whole treaty of 1792, but in direct breach of the letter of one of it's most important articles, the 10th, which expressly stipulates, " that the Nabob shall not " enter into any negotiations, or political cor- " respondence, with any European or native " Power whatever, without the consent of the " Company."

That this article (which every person who consults the treaty of 1792 must consider as the most essential of the whole treaty, as it relates to the security of the British Government,) was completely violated, there could not remain a doubt; and as it is established, by the law of Nations, that the violation of any one article, but more particularly of a fundamental one, of a treaty, overthrows the whole, the treaty of 1792 was of course to be considered as dissolved;

and the line to be pursued by the injured party was that, which a due regard for it's own safety and interests, combined with a respect for the law of Nations, demanded.

The relation in which the Nabob stood to the British Government, was that of a dependent Ally, whose rank and power had been preserved from motives of justice, not of policy; and who owed his accession to the Musnud (upon the same conditions which his father enjoyed it) to the honourable adherence of the English Nation to it's engagements, even when they were evidently in opposition to it's interests.

The conduct which the Nabob had pursued from the commencement of his reign, has been already stated; and proves what sacrifices the English Government made, rather than violate in the slightest degree their good faith with his Highness. To preserve that faith, the Company had, indeed, been exposed to great loss; and the Nabob had been permitted to destroy those resources, on which not only his own safety, but that of the Company, might eventually depend; and to impoverish and render miserable, by his mismanagement, the Country and inhabitants subject to his authority.

The conduct of Omdut-ul-Omrah, in several instances, previous to the discovery of his treachery, though not of a nature to absolve the Company from the obligation of an engagement into which they had deliberately entered, could not but operate unfavourably for him, in the situation in which his own perfidy had placed him, by diminishing his claim to a confidence and generosity which he had so systematically abused.

The light in which the Secret Committee of the Court of Directors had viewed the conduct of the Nabob, previously to the discovery of his treachery, appears from their despatch to Lord Wellesley under date the 18th of June 1799, in which they express themselves as follows:

"In the event of a war with Tippoo Sultaun, "the respective Countries of the Nabob of "Arcot, and the Rajah of Tanjore, will of "course come under the Company's management; and we direct, that they be not relin"quished without special orders from us, or "from the Court of Directors, for that purpose, "in order to afford sufficient time for the for"mation of arrangements for relieving those "respective Princes from all encumbrances on "their revenues."

This order from the Secret Committee showed, that the Indian Government in England considered the general conduct of Omdut-ul-Omrah, previously to the discovery of his treachery, of a nature to warrant their directing a departure from the stipulations of the treaty of 1792, of which the restoration of the Nabob's Country, *at the conclusion of the war*, unless in certain cases, (which are afterwards specified, and which had not occurred at the date of the Committee's order,) is an express condition.

This instruction, though it did not directly apply to the precise case under the consideration of the Governor General, was conclusive as to the principle upon which the Court of Directors desired that all transactions with the Nabob should be regulated.

Lord Wellesley, though aware of the risk which might attend any delay in a case of so delicate and dangerous a nature, a risk which was rendered more serious by the disturbed state of most of the territories under Fort St. George, preferred incurring that danger to the adoption of any measures which might be deemed precipitate, in an affair where the honour of the British Nation was so much concerned. Acting upon that principle, he contented himself, in the first instance, with writing to the Government of Madras to prosecute their inquiry into the Nabob's conduct, by a personal examination of the Vakeels, Gholaum Ally and Ally Reza Khan, and some other Officers of the late Tippoo Sultaun. He transmitted at the same time to England all the documents which had been discovered at Seringapatam, with the Persian translator's report: and stated his opinion, that though the proofs obtained were, no doubt, sufficient to justify the British Government in immediately depriving the Nabob of the means of abusing the protection of the Company, yet he had judged a cautious and moderate proceeding to be more consistent with the character and reputation of the British Government.

Lord Wellesley had directed, that the Government of Madras should take no decisive steps in this affair, unless the Nabob died, (an event rendered probable from the bad state of his Highness's health); in which case, the Madras Government was directed to raise one of two persons to the Musnud; either Hoossain Ally, the reputed son of Omdut-ul-Omrah; or Azeem u Dowlah, the acknowledged son of Ameer-ul-Omrah, under the previous condition, of their resigning to the Company, on consideration of receiving an annual stipend for the support of their rank, the civil and military Administration of the Carnatic.

The elevation of either of these Princes was, agreeably to his instructions, to be considered as a measure of expediency, not of right, the Governor General considering the right of the family as forfeited by the conduct of Omdut-ul-

Omrah. The Government of Madras was directed to make the first offer to the reputed son of Omdut-ul-Omrah; and in the event of his refusing to subscribe to those conditions, which were thought indispensably necessary, to make a similar proposition to Azeem u Dowlah; and if that Prince rejected the offer, the Madras Government was to refer for farther orders to the Governor General.

A remarkable fact is proved by this letter of instructions to the Government of Fort St. George, which is dated the 28th of March 1800, long before any question of the respective claims to the succession was agitated. It appears from the contents of this document, that the impression upon the Governor General's mind then was, that the right of inheritance (if any such had existed) belonged to Azeem u Dowlah, and that the elevation of Ally Hoossain, the reputed son of Omdut-ul-Omrah, would probably give great disgust to the Mahomedans, and induce efforts to defeat the succession.

The Governor General's reasons for directing the first option to be given to Ally Hoossain, are expressly stated, in this letter, to proceed from causes unconnected with any admission of his claim or title to the Musnud.

The result of the inquiry, which Lord Clive instituted in consequence of the Governor

General's orders, went to establish the principal facts of the treachery both of Wallajah and Omdut-ul-Omrah. The evidences examined, were Gholaum Ally Khan, and Ally Reza; and though some parts of the former proofs were invalidated, all the chief points, upon which the proof of the Nabob's violation of the treaty of 1792 rested, were fully confirmed by their depositions.

The whole of these voluminous examinations, accompanied by a report from Colonel Close and Mr. Webbe (the gentlemen who conducted the inquiry), were transmitted to the Governor General by Lord Clive; with a letter from himself, under date the 23d of May. The impressions which this farther prosecution of the inquiry into the conduct of the Nabob Omdut-ul-Omrah made upon Lord Clive's mind, will be best judged from the two following paragraphs, which concluded his Lordship's official address upon this occasion.

" With this strong evidence of internal trea-
" chery, and of open opposition to our interests
" in the Carnatic, established by treaty, it is my
" deliberate opinion, that a farther adherence
" to the letter of the treaty of 1792, while the
" Nabob Omdut-ul-Omrah has been, and now
" is, perfidiously betraying the spirit and sub-
" stance of the alliance between him and the

"Company, would be as inconsistent with the "true principles of public faith, as it would be "obviously incompatible with the preservation "of our just rights and interests.

"On these grounds, I have no hesitation in "recommending to your Lordship the imme-"diate assumption of the civil and military "Government of the Carnatic, under such "provisions as your Lordship may be pleased to "authorize for his Highness the Nabob, his "Highness's family, and the principal Officers "of his Government."

Upon the receipt of this despatch, the Governor General resolved to proceed to Fort St. George, as soon as the season permitted, for the purpose of settling in person an arrangement, which should effectually secure the interests of the Company in the Carnatic. In consequence of this determination, he gave no farther instructions to Lord Clive upon the subject, until the month of March 1801; when finding that the state of affairs in Oude, combined with other circumstances relative to the general Government of India, made it impossible for him to leave Fort William, he directed Lord Clive to send Mr. Webbe, the chief executive Officer of the Madras Government, to Bengal, in order to have the fullest communications with that Officer previously to issuing his final instructions for the settlement of the Carnatic, and several other important points intimately connected with that arrangement.

When Mr. Webbe was at Fort William, to which he had proceeded in consequence of the above orders, the alarming state of the Nabob's health induced Lord Clive to address a letter to Lord Wellesley, stating the conduct which he had resolved to pursue, if the Nabob died previously to his receiving final instructions.

In this letter, which is dated the 21st of May 1801, Lord Clive states, that though the Governor General's letter of the 26th of March 1800, prescribes the line of conduct which he is to follow, if the event apprehended should occur previously to his receiving farther orders, he cannot but think that the circumstances which have occurred since that letter was written, may so materially have altered the whole case under consideration, as to render it probable, that any measures grounded upon the Governor General's instructions of that date, would be more likely to defeat than promote the objects which he might contemplate, in consequence of the full information that he had subsequently obtained. Lord Clive in the same letter stated, that if the Nabob should die previously to the arrival of further instructions, he should not follow the instructions which he had before received, but assume the civil and military Government of the Carnatic, in the name of the Company, until a plan for it's Government should be finally arranged.

Lord Wellesley was, at the period of receiving this despatch from Lord Clive, in possession of every information, and of every opinion, which could guide or influence his judgment on the decision of this important and delicate question.

A letter had reached him from the President of the Board of Control, who fully coincided in the conclusions which he had drawn from the documents found in Seringapatam, and in the measures which he had declared it was his intention to adopt; and a despatch from the Secret Committee of the Court of Directors, dated the 4th of December 1800, expressed their entire approbation of the resolution, which the Governor General informed them (in a letter dated the 9th of June) he had taken, of demanding some more certain pledges of the fidelity of Omdut-ul-Omrah, than the Company then possessed. The Secret Committee distinctly state in this despatch, that many other circumstances might, in their opinion, be urged, besides those adduced by Lord Wellesley, to strengthen the doubts of the Nabob's fidelity to the fundamental principles of his engagements with the

Company: and they particularly instance the mode in which he evacuated the Fort of Chandnagerry in 1796, on which they remark, " that " a more decided instance of disaffection to the " Company can scarcely be imagined."

In the full possession of the general sentiments of his superiors in England, and with an improved knowledge of every particular which had attended this important affair, Lord Wellesley sent his final instructions with respect to the measures which were to be pursued by Lord Clive.

These instructions, which were dated the 28th of May, after taking a complete review of the whole affair, and showing in the most incontrovertible manner, that his Highness the Nabob was reduced by his own conduct to the condition of a public enemy, that he had forfeited every claim to the confidence of the Company, and that it was neither conformable to the dictates of wisdom or prudence, nor reconcileable to justice or policy, to permit him to retain the possession of actual resources, greater than were requisite for the support of the rank which it should be judged proper to permit him to hold in the Carnatic, directed Lord Clive to stipulate with his Highness for the complete resignation of the civil and military Government of that Province, and to grant him (upon his agreeing to that and some other conditions) a stipend not exceeding three, and not under two, lacks of pagodas annually; independent of a provision for the other branches of the family, and for his principal Officers, which was to be made from the revenues of the Carnatic.

Upon this basis Lord Clive was instructed to negotiate a treaty with the Nabob; and he was authorized, for the purpose of obtaining his Highness's consent to the terms proposed, to make him acquainted with the proofs of his treachery, which were in the possession of the British Government.

Lord Wellesley expressly stated, that the proposition of forming a treaty on this occasion, was dictated by a desire to consult the dignity of the British Government, and not from any disposition to admit the claims of the Nabobs, Mahomed Ally Khan and Omdut-ul-Omrah, to either forbearance or generosity; though, he confessed, it would be painful to be compelled to expose the humiliating proofs of the ingratitude and treachery with which these infatuated Princes had acted towards that Power, which had uniformly proved their guardian and protector.

In the event of the Nabob's refusal of the treaty offered, Lord Clive was directed to assume the Country under a proclamation, which accompanied the letter of instructions, and which fully exhibited the causes of that measure. If matters came to this extremity, his Lordship was instructed to pay no attention to any appeal, which the Nabob might desire to make to the Court of Directors, as it was both injudicious and unnecessary to listen to such; more particularly as the Governor General was in possession of the sentiments of the Secret Committee, founded on the discovery of the Nabob's faithless conduct. The admission of any such appeal, the Governor General stated, would be entering upon a formal trial of the Nabob's criminality; whereas the case was one, which demanded an immediate exercise of those rights and privileges, which every Power possesses, by the law of Nations, to secure itself against the proved machinations of a faithless Ally. Lord Clive was, however, directed, even under the extremity of assuming the civil and military Government of the Carnatic, to provide for the Nabob's support in a liberal manner; and also to make a suitable provision for the different branches of his family, and the various Officers of his State.

At the period when Lord Wellesley's instructions, bearing date the 28th of May, reached Madras, the state of the Nabob's health was so bad, as to prevent Lord Clive taking any immediate measures on their receipt. When his Highness's malady had attained a height that left no hopes of his recovery, intrigues were commenced among the different branches of his family, which disturbed the tranquillity of his palace; and a body of men were secretly introduced into it, by his brother Hissam ul Mulk, who was loud in asserting his pretensions to the succession. These circumstances obliged Lord Clive to send a detachment of the Company's troops, to occupy the chief entrance into the palace, and to preserve order and tranquillity within it's walls; as also to guard against the seizure of any treasure, or the dilapidation of any property, belonging to the Nabob; both of which, it was thought, would probably be attempted at the moment of his death.

This step was taken with a degree of delicacy and precaution, which perfectly reconciled it to the Nabob, who was fully satisfied, by the explanation made to him by Lord Clive, and by the conduct of the troops, that the object of this measure was no more than what was professed. Indeed it's expediency and necessity could only be arraigned by those, whose sinister views were defeated by it's adoption.

On the 15th of July, 1801, the Nabob expired; and the dangerous intrigues which had been carried on in his palace, the state of several

Provinces* under the Government of Fort St. George, and a variety of other cogent reasons, forbade (in Lord Clive's opinion) a moment's delay in effecting a settlement of the Country. He, in consequence, a few hours after he heard of his Highness's death, deputed Mr. Webbe, and Lieut. Colonel Close, to confer with the principal Officers of the Court, in order to effect an immediate arrangement for the Administration of the Carnatic.

These gentlemen had an immediate conference with the two guardians of the young Prince Ally Hoosain. But, though their negotiation was continued several days, and was conducted with the greatest temper and judgment, it entirely failed; and they found themselves obliged, after the guardians had formally refused their assent to enter into any treaty which was grounded on the basis of the civil and military Government of the Carnatic being vested in the Company, to express their desire to see Ally Hoossain, and to receive from him in person the final answer to a proposal in which his interests were so deeply concerned.

To their request for this interview, the Khans made many objections, grounded on the alleged

* A very serious civil war at this period existed in the southern Provinces of Fort St. George.

incapacity and inexperience of the young man; but, these being overruled, they were at last obliged to give a reluctant consent to the meeting.

On the 19th, Colonel Close and Mr. Webbe were introduced to Ally Hoossain, the reputed son of the Nabob (a youth of 18 years of age), and stated to him, in a summary manner, all that had passed with his guardians; adding, that on a point, which so materially involved his interests, they were naturally desirous of hearing his own sentiments and resolution, before they terminated a negotiation with which all his prospects of elevation must close. The young man answered (the guardians being present), that he considered the Khans to have been appointed by his father for the purpose of assisting him with advice; and that the object of his councils, and theirs, could never be separated.

On receiving this answer, Colonel Close and Mr. Webbe informed the Khans, that Lord Clive had resolved, previously to the adoption of final measures on a subject of such importance, to have a personal interview with Ally Hoossain; and that his Lordship would come to the tent of the Officer commanding the troops stationed at the palace, for that purpose. This proposal was unexpected; and the Khans endeavoured to evade it, by objections similar to those which they had before urged relative to the incapacity and inexperience of the young man: but finding their arguments of no avail, they consented; and both went to prepare Ally Hoossain's equipage and retinue. The young man, taking advantage of their momentary absence, whispered, with much apparent anxiety, to Colonel Close and Mr. Webbe, that he had been deceived by his guardians; and, after this communication, he proceeded, without attending to the Khans, to the tent where it was fixed he should have an interview with Lord Clive.

When the ceremony of his introduction to his Lordship was over, Ally Hoossain's attendants (including the guardians) being desired to withdraw, Lord Clive, after adverting to the whole of the negotiation, which had passed, informed him of the serious consequences of any resolution he might take; and stated the personal anxiety which he felt, that Ally Hoossain should be clearly apprized of his situation, and determine with caution on a point of such importance to his individual interests and reputation, as well as to those of his family.

Ally Hoossain, without hesitation, declared in the most explicit manner, that the conferences had been conducted by the Khans without his participation, and that he much disapproved of the termination to which they had been brought.

Upon this declaration, it was judged proper to recapitulate, in the most distinct manner, every part of the transaction; and, after the fullest comprehension of the whole subject, the young man declared his readiness to enter into an arrangement grounded upon the basis of the Company exercising the civil and military Government of the Carnatic.

He was very particular as to the secondary parts of the arrangement; such as the provision for his personal expenses, and the extent of his power over the treasure of the late Nabob, which he evidently considered to be large.

This conference, which was frequently interrupted by the importunity of Nejeeb Khan, terminated by the young man's desiring, that a treaty should be made out, resting upon a basis which vested the entire civil and military Government of the Carnatic in the Honourable Company; which, he said, a conviction that it was for his benefit, and that of his family, would lead him to execute with, or without, the consent of his guardians.

On the 20th, Colonel Close and Mr. Webbe again went to the palace, where they were met by the two Khans and Ally Hoossain. The latter began the conference, by retracting every thing which he said to Lord Clive at the private interview, and declaring his fixed resolution to abide by the opinion of his guardians.

This extraordinary change was supposed, at first, to have proceeded from fear; and an adjournment to the tent, to meet Lord Clive, was proposed, and carried into execution. On their arrival there, the young man's attendants and guardians were dismissed, and he was left in private with his Lordship. He there repeated, in the most firm tone, his resolution to abide by the advice of the Khans, and his unalterable determination to accept of no engagement, which had for it's basis the cession of the civil and military Government of the Carnatic. He had spoken the day before, he said, under the impression of the moment; but he had since received full information, and he now acted agreeably to his own sentiments, and to those of the whole family, who had been convened for the purpose of assisting his judgment. He was fully convinced, he added, of the risks he encountered, having received communications, the truth of which he could not doubt, respecting the Governor General's orders. But he was prepared to meet every danger, rather than subscribe to the conditions proposed.

No argument was left untried by Lord Clive, which could persuade or convince this young

Prince that he was misled to his ruin, and that his prosperity depended upon a compliance with the demands of the Company's Government. It was in vain that his Lordship pointed out, in the most clear manner, the situation in which he stood; the motives which influenced his adherents in persuading him to a course incompatible with his true interests; and the certain distress into which he must inevitably bring himself, and all those dependent upon him, by a perseverance in his refusal of the terms proposed.

Ally Hoossain remained unmoved; and Lord Clive was at length reluctantly obliged to inform him, that he had forfeited all claim to consideration, and must await the extreme measures, which his conduct had rendered unavoidable.

All hopes of concluding a treaty with the reputed son of Omdut-ul-Omrah were now at an end; that young Prince had, in the most deliberate manner, terminated a negotiation, which had been conducted throughout with a degree of temper and moderation, that reflected the highest credit upon those to whom it was intrusted; and which had been marked, at it's most important stages, by the extreme of kindness and humanity, on the part of Lord Clive; by refusing his assent to any engagement founded upon the principles, which had been stated, from the first, as indispensable; viz. "The Company being vested with the civil "and military Government of the Carnatic."

The situation of the territories under Fort St. George (part of which were in rebellion) was unfavourable to any measure, however grounded on justice, that excluded the family of Mahomed Ally Khan altogether from the dignity of Nabob; and the Governor therefore resolved on raising Azeem u Dowlah to the Musnud.

The right of this Prince to the succession (if all right had not been forfeited) was perhaps stronger than that of the reputed son of Omdut-ul-Omrah. But this was not investigated; the act being declared one of expediency and grace, not of right or of justice. His claims were only to be considered of consequence, as they served to reconcile the great body of the Mahomedan inhabitants of the English territories, and the Mahomedan Rulers of neighbouring States, to the measure.

When Lord Clive adopted this resolution, he deputed Colonel Close and Mr. Webbe to negotiate, with the Prince Azeem u Dowlah, a treaty founded on the same basis as that which they had been directed to propose to Ally Hoossain. Difficulties of a serious nature occurred, as to their seeing this Prince, for he was kept in a most rigorous confinement; and it was feared, that, should any idea be entertained of his intended elevation, it might prove dangerous to his life. The difficulties, however, were removed by an occurrence, which evinced a contempt for the Company's authority, that required immediate check and interference. The guardians of Ally Hoossain, impatient of the delays which had occurred, privately placed that Prince upon the Musnud; and it was reported to Lord Clive, that they proposed performing that ceremony publicly next day. As there was no calculating the confusion which such a proceeding might occasion, his Lordship gave immediate orders for the Company's troops to take possession of the whole palace, and to remove all the Nabob's guards.

One effect of this measure, was to bring Azeem u Dowlah under the protection of the English troops; and on the 23d and 24th he had interviews with Colonel Close, and Mr. Webbe, at which he settled with those gentlemen the basis of a treaty, which was finally concluded on the 25th of July: and on the 26th this Prince was introduced to Lord Clive, and conducted to the palace of Ameer Bagh, the former residence of his father.

In the course of the interview, which Azeem u Dowlah had with Colonel Close and Mr.

Webbe, a good deal of discussion took place on the subordinate articles of the treaty; and the Prince showed, on this occasion, that he was neither deficient in quickness nor good sense; and that he was fully equal, as far as depended on personal qualifications, to the support of the rank to which he had been elevated.

This treaty, which vested the whole civil and military Government of the Carnatic in the Company, provided for the Nabob's enjoyment of a clear revenue of from two to three lacks of pagodas annually,* unencumbered by any charge; and also for the liberal support of all the different branches of the family of Mahomed Ally Khan. It also settled for a gradual liquidation of such, as were deemed just, of those large debts, with which a long system of usury, extravagance, and oppression, had encumbered the revenues of the Carnatic; and which was rapidly involving this Country in ruin.

Lord Wellesley left India on the 20th of August 1805, soon after the Marquis Corn-

* The sum fixed for the support of the Nabob was one fifth of the revenues of the Carnatic: and the Company agreed that he should, under all circumstances, receive, in advance of the fifth to which he was entitled, twelve thousand pagodas per month for his personal expenses.

wallis, who had been appointed to succeed him, had reached Fort William. I shall conclude the narrative which I have given of this Nobleman's Administration with some general observations upon the leading political measures which he adopted, the impressions they made, and the general result of his Government to the British interests in India.

The state of India, at the period of Lord Wellesley's arrival, compelled him (as has been before shown) to the immediate employment of all the resources of the great Empire committed to his charge. The restoration of the alliance with the Nizam, and the complete destruction of the formidable French party at his Court, were objects, the necessity as well as policy of which have never been denied. Their accomplishment was necessary, not only to enable us to engage in a war, which we could not avert, with Tippoo Sultaun; but to crush a rising danger of perhaps the most serious magnitude that ever threatened our dominions in India.

The most serious alarm had arisen in England respecting the intentions which the French were supposed at this period to cherish against our Eastern possessions; and the connexion of their efforts in India with their invasion of Egypt, was doubted by none. Buonaparte's letter to Tippoo Sultaun* was of itself conclusive evidence on this point; and it was evident that the French had, at the commencement of Lord Wellesley's Administration, those means, which were of all others the best calculated to give success to the designs which they were known to cherish against the British Government. Their influence at the Court of Tippoo was decided. His union with them was grounded upon a congenial feeling of hatred to the English name. At the Court of Scindiah, who was still more powerful than the Sultaun, the French had more than influence: they had power. They had founded an Empire of their

* This letter, which was dated Head Quarters at Cairo the 7th of Pluviose, and 7th year of the Republic, was as follows:

"You have already been informed of my arrival on the borders of the Red Sea, with an innumerable and invincible army, full of the desire of releasing and relieving you from the iron yoke of England.

"I eagerly embrace this opportunity of testifying to you the desire I have of being informed by you, by the way of Muscat and Mocha, as to your political situation.

"I could even wish you could send some intelligent person to Suez or Cairo, possessing your confidence, with whom I may confer. May the Almighty increase your power, and destroy your enemies!

"Yours, &c. &c.

"BUONAPARTE."

own within the dominions of that Prince. The whole of Hindoostan, from the River Sultege to the borders of the unsettled Country of the Vizier of Oude, was in possession of an army of nearly forty thousand infantry, with an immense train of artillery, and every military resource; commanded by a body of about three hundred European Officers, of which not more than forty were British subjects; and these (who were for the most part in subordinate stations), it was the evident object of their French superiors to disgust, that they might make way for others on whom they could better depend, when that crisis, which they always contemplated, arrived.

At Hyderabad the power of the French was considerable, as they had an army of fourteen thousand disciplined troops, with a large and well-appointed train of cannon at their devotion; but their influence had not yet conquered that of the English at the Court of the Nizam. That Prince had too just a dread of Tippoo Sultaun and the Mahrattas, to listen readily to councils which were calculated to involve him with the only State that had the power of protecting him from such enemies: and, though he was too wise to resign those means of defence, to which the neutral policy of the British Government had compelled him to resort, without an adequate security against danger, he did not hesitate to make every sacrifice which was required of him, the moment he received a decided pledge of protection against the Mahrattas. It must here be recollected, that it was impossible for Lord Wellesley either to engage in that war with Tippoo, which was then inevitable, or to expel the French from the Deckan (which was an act of equal, if not greater necessity), without agreeing to give the Nizam that promise of protection against the future unprovoked aggressions of the Mahrattas, which he had constantly solicited from the first hour of his intimate alliance with the English in 1788, and which Lord Cornwallis had only declined on the ground, that such a measure would be offensive to the Mahrattas, who were at that moment as cordial in their alliance with the English Government against Tippoo, as the Nizam was. The consideration, which had chiefly influenced Lord Cornwallis's determination, no longer existed; the power of the Poonah State, with whom the triple alliance had been formed, was almost extinct; and it's resources were at the direction of a Chief (Doulut Row Scindiah), who was more likely to join in a combination against the British Government, than to aid it to repel the attack, or frustrate the plans, of it's enemies.

Under such circumstances, Lord Wellesley could not have rejected the just demand of the Nizam, without incurring the most serious dangers; and, indeed, exposing the Empire under his charge to all the consequences of meeting, without Allies, a war with Tippoo Sultaun, and a combination of all the means which France could bring in aid of that attack upon our power. He was compelled, therefore, by attention to the safety of the British territories, to conclude the treaty of Hyderabad. This measure gave rise to a series of events, which completely changed the condition of the British Government in India. It's first consequence, was the overthrow of Tippoo Sultaun, and the establishment of the Government of Mysore; and it's second, was to effect such a complete alteration of our political relations with the Mahratta States, that it was early evident we must either retract the engagement which we had formed, and abandon the territories we had acquired; or endeavour, by negotiation, to make the principal Mahratta Chiefs modify their policy, and habits of rule, to the altered situation of the political state of the Peninsula.

The Mahrattas, it is true, had, from the period of the conclusion of the treaty of Salbhye, respected our territories, and those of the Allies which we were bound to protect; but these, it is to be observed, had before only joined theirs in one quarter, that of Oude; and, from the date of the treaty of Salbhye, both Madhajee Scindiah, and his successor Doulut Row, had been too intently fixed upon consolidating a power in Hindoostan, which would make them masters of the Mahratta Empire, to think of offending the British Government by any predatory attack upon the territories of it's Ally, the Vizier of Oude. But the causes of this forbearance were hourly generating a more serious evil to the British power: and that neutrality, which we thought recompensed by this temporary exemption from attack, left us, in it's result, exposed to a more imminent danger than the British arms in India have ever had to encounter.

In other quarters of India our territories were remote from those of the Mahrattas. We had interposed the Countries of the Nizam, and those of Tippoo Sultaun, between us and those freebooters. But, when a course of policy, the expediency, justice and necessity of which have never been questioned, led us to form an intimate alliance with the Nizam, by which we became bound to defend his territories as we would our own; when a Government was established in Mysore under our immediate guarantee and protection; we, of course, virtually succeeded to all the local and political relations which subsisted between the Mahrattas and those States.

The previous history of these Countries will show, that a year had hardly ever passed without some dispute arising between them and the Mahrattas; and, as the causes of such quarrels were interwoven in the system of the Mahratta Government, we could only hope for exemption from the constant disputes and wars with which we were threatened, by the adoption of one of the courses which I have before stated. The first was: to retract our pledged faith to the Nizam and the Government of Mysore, and to abandon our conquests. The second: to endeavour to effect, by negotiation, a change in the constitution of the Mahratta Government, and to render that more favourable to the maintenance of the general peace and tranquillity.

To adopt the first of those measures would have been as disgraceful as it was ruinous; and it could not, therefore, under any modifications, have been attempted. The second, was the safest, as well as the most moderate course: and the divided state of the Mahratta Empire gave some reason to hope, that it might be accomplished without the extreme of war. But as that, at an early period of our negotiations, appeared almost unavoidable; and as it was evident nothing but their fears could prevent the Mahratta Chiefs from immediately commencing hostilities, it seemed wise to seize every political advantage, which was likely either to add to their motives for avoiding a contest, or to increase our means of making that successful, if it became inevitable. These were the grounds of our negotiations with the Court of Poonah: without an alliance with which, it was evident, from the state of India at the moment, we could not maintain our engagements with the Court of Hyderabad or the Rajah of Mysore; unless we had resolved on assembling an army on the frontier, to secure the system of neutrality, which we had adopted, being respected: and as we could place no reliance on their faith, this expensive precaution against the designs of the Mahrattas must have been repeated whenever the armies of that Nation were in the field; or, in other words, every year. We should, in short, have had to preserve an armed neutrality when the Mahratta Chiefs were contending with each other, and to have made still greater preparations against danger, when those contentions were ended, either by their union,* or by the establishment of the paramount power of

* Their attack of the Nizam, in 1795, affords a remarkable instance of their uniting, when an object of plunder was in view.

one Chieftain. Our finances must have sunk under this ruinous system; and we could have indulged no hopes of it's termination, as our views and those of the Mahrattas were irreconcileable. They desired power, for no object but that of extending their depredations: we, for that of maintaining tranquillity. Under such circumstances, it appeared alike indispensable for the safety of our own territories, and those of our Allies, to conclude an alliance with the Paishwah, which should not only secure him in the enjoyment of his hereditary possessions, but give him an interest in the preservation of the peace of the Deckan.

From these observations it will appear, that Lord Wellesley was more governed by considerations of necessity than of choice, in his anxious pursuit of an alliance with the Court of Poonah. It was a desire to avoid, not to provoke war, which stimulated him to the efforts which he made. His policy in this instance, as in all others, was directed to the permanent security of the State he ruled; and though most solicitous for an amicable termination of the different negotiations which that course led him into, he accounted no measure worthy of his adoption, which obtained a temporary exemption from danger, at any hazard to the fame or future tranquillity of the British Government.

The ultimate success, in forming a defensive alliance with the Paishwah, and the glorious termination of the war with the Mahratta Chiefs, have been already related. The actual result of those events soon refuted all those prognostications, which men, who took a limited or prejudiced view of this great question, had hazarded respecting it's consequences: and Lord Wellesley had the gratification to see, before he left India, almost every hope which he had formed, from the wise and enlarged measures that he had adopted, completely accomplished.

To show this in a more clear point of view, it will be necessary to glance at the actual state of India at the period of his departure.

The designs of the French against the British Government, as far as those depended upon the great aid which that Nation might have expected from it's subjects in India,* were com-

* The nature and extent of these designs are now generally understood. The quality and numbers of the military staff sent to Pondicherry with General De Caen, was of itself conclusive as to the hopes which the French Government entertained from adding to the strength and efficiency of this means of attacking our power.

pletely frustrated. The old and venerable Emperor of Dehli, who had been in the hands of the Mahrattas, and latterly of the French party established in Hindoostan, was relieved from all his distress, and enjoyed, under the protection of the British Government, an affluent repose.

Secunder Jah,* the Soubahdar of the Deckan, who had succeeded his father in the year 1803, was completely confirmed in his alliance with the Company; and maintained permanently, within his territories, a subsidiary force of one regiment of Europeans, two corps of native cavalry, six battalions of Sepoys, and a proportionate train of artillery; and the expense of this large field force was defrayed by a territorial cession, which consisted of Provinces that had been conquered from Tippoo and ceded to this Prince; whose revenues had, subsequently to the last treaty, received a considerable accession, from the conquest of Berar, and the

* The British Resident at Hyderabad was directed to give this Prince, who was the eldest son of the Nizam, the full and unconditional support of the British Government. Secunder Jah, in gratitude for this aid, made a cession of an annual tribute of seven lacks of rupees, which the Company have long paid the Soubahdar of the Deckan for the Northern Circars. This cession was not received by Lord Wellesley, who considered it at variance with those principles of disinterested policy on which it had been resolved to support Secunder Jah in his succession to the throne of his father.

cession to him of the share held by the Rajah of Berar in that rich Province.

The complete reduction of the Mahratta Chiefs,—Scindiah, Ragojee Bhonslah, and Holkar,—had freed the Soubahdar of the Deckan from every alarm respecting his future safety; and had given to his subjects a tranquillity, which they had never before enjoyed.

The Government of Tippoo Sultaun was annihilated; and the family of the former Rajahs of Mysore were raised, by the magnanimity of the British Government, to that throne, of which they had been thirty-eight years deprived by the usurpation of Hyder Ally Khan and his son. The considerations which led Lord Wellesley to make this arrangement, have been noticed; but it will be useful to say a few words on it's operation.

The general theory of this Government is, that of a Prince exercising an independent authority over his own Country, and maintaining sufficient force to preserve it's internal quiet, and to contribute eventually to the aid of an Ally, which charges itself with the defence of his territories from all foreign attack; and which, to enable it to fulfil this stipulation, has a large body of subsidized troops stationed within his territories, and is vested with the sole and exclusive conduct of all foreign relations.

The success of reducing this theory into practice, would evidently depend upon the care and wisdom with which the connexion was watched in it's infancy; and this point received, as it merited, all Lord Wellesley's attention. The example of the Courts of Lucknow, of Chepauk,* and Tanjore, furnished an ample chart to show the rocks which were to be avoided on this occasion: and, though the origin of our connexion with Mysore differed widely from that which we had formed with those Princes; as our task with the former was establishment, with the latter reform; there was still cause to fear, that, if the greatest caution was not used, the young Rajah of Mysore, and his Ministers, would soon fall into a course of intrigue and corruption, which would bring ruin on his Country and it's inhabitants, and consequently defeat all those objects which had been expected from the establishment of this Government.

There appeared another obstacle of still greater magnitude to the happy operation of this arrangement. The State of Mysore was so really dependent upon the British Government,

* Nabobs of the Carnatic.

that it appeared difficult, if not impossible, consistently with the check which it was necessary to maintain over it's Councils, to raise those, by whom it was ruled, into that estimation and rank, with themselves and others, which was necessary to enable them to perform the important functions with which they were trusted. This condition of the young State required, that the first public Officers of the Power by whom it had been created, should, while they exercised a firm but delicate, and, as far as possible, unseen control, make it their particular duty to support, in the most public and decided manner, it's power; and to raise, by every effort, it's consequence and reputation, as an efficient and separate State.

The early and successful accomplishment of all the objects, which the establishment of this Government was meant to effect, "is," (as Major Wilkes observes, in his clear and able Report on the affairs of Mysore,) "next to those "measures of a general nature, which directed "the great arrangements of that period, to be "attributed to the energy, the talents, and "cordial co-operation, of the uncommon men,*

* The name of the able writer of this Report must ever occupy a distinguished place among those, who have contributed, by their integrity and talents, to the happy operation of this great arrangement.

"who were selected for the execution of the "civil and military duties; and to the fortu- "nate choice of a Dewan,* who, to a mind of "singular vigour, added an extensive acquaint- "ance with the resources of the Country, and "an intimate knowledge of characters; and "was thus capable of collecting and combining, "at once, all that had been useful in the esta- "blishment of the late Government."

Our relations with the Government of Mysore, though admirable, are of that delicate texture, which must make them require constant attention. The smallest departure from any of those fundamental principles upon which they are grounded, will infallibly lead to their ultimate dissolution: but, while those are respected, this connexion will form the bulwark of our strength in the south of India; and it may, in the course of events, be a consideration of policy to increase, instead of diminishing, the wealth and limits of a State, which, while it affords us resources fully equal to the same extent of our own dominions, is exempt from some of the objections of rule to which those are subject; and particularly to that popular,

* Poorneah, a Brahmin, who was Minister of finance under Tippoo Sultaun, and was selected by Lord Wellesley as the fittest person to fill the office of Prime Minister to the young Rajah of Mysore.

and, to a certain degree, true one, of not giving sufficient employment to the different classes of military inhabitants.

Superficial observers have been too ready to compare our connexion with Mysore, to that with the Nabob of Arcot, the Vizier of Oude, and the Rajah of Tanjore; and to conclude on general, but erroneous principles, that it would soon run it's course; as it carried, like them, the seeds of it's own destruction, and was (from it's very nature) at variance with duration. But a very little reflection will show the radical difference, which subsists in those connexions. Our relations with the Nabob of Arcot, the Vizier of Oude, and the Rajah of Tanjore, were gradual in their formation; and they were, from their origin, marked by intrigue and corruption. The revenues of those States were anticipated by usurious loans; and individuals (often high in rank in the English Government) benefited too largely by this usage, to attend to those dictates of public virtue, which must, if they had been attended to, have taught them, that such a system must not only prevent the State by which it was followed from ever being an useful Ally, but accelerate it's destruction. And when at last this obvious result was forced upon our observation, it was too late for remedy; the deep-rooted evil could not be eradicated:

and the Governments above mentioned have, from the occurrence of different emergencies, naturally sunk into that condition of complete dependence on the British Government, in which (considering the vitious principles of their constitution) they could alone be allowed to exist.

It is also of importance to remark, that these Governments have, from the causes stated, progressively declined in power and splendour from the period of their connexion with the English: and though there can be little doubt but they would, if that connexion had not been formed, have long ago been subdued by their powerful neighbours, the probability of that event has in all likelihood seldom entered their imagination. It was indeed natural, that the minds of the Nabobs of Arcot, the Viziers of Oude, and Rajahs of Tanjore, and their dependents, should have dwelt chiefly upon their past glory; and the sentiments they have entertained of the English Government have been such, as were likely to arise from a comparison of that, with their actual condition; and a conviction as strong, as it was erroneous, that the great reverse was solely produced by their connexion with that State.

The Mysore Government presents a perfect contrast to this picture. It has been created by the generosity of the British Government; and that weight of original obligation must long operate, and attach* it to the State to which it owes it's existence. It must also give popularity, and the appearance, as well as the reality, of justice to that right, which the English Government has acquired (and which is sanctioned by the form of treaty), of exercising a liberal control over the Administration of the affairs of Mysore; and of directing, in a general way, the disposal of it's revenue, the organization of it's army, and the employment of it's resources. Hitherto that right has been exercised in a manner, that has added to the wealth, population and prosperity, of Mysore. The attachment of that State has been tried, and it has exceeded expectation. Throughout the whole of the Mahratta war, no part of the Company's territories, of the same extent, afforded such resources in men, money and grain, as Mysore: and these were supplied with a voluntary and forward zeal, which stamped practically, and

* During the late mutiny at Vellore, though the name of the family of Tippoo Sultaun was the watchword of revolt, not a man in the army of Mysore (upwards of 10,000 in number), not an inhabitant of that country, was convicted of either mutiny or treason:—a proof (beyond all opinion) of the vigilance, vigour, and excellence of the existing Government, as well as of the general attachment of it's subjects.

therefore incontrovertibly, the happy operation of the alliance.

This Government has, no doubt, it's defects: but it is as good, I believe, as it is possible for a native Government to be: and it is, as far as we are yet concerned with it's Administration, pure. There have hitherto been no intrigues at the Rajah's Court, no clashing of authorities, no corruption, no usurious loans; and consequently no anticipation of revenue, that fruitful source of ruin and oppression.

These are the great and radical points on which this connexion differs from those we have formed with the Nabob of Arcot, the Vizier of Oude, the Rajah of Tanjore, and many of the inferior States in India. And, if we have wisdom and courage to defend those principles of purity from every attack, we may promise ourselves a continued source of improving strength from our alliance with Mysore. It is, however, the misfortune of this connexion (as I before stated), that it's nature, though excellent, is so delicate, that it is perhaps more liable to injury from inattention, or from a cessation of active and spirited support, than it is from a bold and unblushing attack. The Mysore State is, in fact, so actually dependent upon us; and that dependence is so marked by the number of British troops stationed in it's territories, that nothing but the English Government being constantly alive to the character and value of the connexion, can keep it in that state of elevation and respectability, which appear to be absolutely necessary for it's existence.

As the revenues of Mysore have greatly increased, from it's ameliorated system of management, and the internal tranquillity which it has enjoyed; that State has had, after the payment of the Company's subsidy, and of it's own civil and military establishments, a considerable surplus revenue; part of which has been annually employed in great and useful works. It's canals, public roads, and bridges, already surpass those of any Province in India; and will (if the same active spirit of improvement continues) soon rival those of the most civilized parts of Europe.

Such was the change which Lord Wellesley, on his departure for England, had to contemplate in a Country, which, when he arrived in India, was in possession of a tyrant, who had no object but that of collecting means to annihilate the British power in India.

The authority of the Company had, as I have before stated, been completely introduced into the Carnatic; and that fine Country, no longer a prey to a system of usury and oppression, was rising rapidly into prosperity. Even those, who questioned the justice of the arrangement with the Nabob, could not deny the great amelioration of the condition of the inhabitants and the Country.

The conquest of Cuttack had connected the territories of Madras and Bengal; and, combined with the important cessions we had before obtained in Guzerat, Malabar, and Canara, gave the Company the possession of almost the whole line of sea-coast, from the mouths of the Ganges to those of the Indus.

The subordinate Government of Bombay had obtained, during the Administration of Lord Wellesley, a great and essential addition to it's resources, by the territories in Guzerat ceded by the Paishwah and Scindiah, and by the Guickwar, with whom the Government of Bombay, acting under that nobleman's orders, had formed a subsidiary alliance: and this important Presidency had become, from this acquisition, more equal to answer those calls, which it appeared likely, from the state of Europe, might be eventually made on it's military resources.

The Paishwah, whose natural weakness of character had led him to hesitate at entering into a defensive treaty with the British Government, had proved a most faithful and useful Ally. Early sensible of the advantages which the connexion brought to him and his subjects, he endeavoured, by every means within his power, to evince his fidelity to the engagements that he had formed: and his territories, which had been, from the day of his accession till that on which the treaty of Bassein was concluded, annually wasted by his rebellious Feudatories, had enjoyed from that date uninterrupted tranquillity. The subsidiary corps, in the territories of this Prince, was stationed forty miles to the northward of Poonah; and formed, with the subsidiary force at Hyderabad, a complete chain of defence against any possible attack, which could be made; and not only covered the frontiers of the Paishwah and Nizam, and secured the internal tranquillity of the Countries of these Princes; but gave permanent security and peace to all the southern parts of the Peninsula.

The power of Doulut Row Scindiah had been completely reduced; and at the period of Lord Wellesley's departure, though that Prince continued discontented at the alienation of Gohud and Gwalier, which he continued to hope he might regain through the liberality of that State by which he had been vanquished, he was nowise inclined to a renewal of hostilities. He had, indeed, shown a decided aversion to the violent councils of his Minister and father-in-law, Surjee Row Gautka, who had endeavoured, by every means, to involve him with the British Government; and, among others, had recourse to the disgraceful and cowardly expedient, of attacking the escort, and plundering the baggage, of the acting British Resident with Scindiah's camp.

Jeswunt Row Holkar was at this period reduced from the condition, which he had once enjoyed, of a Chief at the head of a State with regular resources, to that of a freebooter commanding a body of dispirited troops, who had nothing but plunder to depend upon; but whom, it was evident, he never could again persuade to meet the British armies in the field, or indeed to trust themselves within fifty miles of an English force.*

In the quarter of Hindoostan, all those great prospects, which Lord Wellesley had contemplated at the commencement of the war, had been completely realized. The French party had been annihilated, the Mahrattas expelled, the British Government established over the whole of the Duab, and along the right banks of the Jumnah; and a line of petty States, from

* The last campaign this Chief made, was literally a rapid flight before the British troops, from the day he entered their territories to the westward of Dehli, to that of his arrival at Amrutsir, in the Punjaub, where he concluded a treaty with Lord Lake.

the mountains of Cumaoun to Bundlecund, under the protection of the British Government, were established, as a barrier between it's most fruitful Provinces and the future predatory encroachments of the Mahrattas. The rich Province of Bundlecund was subdued, and occupied by British troops; and the Countries ceded by the Vizier in 1801, were completely settled, and greatly improved in revenue; while that Prince was not only reconciled, but happy, under a change, which left him undisturbed, and in perfect security to pursue his favourite pleasures, and to amass treasure.

It would be endless to attempt to take a view of the minor arrangements of Lord Wellesley's Government: it will be sufficient to observe, that they were all made in the same spirit of radical and substantial improvement, as those which have been described; and were all equally attended with permanent benefit to the public interests. The general result of his Administration changed the face of India: and a course of events, as extraordinary as they were important, gave an entire new character to the British power in that quarter of the globe; which, at the close of this nobleman's Government, was completely paramount to that of all the States in India; and at liberty to choose, as it's wisdom should direct, that course of policy which seemed best suited to it's new condition. It had, from the nature of the events which had occurred, and the manner in which it's power was established, no danger to fear, either from the efforts of any one State, or a confederacy. The discontent of Scindiah, and the continued hostility of Holkar, at the period at which I write, cannot affect this conclusion; as it has been shown, that the condition of these Chiefs was such, as to prevent the apprehension of any evil from their attack, beyond a short continuation of that embarrassment in our finances, which had been the unavoidable consequence of the great exertions which had been made; but which, it is evident, was of a very temporary nature; as the improvement of our own revenues, the receipts from the conquered Countries, and those reductions which Lord Wellesley had commenced before he left India, not only promised a speedy relief to this pressure, but gave a prospect of an early and large surplus revenue from our possessions in India.

The great success which attended Lord Wellesley's Administration of British India, is, on a general view, calculated to excite astonishment: nor will that be diminished by a nearer contemplation of the manner in which he ruled the large Empire committed to his charge. His great mind pervaded the whole; and a portion of his spirit was infused into every agent whom he employed: his authority was as fully recognised in the remotest parts of British India, as in Fort William; all sought his praise; all dreaded his censure: his confidence in those he employed was unlimited; and they were urged to exertion by every motive that can stimulate a good or proud mind to action. He was as eager to applaud, as he was reluctant to condemn, those whom he believed conscientious in the discharge of their public duty. It was the habit of his mind to be slow in council, but rapid in action; and he expected the greatest efforts from those he employed in the execution of his measures, whom he always relieved from every species of vexatious counteraction and delay, which could arise from the untimely intrusion of official forms, or the unreasonable pretensions of lesser authorities. It was, indeed, with him a principle, to clothe them with all the power they could require, to effect those objects which they were instructed to attain; and though there can be no doubt of the great and extraordinary merit of the distinguished Officers, who commanded the British armies during his Administration, it is to that liberal confidence, which gave them all the impression of the fullest power, and the most complete scope for the exercise of their judgment, that their unparalleled success is chiefly to be ascribed.

It could not be a matter of surprise to those, the least acquainted with the clashing of opinions that prevailed in England with regard to the Government of British India, and knew the various interests which are affected by the changes in that Country, to find that a strong and violent prejudice had been excited against Lord Wellesley; and that numbers were for a moment led, by partial and distorted statements of his Administration, to conceive that it had been as ruinous, as it was in fact glorious, to the British Government. Truth has already obtained a victory; and that nobleman now enjoys, in the just admiration of his Country, the highest reward that can attend eminent public service.

CHAPTER V.

SECOND ADMINISTRATION

OF

MARQUIS CORNWALLIS;

AND

ADMINISTRATION

OF

SIR GEORGE BARLOW,

Till the Conclusion of Peace with

JESWUNT ROW HOLKAR.

CONTENTS.

Cornwallis.—Character of that Nobleman.—Succeeded by Sir George Barlow.—Treaty concluded with Scindiah.—Correspondence respecting some Articles in it.—Treaty of Peace with Holkar.—Despatch from Lord Lake respecting the Rajah of Jypore.—Dissolution of the Alliance with that Prince.—General Reflections arising from a View of the Line of Policy pursued in these Transactions.

THE nature of the public feeling in England has been noticed in the last Chapter. Much alarm was excited by an indistinct and exaggerated apprehension of the evils, which it was imagined would result from the system of policy pursued by Lord Wellesley, and the ruinous wars in which the Government of India was thought to be involved. This feeling was rendered more general and popular among all persons in England, connected with the Company, from the increase of the Indian debt; the interest of which, combined with the want of sales for their accumulated investments, threatened that body with immediate distress, which many were desirous of exclusively ascribing to the political measures of the Governor General of India; and not, in any degree, to that immense loss, to which, from the nature of the war in Europe, the commerce of the Company was at this period subject. The little knowledge, which many of the most liberal and best informed persons in England have of the detail of Indian politics, added to the remoteness of the scene, and the general nature of the accounts from that quarter, gave the greatest advantage to those, who desired at this period to make impressions upon the public mind unfavourable to the Administration of Lord Wellesley. But it is only just to observe, that many, who were most violent against that nobleman's measures, were perfectly conscientious in the sentiments which they entertained and expressed on this subject; for it required the most complete, and indeed minute, information with respect to the changes which had occurred, before even men of enlarged and liberal minds (who had to view this question at a distance) could be competent to pronounce with justice on a revolution so great and extraordinary, and so inconsistent with established opinions and rooted prejudices, as that which had taken place within the few years during which Lord Wellesley presided over the British interests in the East.

To minds acting under the influence of such feelings as those I have described, it was natural to look round for a remedy for those great evils which they apprehended; and no one can be astonished, that the choice of Lord Cornwallis, as a successor to Lord Wellesley, was a measure which met, at such a moment, with almost general approbation in England: and to those acquainted with that venerable nobleman's character, it will be a subject of still less surprise, that his accumulated years and infirmities did not render him insensible to such a call. Though his health was in a most declining state, he caught, with that enthusiasm which belongs only to good and great minds, at the prospect of performing one more important service to his Country, before he died; and he listened, as was natural, with avidity to those who, desirous of the authority of his great name to their plans, represented to him, that his presence alone could save from inevitable ruin that Empire, which he had before ruled with such glory. It is to the impression made upon his mind by such representations, and to the infirm state of this nobleman's health, which could not but in some degree impair the strength and vigour of his mind, that we must ascribe the difference in character of those few political measures, which he adopted during his last short Administration of the affairs of British India, from those which distinguished his first Government.

The Marquis Cornwallis arrived at Fort William in July 1805. The state of all the native Powers, at this period, has already been minutely described. It is only necessary to add, that the acting Resident* at the Court of Doulut Row Scindiah was still detained in the camp of that Chief, though Lord Lake had not only required his release, but had informed Scindiah, that a recommencement of hostilities would be the certain consequence of his non-compliance with this demand. As this communication had produced no effect, Lord Lake, in a letter to that Chief, dated the 18th of July, informed him, that he had, by his conduct in this instance, not only dissolved the treaty of peace and of subsidiary alliance, but violated, in the grossest manner, the law of Nations; and that he considered the British Government was at liberty to act towards him in such manner as it's interests and security might dictate. Lord Lake concluded this letter by remarking, that the release and safe conduct of the British Residency to his camp, was an indispensable preliminary to any renewal of amity or intercourse between the two States.

The proceedings of Lord Lake upon this occasion had been confirmed by Lord Wellesley, in a despatch dated the 25th of July, which gave cover to a letter to Scindiah, signifying the complete acquiescence of the Governor General

* Mr. Jenkins.

in all the measures which Lord Lake had taken; and informing him, that that nobleman was vested with the fullest military and political powers, and that his acts were as valid as if they proceeded direct from the Supreme Government.

In this stage of the proceeding Lord Cornwallis arrived; and immediately addressed a letter to Scindiah, in which he stated, that it had not been his intention to write to him before he heard of his compliance with the request which Lord Lake had made, respecting the release of the acting Resident; but, wishing to manifest an inclination for peace, he had been induced to address him, in consequence of a letter from the acting Resident, which stated, that his Highness had declared his intention to permit him, accompanied by two confidential agents, to join the camp of Lord Lake. That Officer, Lord Cornwallis observed, was fully authorized to communicate with these agents on all points connected with the welfare of both States.

A letter from the acting Resident at the Court of Scindiah, under date the 11th of September, stated, that that Chief, though he had received the letter of Marquis Cornwallis, still hesitated in granting him permission to leave camp: and, in a letter dated the 16th of the same month, he transmitted a reply from Doulut Row Scindiah to Lord Cornwallis's letter; in which, after many professions of friendship, Scindiah observed, that the dismissal of the acting Resident was, agreeably to usage, delayed until a successor arrived in his camp.

Though Lord Cornwallis continued for some time to think, that the release of the Residency with Doulut Row Scindiah was, after the great insult which the English Nation had received from it's being plundered and forcibly detained, an indispensable preliminary to any negotiation with that Chief; his anxious desire for peace subsequently led him, first to a modification, and ultimately to a complete alteration, of this sentiment. In a letter addressed to Scindiah, he informed that Chief, at the same time that he urged him to allow the acting Resident to depart, that Lord Lake had been authorized to enter into a negotiation with him, on the basis of restoring the fortress of Gwalier and the territories of Gohud; and in his despatch to Lord Lake, under date the 19th of September, which accompanied the letter to Scindiah, Lord Cornwallis expressly states, that though aware of the disadvantages of immediately relinquishing, or even compromising, the demand so repeatedly made for the release of the British Resident; yet, that as he considered it a mere point of honour, he would certainly be disposed to do so, should it ultimately prove to be the only obstacle to a satisfactory adjustment of affairs with that Chieftain. No opportunity was afforded of judging of the impression which this extreme solicitude for peace would have had upon Doulut Row Scindiah, as a measure adopted by Lord Lake had effected the release of the acting Resident before these instructions from Lord Cornwallis, upon this point, were received.

Lord Lake had authorized the political Agent* of the Governor General, in his camp, to send for Moonshee Kavel Nyne from Dehli. That respectable native had long been one of Doulut Row Scindiah's favourite and confidential servants; but had fled from the temporary tyranny of that Chief's father-in-law, Surjee Row Gautka, into Hindoostan. When he arrived in Lord Lake's camp, he was instructed to depute one of his relations to Scindiah, to explain to that Chief the manner in which he could best open a negotiation for an amicable adjustment of differences between him and the British Government; and Scindiah, as had been expected, caught at this new and unexpected channel of communication, and sent proposals for a settlement, to be laid before the Commander-in-Chief by Kavel Nyne. In answer to this overture,

* Lieutenant Colonel Malcolm.

Lord Lake observed, that he could not attend to any proposition whatever till the British Residency was released. The consequence was the immediate accomplishment of that object; and Mr. Jenkins was on his march to the British territories before the last letter of Lord Cornwallis to Scindiah, upon that subject, reached the British camp; and it was, in consequence, not forwarded.

Lord Cornwallis gave Lord Lake the fullest instructions, with respect to the treaty which he wished to be concluded with Doulut Row Scindiah, in his despatch dated the 19th of September.

In this letter Lord Cornwallis stated his decided opinion, that it was desirable to abandon the possession of Gwalier and Gohud, independently of any reference to the settlement of differences with Scindiah; and that he consequently had no hesitation in transferring these possessions to Scindiah, after having secured a suitable provision for the Ranah of Gohud. The Governor General, however, stated, that he did not wish to make an unconditional surrender of these Countries, but was desirous that Scindiah should be induced, by this measure, to relieve the Company from the burden of the Jagheers and pensions granted by the treaty of peace; to bear the charge of a suitable establishment for the Ranah of Gohud, and to reimburse the public and private losses occasioned by the plunder of the British Residency. It would, the Governor General stated in this letter, be in the option of the British Government to augment the cession to Scindiah by a portion of the territory in our possession to the westward and southward of Dehli. The expediency of this measure must, he observed, be determined by political considerations; and if circumstances would admit of it, he added, the dissolution of our alliance with the Rajah of Jypore, and the amount of tribute which Scindiah would then be at liberty to demand of that Chief, might be considered as an additional benefit, which he would derive from the general arrangement.

Lord Cornwallis, who had appeared from the first resolved upon making the Jumnah the boundary* of the Company's possessions, stated

* Retaining Dehli and Agra, and a small district near the latter fortress; but, as his Lordship was anxious to remove the old Emperor from his capital, he probably contemplated, at one period, the eventual abandonment of Dehli. An erroneous idea had been entertained, that the Jumnah river was in itself a strong barrier. This Lord Lake corrected in a communication to Lord Cornwallis, in which he transmitted the most particular information upon this subject; the result of which was, that the Jumnah was only useful as a barrier during the rainy season, when military operations were, from the gene-

in this letter his opinion, that though it would be advisable to establish any other than a Mahratta Power to the westward and southward of Dehli; yet he should consider even that arrangement more expedient, than our maintaining any further connexion with the territories in question ourselves. The following is the basis upon which Lord Cornwallis desired this treaty with Scindiah to be concluded.

"1st. To make over to Scindiah the possessions of Gwalier and Gohud.

"2d. To transfer to him, according to the provisions of the treaty of peace, the districts of Dhoolpoor, Baree, and Rajah Kerrah; and to account to Scindiah for the collections from those districts, since the peace. I am aware, Lord Cornwallis states, that this is not to be considered in the light of a concession; but I am willing to relinquish that stipulation of the treaty, which prohibits Scindiah from stationing a force in those districts; an object which I should suppose to be highly desirable to that Chieftain.

ral state of the Country, almost impracticable. It was fordable in several places above Agra, even before the 1st of October; and could not be looked upon as a boundary of any strength, at any place above it's junction with the Chumbul, for more than a few weeks of the wet season.

"3d. The eventual restoration of the Jynegur "tribute, amounting to the annual sum of "three lacks of rupees.

"4th. To require from Scindiah his consent "to the abrogation of the pensions, and to the "resumption of the Jagheers in the Duab, esta-"blished by the treaty of peace.

"5th. To require from Scindiah the relin-"quishment of his claim to the arrears of the "pension.

"6th. To demand a compensation for the "public and private losses sustained by the "plunder of the Residency.

"7th. To require Scindiah to make a pro-"vision for the Ranah of Gohud, to the "extent of two and a half, or three lacks "of rupees per annum."

But although Lord Cornwallis desired the negotiations should be commenced upon this basis, he declared his intention of relaxing in some of the demands in favour of the Company, rather than delay the conclusion of peace; and to attain that object, he was, he said, ready to extend the cessions to Scindiah, should such appear necessary for the satisfactory adjustment of affairs between the two States.

It was not, he observed in this communication, his intention to renew our defensive engagements with Scindiah, though he was ready to act in concert with that Chief, as an Ally, against Holkar, until the latter should be brought to reasonable terms. He stated, in these instructions, the grounds upon which he was disposed to make that arrangement which annulled the alliance with the Ranah of Gohud. These were;—the utter incapacity of that Chief to rule, and his inability to perform the engagements which he had contracted with the Company: but he, at the same time, conceived it just, to make a suitable provision for the future liberal support of this inefficient Prince.

Lord Cornwallis also communicated to Lord Lake, in this letter, the plan which he had contemplated for disposing of the conquered Countries southward and westward of Dehli; which was, to give part of them to the several Chieftains* for whom we were bound to provide, on condition of their not claiming our protection; and dividing the remainder between the Rajahs of Macherry and Bhurtpore, on their agreeing to relinquish the alliances which they had formed with the British Government.

The territories of these Chieftains would, his Lordship thought, so extended, constitute the desired barrier between the possessions of Scin-

* Commanders of corps of native horse, and others, who had, by their defection from our enemies, or by their services during the war, entitled themselves to reward.

diah in Hindoostan, and those of the Company in the Duab; and, in the reduced state of Scindiah's power, he thought it not improbable that these Rajahs might be able to oppose him; particularly if aided by the independent Jagheerdars. At all events, his Lordship declared, that he was satisfied of the expediency of even admitting the power of Doulut Row Scindiah into the territories in question, rather than that we should preserve any control over, or connexion with them. "But Scindiah's endea-
"vours," his Lordship adds, "to wrest those
"territories from the hands of the Rajahs of
"Macherry and Bhurtpore, may be expected to
"lay the foundation of interminable contests,
"which will afford ample and permanent em-
"ployment to Scindiah: and, under any cir-
"cumstances, I cannot," he adds, "admit the
"apprehension of any hostile attempts on the
"part of Scindiah against the British posses-
"sions in the Duab; still less should I deem it
"probable, in the event of his rendering the
"Chiefs of Macherry and Bhurtpore his per-
"petual enemies, which must be the conse-
"quence of his endeavours to deprive them of
"a portion of their dominions."

Lord Lake, in his reply to these instructions, referred to a letter which he had before written to Lord Cornwallis, on the subject of the great benefits which must result to the Company's territories from the complete expulsion of the Mahrattas from Hindoostan: and stated his perfect conviction, (founded upon his local experience,) that the maintenance of the strong boundary, which we possessed, would soon cause the Mahrattas to abandon every idea of attacking our Provinces in that quarter; which he was fully persuaded they never would do, if permitted to possess territory in Hindoostan, or to employ their armies against the petty States or Jagheerdars immediately west of the Jumnah. Lord Lake, in this despatch, stated the numerous reasons, which convinced his judgment, that, if the British protection was withdrawn from those petty States, they would either be subdued by Doulut Row Scindiah, or some other Chief; who would found on their ruins a Power, formidable, from it's strength and local situation, to the British Government.

Lord Lake observed in this letter, that the armies of Scindiah and Holkar had comparatively few Mahrattas* in them, and were mostly

* This extraordinary composition of the armies of the different Mahratta Chiefs, while it led to very false conclusions respecting the actual military strength of that Nation, was one, among many other causes, which prevented their combination. It was, indeed, a radical cause of their division and ruin: for the fact was, that the Mahrattas, originally inhabitants of one of the

composed of Rajpoots and Mahomedans, natives of Hindoostan; most of whom had returned to their homes, or entered into the service of the British Government: and he was satisfied, that they might, by a liberal line of policy, be, within a very short period, detached from their habits, and rendered useful subjects. But every plan of this nature would, he conceived, be completely frustrated, if the territories west of the Jumnah were permitted to become a scene of perpetual warfare and contest; or if they fell under the dominion of any one native Prince, whose views were directed to plunder and conquest. In either of those cases, the habits of this tribe of men would be perpetuated, and hordes of plunderers would be formed, ready to join the first bold adventurer, who offered to lead them from the Countries which their ex-

divisions of India, taking advantage of the decline of the Moghul Empire, had spread their power over the greatest part of that vast Peninsula; but, like every barbarous Nation, which carries with it nothing but force to effect conquest, it was weakened by extension; and the descendants of those Chiefs, who first led Mahratta armies into distant Countries, have of late led bands of foreigners, to plunder and desolate the Provinces of their ancestors: and all the ravages, which this race formerly committed on other parts of India, have, within these few years, been amply revenged upon their own Country by armies of Mussulmanns and Rajpoots, led by Mahratta Chiefs.

cesses had wasted, into the neighbouring rich and fertile Provinces of the Company.

These, Lord Lake observed in this letter, were his sentiments upon this subject, in a political point of view. He next proceeded to consider it's practicability, and whether it could be carried into execution, without a violation of the faith of the English Nation, and the deepest injury to the honour and reputation of that State. After a full explanation of the grounds upon which his opinions on this head were founded, he stated his conviction, that the plan, which Lord Cornwallis had in contemplation, was impracticable, by other means than that of loading the revenues of the Company's territories to a great amount, with the compensations which must be made to those, from whom considerations of policy had made that Government to withdraw it's protection.

" I am fully satisfied," Lord Lake remarks in this letter, " that no inducement whatever " would make the lesser Rajahs in this quarter " renounce the benefit of the protection of the " British Government: such a proposition, " even, would excite in their minds the utmost " alarm; they would, I fear, consider it as a " prelude to their being sacrificed to the object " of obtaining a peace with the Mahrattas; nor "would it, as far as I can judge, be possible, by "any explanation, to remove from their minds "an impression so injurious to the honour and "reputation of the British Government.

"Not one of the Chiefs," his Lordship adds, "who have claims upon the British Government, and whom it appears to be your Lordship's intention to settle to the west of the "Jumnah, would ever consent to be provided "for in the Country of any of the Rajahs, except under a guarantee, that would prove a "thousand times more embarrassing than their "settlement under the direct authority of the "British Government: and, on the other hand, "I do not believe that any of those Chiefs "would be able to maintain themselves, for "even a short period, against the more established local authorities, if the protection of "the British Government was withdrawn."

Lord Lake, in this letter, reported the progress made in the negotiation with Scindiah; and expressed his regret, that the personal incapacity of the Ranah of Gohud should have defeated all the objects which were anticipated from the arrangement made regarding him; and fully concurred with the Marquis Cornwallis in the opinion, that, though just grounds existed for the abrogation of that alliance, it was better to obtain the consent of that Chief to a change of his condition, from a power he was unequal to exercise, to one more suited to his weak and inefficient character.

As some serious discussions took place, at this period, respecting our connexion with the Rajah of Jypore; it will be necessary to trace, in a few words, the rise and nature of that alliance.

The Rajah of Jypore, who is one of the principal Rajpoot Chiefs who possess that tract of Country which divides Malwah from Hindoostan, entered very early in the war with Scindiah into an alliance with the English Government. The general conditions of this alliance have been described. The Rajah had certainly on many occasions deviated from both the letter and spirit of this engagement. But, at the moment when both Scindiah and Holkar were on the frontiers of Jypore, and the Bombay army had marched to Tonk Rampoorah, a place immediately in the vicinity of the capital of the Rajah, from whose territories it drew most of it's supplies, Lord Lake conceived it consistent with good policy to relieve the solicitude which the agent of the Rajah of Jypore, residing in his camp, expressed respecting the consequences which might attend the wavering part that his master had pursued; and he directed him to inform the Rajah, that he had now an opportunity, which he hoped he would not neglect, of proving himself worthy of the friendship and support of the British Government.

After Lord Lake had made this communication to the agent of the Rajah of Jypore, he received a letter from Lord Cornwallis, under date the 3d of August, on the subject of this alliance. Lord Cornwallis stated in this despatch his opinion, that the Rajah of Jypore, so far from performing his engagements with the Company, had favoured the cause of the enemy; and he, therefore, considered the alliance dissolved: and as he saw nothing but inconvenience and embarrassment from the connexion, it had, he observed, been resolved by Government, not to repel any aggression that Scindiah or Holkar might make on the territories of Jypore.

Lord Lake was instructed to transmit orders to Major General Jones, who commanded the Bombay army, (then cantoned on the frontiers of the Jypore State,) not to give the Rajah any aid, in the event of an attack from the Mahrattas, as the Governor General in Council had resolved to abandon the connexion. But Lord Cornwallis stated in these instructions, that it was thought impolitic to declare to the Court of Jypore the dissolution of the subsisting engagements, as such a declaration might, under the actual situation of affairs, be productive of great disadvantage to the interests of the British Government. The Resident at the Court of the Rajah of Jypore was therefore to be informed of the resolution, which the Governor General in Council had taken respecting the alliance, and desired to make no communication whatever upon the subject; but he was instructed not to give the Rajah of Jypore any promise of aid from British troops, in the event of his territories being invaded by Scindiah, Holkar, or any other Chief.

Lord Lake, after the measures which he had adopted, felt the greatest embarrassment on receiving these orders; and immediately communicated to Lord Cornwallis the nature of those assurances of continued support and friendship, which circumstances had induced him to make to the Rajah of Jypore, on the condition of that Prince meriting, by his future conduct, the protection of the British Government.

When Lord Lake, subsequently to this communication, received information, in a letter dated the 1st of October, from the Resident at Jypore, that Holkar was advancing through the territories of Jypore towards the Company's frontier; and that the Rajah did not seem inclined to oppose him, but was employing the principal part of his army towards effecting the subordinate object of his marriage with the daughter of the Ranah of Oudepore; he addressed a letter to the Rajah, in which, after recapitulating the various instances in which he had violated his engagements, and informing him, that it was probable the Governor General would issue immediate orders for the abandonment of such an useless and burthensome connexion, he stated, that it was probable General Jones's army would soon move against Holkar; in which case the Rajah might yet retrieve his credit, by a hearty co-operation with that Officer, and by adopting the most active and efficient measures for securing him those supplies which were necessary to his army.

This measure was not only in consistency with the line of proceeding, which Lord Lake had adopted towards the Rajah of Jypore; but was, from the actual situation of the enemy and of our forces, quite essential to the success of the opening campaign; and it was attended with the completest effect. The Resident at the Court of Jypore informed Lord Lake, in a despatch under date the 16th of October, that the Rajah, as soon as he received his Lordship's letter, had abandoned his favourite project of marching a force towards Oudepore, and prepared a detachment to join General Jones's army, with which he co-operated in the most zealous and decided manner during the remainder of the war with Holkar.

Lord Cornwallis had, upon Lord Lake's report, suspended the execution of the measures which he had taken regarding the dissolution of this connexion. It was concluded, therefore, by Lord Lake, that the Rajah of Jypore had, by his complete fulfilment of the conditions proposed to him, fully entitled himself to the rank which he before held, of an intimate and faithful Ally of the British Government.

Lord Cornwallis took, during his last Administration of British India, no measures of any importance with the Courts of Hyderabad, Poonah, and Berar. He addressed, on his arrival at Fort William, letters to each of these Rulers, reminding them of the principles of his former Government; professing the greatest moderation, and a desire to remove from their minds those impressions, which late events might have produced. The general tenor of these letters was no doubt calculated to convey a belief, that the measures of Lord Wellesley had been condemned, and that another system was to be pursued: and in one instance, at the Court of Berar, this proceeding gave rise to a long and vexatious discussion between the Rajah and the British Resident; the former contending, that it was evidently Lord Cornwallis's intention, from the expression of his letter, to restore affairs in India to that posture in which he had left them in 1793,* which included the restoration of Berar, Cuttack, and all the possessions which this Chief had lost since that period.

No negotiation was carried on with Jeswunt Row Holkar while Lord Cornwallis lived; but that nobleman gave general instructions to Lord Lake respecting the conduct of any settlement with that Chief, which he desired should be made upon the general basis of leaving him in possession of the territories of the Holkar family, on his affording the British Government reasonable security for his future conduct. But no opportunity occurred, even of making any proposition to this Chief; who, accompanied by a comparatively small number of distressed and disheartened adherents, advanced through the barren Provinces to the north west of Dehli, into

* The Rajah of Berar, in speaking upon this subject, distinctly stated, that when Lord Cornwallis had, of his own free will, written to him, expressing great grief at his reduced condition, and a desire to renew the ties of friendship with him on the ancient footing, and a determination to make restitution to the utmost extent which good faith would permit; that he had, on the strength of this declaration, expected the restoration of all his lost territories.

the Provinces of the Punjaub,* about the period of Lord Cornwallis's death.

Lord Cornwallis appears, from his first despatches to the Court of Directors, to have been very anxious to adopt such measures as he deemed calculated to relieve the finances of the Company from that embarrassment, which was the inevitable consequence of the wars in which we had been, and were, engaged; but it was of course impossible to make any reductions of consequence in our military establishments † before the war was completely at an end, as it's suc-

* This extensive and fertile Country is inhabited by Sieckhs, an extraordinary race; of whom a very full account is given in the eleventh volume of the Asiatic Researches.

† Much has been said respecting the enormous expense of the irregular horse with Lord Lake's army; and this large item in the military disbursements attracted the early attention of Lord Cornwallis: but it is to be recollected, that it only began to be heavy when the retreat of Holkar from Hindoostan occasioned the defection of almost all the Chiefs belonging to that Country; who, with their numerous followers, joined the British army. The heaviest amount of this temporary disbursement was five lacks and eighty-three thousand six hundred and sixty-nine rupees four anas and three pice per month, which did not continue for more than three months. It's reduction was in progress before Lord Cornwallis's arrival: and this charge was, in September 1806, reduced to three lacks and ninety thousand four hundred and fifty-five rupees nine anas; in December, to two lacks nineteen thousand six hundred and

cessful termination depended upon the efficiency of the army, and it's equipments.

The health of Lord Cornwallis, which was in a declining state when he left England, became worse from the period he left Fort William to join the army in the upper Provinces,* and his existence terminated at Gazeepore, near Benares, on the 5th of October 1805.

Thus closed the life of this distinguished nobleman; whose memory will be revered as long as the sacred attributes of virtue and patriotism shall command the approbation of mankind. To a dignified simplicity of character, he added a soundness of understanding and a strength of judgment, which admirably fitted him for the exercise of both civil and military power: and his first Administration of the British Empire in India must ever be a theme of just and unqualified applause. His second was of too short a

sixty-seven rupees and ten anas; and in February, 1807, to a sum under one lack of rupees.

* In the weak state in which he was during the last month of his existence, it is hardly possible to conceive how he was able to transact any business of importance. He continued the greatest part of the morning in a condition of weakness approaching to insensibility: towards the evening he revived so much, as to be dressed, to hear the despatches which had been received, and to give instructions respecting such as were to be written; and his mind is stated, by those who attended him, to have retained, even in this state, much of it's wonted force.

duration to make it possible to judge of the consequences with which it would have been attended; and it is perhaps probable, that the evil effects of those concessions, which he seemed disposed to make, would have been corrected by his great personal reputation; as every State in India was aware of his character, and of that spirit and promptness with which he had formerly asserted the honour and interests of the British Government. But however much many may question the policy of some of the last acts of this nobleman, or speculate upon the causes which produced such an apparent deviation from the high and unyielding spirit of his former Administration; no man can doubt the exalted purity of the motive, which led him to revisit that Country. Loaded with years, as he was with honour, he desired that his life should terminate, as it had commenced; and he died, as he had lived, in the active service of his Country.

After the death of Lord Cornwallis, Sir George Barlow* succeeded, by a provisional

* Sir George Barlow is a civil servant of the Honourable Company. He recommended himself to the notice of his superiors by an able and honourable discharge of the various subordinate offices which he filled before he reached the high station of Governor General. He was actively employed, under Lord Cornwallis, in introducing the code of regulations for the civil

appointment, to the Administration of the affairs of British India. It is not intended to give a narrative of his Government further than to the termination of the treaties of peace with Doulut Row Scindiah and Jeswunt Row Holkar; which engagements I shall proceed to notice; stating, at the same time, such facts as are calculated to elucidate the principles upon which they were formed, and the general condition of India at this epoch.*

The instructions which Sir George Barlow gave to Lord Lake, for the conclusion of the treaty with Scindiah, in no respect differed in principle from those given upon the same points by Lord Cornwallis. He indeed expressed, in his first communication to the Commander-in-Chief, his resolution to follow the steps of that nobleman; and his conviction, that the public interests would be best promoted, by our throwing off, at the earliest practicable period, all connexion with the petty States west

Administration of the territories of Bengal; and filled the office of Chief Secretary to Government under Lord Teignmouth and Lord Wellesley, before he was raised to the Supreme Council, of which he was a member during the four last years of the Administration of the latter nobleman.

* Almost the whole of the public correspondence down to this date, is, I imagine, in one shape or another, already before the public.

of the Jumnah, limiting our boundary to that river, and a line of territory not exceeding eight or ten miles in breadth on it's right bank; and trusting, in a great degree, for our future security, to the contests of our neighbours. Upon this principle, while he desired to be free of all defensive engagements with Scindiah, he expressed himself more desirous of a peace with Holkar, than of the complete reduction of that Chief.

On the 23d of November, a treaty was concluded by the political Agent* of the Governor General (acting under the authority of Lord Lake), and Moonshee Kavel Nyne, whom Doulut Row Scindiah had appointed his Agent, and vested with full powers; of which the following are the heads:—

Every part of the treaty of Surjee Anjengaum, except what might be altered by this treaty, was to remain in force.

Although the Honourable Company did not acknowledge that Scindiah possessed any claim to Gohud and Gwalier, under the abovementioned treaty; yet, from considerations of friendship, they agreed to cede to him Gwalier, and such parts of the territories of Gohud as were described in an accompanying schedule.

* Lieutenant Colonel Malcolm.

Scindiah relinquished all claim to the pensions granted to different Officers of his Court by the original treaty of peace, to the amount of fifteen lacks annually.

The Company agreed to pay the arrears of those pensions up to the 31st of December 1805; and the balance due upon the revenues of Dhoolpoor, Barree, and Rajah Kerrah, up to the same date; making deductions on the following heads:—

1st. Pensions forfeited by Bappoo Scindiah, and Sudashes Row, by acts of hostility towards the British Government, to be stopped from the date of their hostility.

2d. Plunder of the British Residency.

3d. Cash advanced by Mr. Jenkins to parties of the Maharajah's horse.

4th. Charges of collection, &c. for the Provinces of Dhoolpoor, Barree, and Rajah Kerrah.

The river Chumbul * was to form the boundary between the two States, from the city

* The Chumbul was not taken as a boundary from it's being of any use as a barrier, but as a distinct line of demarcation; an object of the greatest consequence, to prevent future discussions with a Power of the nature of that of a Mahratta Chief. This article was considered by Lord Lake to be more essential, at the time when this treaty was concluded, from his conceiving that the maintenance of our alliance with the State of Jypore was, under the conduct which the Rajah had lately pursued, a matter of course.

of Kottah to the west, to the limits of the territories of Gohud to the east; Doulut Row Scindiah was to have no claims whatever to the northward of that river; and the Honourable Company, in like manner, to have no claims to the southward of that extent of it's course. The Talook of Bhadek * and Sooseperarah, which are on the banks of the Jumnah, to remain, notwithstanding, in the possession of the Honourable Company.

By the preceding articles, Scindiah resigned all claims and pretensions on the Countries of Boondee, Sumedee, Dhoolpoor, Barree, and Rajah Kerrah.

The Company granted to the Maharajah, personally and exclusively, the sum of four lacks of rupees annually; and assigned within their territories in Hindoostan, a Jagheer, to the amount of two lacks of rupees per annum, to Baezah Bhye, wife to Doulut Row Scindiah; and another, of one lack per annum, to Chumnah Bhye, daughter of that Chief.

The Company also engaged to enter into no treaties with the Rajahs of Oudepore and Joud-

* The small and unproductive districts of Bhadek and Sooseperarah, though to the northward of the Chumbul, were granted to the Company, as being on the banks of the Jumnah, and preserving the communication from the Province of Agra to Bundlecund.

pore, and Kottah, or other Chiefs tributaries to Doulut Row Scindiah in Malwah, Mewar, or Merwar; and in no shape to interfere with the settlement which Scindiah may make with those Chiefs.

In the event of the conclusion of a peace with Jeswunt Row Holkar, the Company engaged not to restore to him, or desire to be restored to him, any of the possessions of the Holkar family in the Province of Malwah, lying between the rivers Taptie and Chumbul, which may have been taken by Doulut Row Scindiah; nor to interfere in the disposal of those Provinces; and consider Scindiah at liberty to make what arrangement he pleases with Jeswunt Row Holkar, or any branch of the family, respecting it's claims to any tribute or territorial possessions north of the river Taptie, and south of the river Chumbul: but it was clearly to be understood, that the British Government would not take any part in any dispute or war, which may be the consequence of such arrangement.

A stipulation was made in this treaty, by which Scindiah agreed never to admit Surjee Row Gautka* to share in his councils, or to

* This atrocious character had been declared a public enemy by the British Government: and this article, which was a complete vindication of our insulted honour, was confirmed; and one of a similar nature was inserted in the treaty concluded with

hold any public employment under his Government.

In addition to the Jagheers given to Scindiah and his family by this treaty, estates to an amount of upwards of three lacks of rupees were given to the chief Officers of his Court: but, calculating the cessions to the northward of the Chumbul, which Scindiah had made by this treaty, at seven lacks of rupees, and the Jagheer or pension which was to be assigned to the Ranah of Gohud, at three lacks, the Company gained by the treaty, in lieu of the cession of Gwalier and Gohud, a revenue of upwards of eight lacks of rupees per annum, which was nearly the amount of the subsidy settled in the treaty with the Ranah of Gohud.

Sir George Barlow did not altogether approve this treaty; and though he expressed his high satisfaction at the readiness with which Doulut Row Scindiah had consented to withdraw from any concern in the affairs of Hindoostan to the northward of the Chumbul, he stated in the most decided manner his conviction, that the actual condition of our affairs confirmed the

Holkar: but a few months afterwards, on a report that Surjee Row Gautka was about to join Holkar, the abrogation of these articles was directed, as it was feared they might lead to an embarrassment, which it was deemed (agreeably to the policy of the day) prudent to avoid.

policy and expediency of the principles upon which he had it in contemplation to effect a final arrangement with respect to the Chieftains and territories west of the Jumnah. He was fully satisfied, he informed Lord Lake, that, when these arrangements were carried into execution, they would constitute a degree of security against all hostile attempts, which could not be augmented, though it might be impaired, by the preservation of our alliances with the petty States west of the Jumnah.

Sir George Barlow thought, that, with the exception of the defensive alliances subsisting between the British Government and the great Powers of India, it was for the interest and security of the Company to limit all relations with the surrounding States to those of general amity and friendship; and to trust the safety of it's territorial possessions to the supremacy of our power, a well-regulated system of defence, and a revival of those contests and commotions which formerly prevailed among the States of Hindoostan.

Under such circumstances, the Governor General conceived that the fifth and sixth articles of the treaty might preclude the accomplishment of this general system, as they imposed upon us an obligation to protect from Scindiah's encroachments all the

States and Chieftains to the north of the Chumbul, from Kottah to the Jumnah.

In order to remedy the inconvenience which the Governor General apprehended from this arrangement, he transmitted, to be annexed to the treaty, declaratory articles, to the following purport:—

1st. That Scindiah ceded to the Honourable Company all the territory north of the river Chumbul, which was ceded him by the 7th Article of the Treaty of Serjee Angengaum; that is to say, the whole of the districts of Dhoolpoor, Barree, and Rajah Kerrah; and the Company gave up all claim to any rule, tribute, or possessions, on the south bank of that river. The Talooks, however, of Bhadek and Sooseperarah, on the banks of the Jumnah, remained in possession of the Company.

2d. That the Company, from friendship to Scindiah, agreed to pay him the annual sum of four lacks of rupees. Also, that they assigned, within their territories in Hindoostan, a Jagheer, amounting to a revenue of two lacks of rupees per annum, to Baezah Bhye, the wife of Scindiah; and a Jagheer, amounting to one lack of rupees per annum, to Chumnah Bhye, the daughter of that Chief.

The intention of these articles was, as has been stated, to supersede the operation of the fifth, sixth, and seventh articles of the treaty:

and they were to be delivered to Moonshee Kavel Nyne with the ratified treaty of peace.

The Governor General was also desirous of ceding the districts of Tonk Rampoorah to Scindiah, in lieu of the four lacks of rupees per annum to which that Chief became personally entitled by the treaty: and he conceived this cession more desirable, as the territory in question was formerly possessed by Holkar; and it's cession to Scindiah would tend to confirm and perpetuate an opposition of interests between those Chieftains.

The remaining parts of the treaty were entirely approved by the Governor General; who stated in this despatch, that he was, after the maturest deliberation, satisfied of the policy and expediency of dissolving the alliance with the State of Jypore; but would defer, to a subsequent despatch, the communication of the line and mode in which this arrangement ought to be carried into execution.

Lord Lake immediately communicated the declaratory articles to Moonshee Kavel Nyne; and proposed the exchange of Tonk Rampoorah for the pecuniary stipend of four lacks per annum, which it was agreed by that treaty to pay Scindiah. To this proposition, however, Kavel Nyne said his master would not agree; and he added his conviction, that he would not accept the districts of Tonk Rampoorah, if given gratis, as such an act would form an insurmountable bar to any reconciliation between him and Holkar. Kavel Nyne earnestly recommended, that the declaratory articles should not be sent to Doulut Row Scindiah till a British Resident had reached the Court of that Chief, who could furnish the requisite explanations respecting them, and satisfy Scindiah's mind with regard to the meaning and intent of that policy by which they had been dictated. As there appeared much good sense in this opinion, Lord Lake informed the Governor General, that he had delayed their transmission; and took this opportunity of again urging to Sir George Barlow the necessity of some modification of the general principles which he had laid down for his guidance. Lord Lake, in this letter, dwelt upon the grounds which had led him to insist upon the Chumbul being the line of demarcation between the two States; and observed, that the territories of the Boondee Rajah, which were immediately to the northward of the Chumbul (opposite to Kottah), though small both in revenue and extent, were very important, as they commanded a principal pass into Hindoostan; and that the Company was, in his opinion, bound to defend and protect that Rajah for his uniform friendly conduct, and particularly for the great aid which he had the courage to give Colonel Monson during his retreat; by which conduct he had exposed himself to the vengeance of Jeswunt Row Holkar, who was known to cherish the most inveterate hostility against this petty Chief. From this fact, Lord Lake observed, that he had always imagined, that under any arrangement which might eventually be made with Jeswunt Row Holkar, it would be difficult, consistently with a due regard for the honour and reputation of the British Government, to give the Boondee Rajah over to the rage of that Chief; and he had therefore thought it would be desirable to release him altogether from Mahratta power and influence.

Lord Lake stated in this despatch, that he had viewed the assent given by Scindiah, to retire altogether from Hindoostan northward of the Chumbul, as an unequivocal and complete acknowledgment of our established power and superiority; and gave it as his opinion, that no secure or honourable peace could be concluded with Holkar, which did not contain a similar concession: for though (his Lordship remarked in this communication) it was possible that the British territories might experience an increased security from the remote contests of the principal Mahratta Chiefs, he was satisfied, that if

Scindiah and Holkar were allowed to renew their claims upon any of the States immediately west of the Jumnah, and to mix in their disputes, there would be a serious danger of reviving ambitious hopes, which were now completely extinguished, and of causing another contest for that supremacy, which was now so fully acknowledged.

These opinions had no effect whatever in changing, or even modifying, the resolutions of the Governor General; who, though he admitted the great attention which was due to the local experience of Lord Lake, deemed it his duty to adhere to those general principles by which he had determined to regulate his conduct in this proceeding; and the declaratory articles were forwarded to Doulut Row Scindiah, with a letter from Sir George Barlow to that Chief explanatory of their nature and object.

Lord Lake was, during the period of these discussions, in pursuit of Jeswunt Row Holkar, whose last campaign was only a flight before the British army; which, leaving our own Provinces, pursued him as far as the banks of the Beeah* (or Hyphases); where Holkar, reduced to the extreme of distress, sent agents to Lord

* One of the five rivers which run through the Country of the Punjaub.

Lake, to solicit peace. The following is an abstract of the conditions which were offered for his acceptance:—

That he should renounce all right to the districts of Tonk Rampoorah, Boondee, &c., and places north of the Chumbul.

The Company would agree not to interfere with any Rajahs, or other dependants of the Holkar family, south of the Chumbul; and to restore, eighteen months after the conclusion of the treaty, Chandore, Gaulnah, and other forts and districts south of the Taptie and Goudavery, belonging to the Holkar family, which we had conquered and occupied, provided the conduct of Jeswunt Row Holkar was such as to satisfy the English Government of his amicable intentions towards us and our Allies.

Holkar was to renounce all claims upon Koonah and Bundlecund; and all claims whatever upon the British Government and it's Allies.

He also engaged to entertain no Europeans in his service, without the consent of the British Government.

Surjee Row Gautka was never to be admitted into his councils or service.

Jeswunt Row Holkar was, on these conditions, to be allowed to return to Hindoostan; but a route was prescribed, by which he was to avoid injuring the territory of the British Government, and it's Allies.

These articles were, with a very few and unessential modifications, after a short negotiation between the Agent* of the Governor General and the Vakeels of Holkar, reduced into a treaty of peace, which was confirmed on the 7th of January by that Chief; to whom, in fact, the Commander-in-Chief dictated this peace, which was of course formed agreeably to the general tenor of the instructions of the Governor General.

Sir George Barlow considered this treaty as highly honourable and advantageous to the British Government; but, though he had before instructed the Commander-in-Chief to insist upon the cession of the Provinces of Tonk Rampoorah, he stated in his communication upon this subject, that a resolution had been taken, with a view to an arrangement with Scindiah, respecting these Provinces; but, as he found that impossible, and that no State or Chief would venture to take them without a guarantee, we were, he conceived, reduced to the necessity of either guaranteeing these districts, or keeping them ourselves; and, as neither of these measures were consistent with

* Lieutenant Colonel Malcolm.

those general principles of policy which he had resolved to pursue, he determined to annul the provisions of the second article of the treaty, and restore them to Holkar: and for that purpose he returned the treaty, with a declaratory article annexed, by which a recession of these valuable Provinces was made to Jeswunt Row Holkar; and the Boondee Rajah was also abandoned. Lord Lake endeavoured, but in vain, to alter the sentiments of the Governor General relative to this principle of concession to Scindiah and Holkar; and to prevail upon him not to withdraw our protection from those petty Chiefs, whom he thought entitled to it by their conduct and attachment. He was particularly desirous, for reasons before stated, to obtain protection for the Rajah of Boondee: but Sir George Barlow was inflexible in the course he had adopted; and considered any deviation from it would be not only inconsistent with that system of policy, which he judged it his duty to pursue, but could not fail of producing at an early period the most serious political embarrassment.

It has been before stated, that the Governor General had signified his intention of dissolving the alliance with the Rajah of Jypore. The moment Lord Lake received this intimation, he represented to Sir George Barlow, that though the Rajah's former conduct had been directly contrary to good faith, and though that Prince had acted, upon the occasion of Holkar's advancing into Hindoostan, in a manner which was at variance with his engagement, the importance of his co-operation in the approaching campaign had appeared so great, that he had been induced not only to promise that he would entirely pass over the former conduct of the Rajah, but had, by continued assurances of friendship and protection, endeavoured to excite him to a zealous fulfilment of his engagements. In the accomplishment of this object, Lord Lake observed, he had fully succeeded; and the consequence was, that a British army, under Major General Jones, was, by the Rajah of Jypore's aid, and the ample supplies which his Country furnished, enabled to maintain a position of the greatest consequence to the success of the general operations of the war: and he had no doubt, from the communications which he had received from General Jones, that had Holkar attempted to retreat, as was expected, in the direction of the position which that Officer's army occupied, the co-operation of the Rajah's troops, who had joined his camp, would have been efficient. The sincerity and good faith with which the State of Jypore had acted at this crisis, was, Lord Lake stated, most strongly corroborated by the letters received from General Jones, which had led to his addressing the Rajah in a style, which he never would have used, had he not conceived that the circumstances he had mentioned would have changed those intentions which Government previously entertained of dissolving the alliance.

Lord Lake stated his opinion, that although there might be sufficient grounds for opening a negotiation for new-modelling the alliance with the Jypore State, or even for effecting a dissolution of all engagements between the two States, he doubted how far the British Government had a right, after what had passed, to dissolve it in a peremptory manner: because, as such a proceeding would expose the Rajah of Jypore to an instant attack from both Scindiah and Holkar, it would, unless it rested upon clear and undisputed grounds, make an impression among the States of India highly unfavourable to the reputation of the British Government. Lord Lake, in this communication, referred the Governor General to the conferences* between his

* Holkar's Vakeels demanded, with no slight degree of pertinacity, the cession of the Jypore and Boondee tributes; and one of them, speaking of the former, stated, that he no doubt would continue to enjoy the friendship of the English, as he had disgraced himself, to please that Nation, by giving up the unfortunate Vizier Ally (who had sought his protection) to their

Agent* and the Vakeels of Holkar, regarding the tribute which their master claimed from the Rajahs of Boondee and Jypore; and stated his expectation, that Sir George Barlow would agree with him, (after he had seen the report of these conferences,) that neither of these points could have been conceded to that Chief in the negotiation, without injury to the character of the British Government. His Lordship concluded this despatch by expressing his earnest hope, that, if the Governor General was ultimately resolved upon the dissolution of the alliance with the Jypore State, he would defer the execution of that measure till Holkar had passed the territories of the Rajah, and reached his own dominions in Malwah; to which he was, by the treaty, pledged instantly to return.

Lord Lake had before communicated his sentiments respecting the policy of this measure; but, as his opinions differed from those of Sir George Barlow, he confined himself upon this occasion to the question of faith, which, he conceived, it involved. His arguments, how-

vengeance. The Vakeel was very severely rebuked by the Agent of the Governor General for this insolent reflection on the conduct of an Ally of the British Government, who had, upon the occasion to which he alluded, delivered up a murderer, whom it would have been infamy to shelter.

* Lieutenant Colonel Malcolm.

ever, made no impression upon the mind of the Governor General, who continued to think, after the receipt of this communication, as he had done before, that we had, from the former conduct of the Rajah of Jypore, obtained a right to dissolve the alliance, which was not at all invalidated by his subsequent adoption of measures, which were more forcibly recommended to him by considerations of his own safety and convenience, than by any returning sense of good faith: and considering the question of faith in this view, he could not, he observed, hesitate in dissolving an alliance, which was likely to include much future inconvenience and embarrassment.

The English Government had given, the Governor General thought, a proof of it's liberality towards the Jypore State, in not dissolving it's alliance pending the negotiation with Scindiah, when it might have derived advantage from the cession of the tribute of Jypore to that Chief; and with respect to the period of adopting this act, he conceived the Company at liberty to choose that which was most convenient; and he had resolved upon it's instant dissolution, from an apprehension that Holkar, upon his return, might, as he passed the territories of Jypore, commit some excesses, which we would be obliged to notice if the alliance was not previously dissolved.

Sir George Barlow, in conformity with this resolution, directed the Resident at Jypore to announce the dissolution of the defensive alliance; informing the Rajah at the same time, that the English Government would be most happy to maintain with him general relations of friendship and amity. The Resident was at the same time desired to deliver to the Rajah a letter from the Governor General, explanatory of the grounds upon which this measure had been adopted. The justice of these grounds, however, was warmly disputed by the Court of Jypore, which, under a lively sense of that imminent danger to which it became exposed from this measure, almost forgot, for a moment, that temper and respect which it owed to the character of the English Nation. In a conference which one of the principal Agents of the Rajah of Jypore had with Lord Lake at Dehli, he had the boldness to observe, after stating all which his Prince had desired him to say upon the occasion, that this was the first time, since the English Government was established in India, "that it had been known to "make it's faith subservient to it's conve- "nience."

Sir George Barlow was equally anxious to dissolve the defensive alliances, which we had contracted with the lesser States of Bhurtpore and Macherry, as he was that with Jypore. But as those Rajahs had given no pretext for adopting this measure without their assent, he directed a negotiation to be opened with them for the purpose of effecting this object; and he authorized Lord Lake to make them a considerable cession of territory, as a means of prevailing upon them to give up that right, which they had acquired by treaty, to the protection of the British Government.

Lord Lake, however, was induced, by a variety of urgent considerations, to defer any mention of such an intention on the part of Government to these Rajahs; and he stated in the most forcible manner his fears, that the very rumour of such a measure being in the contemplation of the English Government, would again involve Countries, which had been settled at such an expense of blood and treasure, in a state of anarchy and confusion. Though the Governor General continued to declare, that he was quite resolved upon the adoption of this measure, he did not desire it should be precipitated. He was induced, by subsequent communications which he received, to suspend it's execution; and fortunately, as it would appear, for the public interests, this question has never since been agitated; and the Rajahs of Macherry and Bhurtpore, with other Chiefs settled in their vicinity, continue, in the faithful fulfilment of their engagements, to form an essential part of that strength which we derive from the maintenance of the territories to the west of the Jumnah.

It will be useful, before this chapter is closed, to make some observations upon that neutral and selfish policy, which, after all the evils that had before resulted from it's pursuit, appears to have been again prescribed by the Authorities in England, to the observation of the Supreme Government in India.

This system had been tried upon a large scale, during the Government of Lord Teignmouth. It was then applied to almost all the principal States of India. A course of events had rendered an exact repetition of this experiment impossible; but it was desired to do it in as great a degree as the actual situation of affairs would admit; and Sir George Barlow endeavoured to carry the wishes of his superiors into execution with a zeal and ability, which was well calculated to have attained success, if that had been practicable.

The events, which I have related, show the

result with which his efforts were attended. And it is only necessary to add, that the Siekh Chiefs to the north-west of the Jumnah and the southward of the Sutledge, who had received and merited our protection by their services during the war, but from whom it was afterwards, in pursuance of this policy, withdrawn, have, under the wise, moderate, and firm Government of Lord Minto, been saved from that destruction to which they were exposed by the ambition of the Rajah of Lahore; and now form, with other Chiefs in dependence on the British Government, a strong frontier to it's territories in Hindoostan. It would also appear, from the manner in which Lord Minto has lately employed the British arms to protect the Rajah of Berar from the attack of that celebrated freebooter Meer Khan,* that he is satisfied that the security of our possessions is more likely to be maintained by using the great and commanding power which we have acquired, to preserve the general peace and tranquillity of India; than by a policy, which declaredly looks to the

* This Chief is the principal Mahomedan leader with Jeswunt Row Holkar: but he appears, on this occasion, to have acted independently, and in combination with some tribes of pundaries, or freebooters, of which there are several in Malwah.

disputes and wars of it's neighbours, as one of the chief sources of it's security; and which, if it does not directly excite such wars, shapes it's political relations with inferior States in a manner calculated to create and continue them.

The professed object of this system is to avoid, by contracting our political relations, that continual embarrassment to which, it is argued, we must otherwise be subject; and all measures pursued are to be conformable to certain general principles, which, like a broad shield, are to save us from every injury, and simplify the whole scheme of our Government in India.

If such a result was really attainable, the task of rule would become easy, and the whole machine of Government might be kept in order by a very moderate share of attention and understanding; but, unfortunately, all experience is against such a conclusion, which is indeed contrary to the nature of man. We must, if we endeavour to fly from those political embarrassments and complex relations, which have been in all ages the conditions of extended power and dominion, always meet with much greater evils than those from which we try to escape. With regard to all general principles of rule, we should recollect, that their value is not in their abstract excellence, but in their seasonable and just application; for it is the great and sole art of Government to adapt principles to the continual changes of human affairs, not to force human affairs into a shape that suits principles. This observation applies with peculiar force to our Empire in India; which, from it's foundation, the nature of it's Government, and the various tribes and nations which it includes, demands more wisdom and more modification of system in it's Government, than perhaps any that ever was established in the universe.

This Empire, though raised by the operation of many and various causes, has been chiefly established, and must be constantly maintained, by the sword. But though we must continue to govern as conquerors, it is our duty to make our rule a benefit to mankind; and to carry among those whom we have subdued, the blessings of peace, knowledge, and improvement in all the arts of civilized life. And at that stage which our power in India has attained, we will probably find the accomplishment of such an object easier, and more conducive to our security, than all the wars and contests in which a selfish and neutral policy can ever involve our neighbours.

The system of trusting, in a great degree,

for our security, to the wars and contentions of the other States in India, has received great strength from a general but erroneous impression respecting the unalterable and hereditary habits of the military tribes of India; who, it is contended, can never be converted to the usages of civil life. The temporary disturbances, which have been created by the discontented of this class, when any great political changes have deprived them of the means of immediate subsistence, have been given as instances of the truth of this assertion; but it has been forgotten, that the Countries of Bengal, Behar, and the Carnatic, abounded a few years ago with hordes of armed men, whose descendants now find a livelihood in cultivating some peaceable occupation; and that the Kingdoms of Mysore, Oude, and the Deckan, are now gradually undergoing the same change. The period of change is certainly one of some danger; but that danger only requires to be watched with vigilance and care, and may be easily averted by measures of large and liberal policy.

To conclude. There would hardly appear to be a greater and more noble object for the exercise of human wisdom, or one more worthy of all the attention of a great State, than that of establishing and maintaining, through the action of it's influence and power, union and tranquillity over a considerable portion of the globe; and of bringing to nations, whom it found involved in continual discord and war, the blessings of harmony and peace. This we may never be able completely to effect; but there is no danger in a course of prudent policy, which keeps so great an object in view: and a state of perfect security against external attack would be the reward of it's accomplishment. When the unparalleled successes, which attended Lord Wellesley's Administration of India, placed the British power upon so commanding an eminence, his ardent mind naturally contemplated the attainment of this great end.

" In the termination of hostilities," that nobleman observed, " my solicitude has been
" directed to the important purpose of effecting
" a general pacification of India on principles
" of reciprocal justice and moderation. The
" power, reputation and dignity, of the British
" Empire in India, will derive additional secu-
" rity and lustre from the establishment of
" peace and good order among the native
" States. In the decline of intrinsic strength,
" inferior States may perhaps have gained a
" temporary safety by fomenting the discord of
" contiguous Powers. In any extremity, such
" a policy is unwarrantable and disgraceful;
" nor can permanent repose be secured upon

"such precarious foundations in the actual condition of this Empire. I am happy to declare, that the concord of the established native States, the independence of their separate authorities, the internal peace of their respective dominions, and the tranquillity and happiness of their respective subjects, will tend to confirm and to fortify the power and resources of the British Government, and must constitute the most desirable objects of the British policy in India."*

* Vide Reply to the Address of the British Inhabitants of Calcutta, on the 29th of Feb. 1804.

CHAPTER VI.

GENERAL REFLECTIONS

ON

THE POLITICAL, CIVIL, AND MILITARY,

GOVERNMENT OF BRITISH INDIA.

CONTENTS.

Regulations introduced in 1796.—Discipline of the Native Army.—Condition and Consequence of the Native Officer.—Measures suggested for the Improvement of the Condition of this Class; and also of the Native Soldier.—Conclusion.

THE reflections, which it is meant to offer upon the political, civil, and military, Government of British India, are submitted with a deference, which proceeds equally from a want of complete knowledge of some parts of the subject, and a sense of it's general magnitude and importance. The considerations, indeed, to which this Chapter is exclusively devoted, are in themselves of so large and complicated a nature, that no person can expect to treat them without falling into frequent error: but the apprehension of this danger is not sufficient to deter me from contributing as much as I can to the elucidation of questions of such vast national importance; and the character of the object which I have in view, will, I trust, plead for any failure in it's accomplishment.

The present constitution of those Authorities in England, which direct and control the political Government of British India, has been already described. It has been stated, that the political authority of the Court of Directors should, by the theory of Mr. Pitt's Bill of 1784, be extinct; but, that the fact is otherwise;

which has been accounted for on the grounds of that Court maintaining, by it's influence in the Country and in the House of Commons, a check upon his Majesty's Ministers, which generally compels them to seek the acquiescence, if they are not guided by the opinions, of the leading Directors; and the operation of this cause must often create delays, if it does not produce contest and collision.

The Court of Directors are the only public body in England, who can be supposed to have any detailed intelligence of the politics of India; and as they possess copies of the records of that Empire, with the Governors of which they maintain, under the direction of the Board of Control, all political correspondence, their knowledge of it is presumed to be drawn from the most authentic sources: and it is further concluded, that this Corporation is formed of men, who, generally speaking, have spent most of their lives in India, or else have devoted themselves to a study of the British interests in that quarter.

From such circumstances, the complete exclusion of the Court of Directors from a share in the political Administration of British India, while that body continues to govern and regulate the commercial branch of that Empire, is a measure which would appear almost impracticable; as hardly any political act of consequence can be adopted, without affecting, in some degree, either the finances or trade of our possessions in India, and of course giving them a pretext, if not a right, of interference.

What has been stated on this head is sufficient to show, that, in considering the Authorities in England by which the political Administration of our Empire in India is directed and controlled, the Court of Directors must be deemed (in spite of the intent or expression of the act of the Legislature) to be one of the principal: because their influence, and the duties they have to perform, give them a power of interference, which enables them, if they are so inclined, to oppose with effect any political acts, which the Board of Control may desire to carry into execution.

The constitution of the Board of Control is such, that it's President and principal Members must be his Majesty's Ministers. The junior members have been occasionally selected from persons who have been in India; but no instance has occurred of any such members being actively employed at this Board; the duties of which, indeed, appear to be chiefly performed by it's President, who becomes conversant with the political interests of India from a perusal of the records of the Company, and from that constant communication with persons of some experience in that quarter, which the duties of his station oblige him to maintain.

The station of President of the Board of Control, is one which cannot be held by any Minister who has not both talents and reputation: and, supposing this public Officer to be even tolerably able, with a mind liberal and free from prejudice, he becomes an instrument every way calculated to perform the duties of his office in a manner suited to the constitution of the Country, and to the act of the Legislature for the better Administration of India. But it is evident, from what has been stated, that he must, under the operation of that act, obtain the consent and approbation of the Court of Directors to those political measures which he sanctions or suggests; or enter into a contest with that body, which would tend to embarrass the Authorities at home, weaken the Administration abroad, and create delays and confusion in the whole system of the Indian Government.

The opposite causes of action, which influence those two Authorities, must often make it difficult, if not impossible, to reconcile them to the same course of action. His Majesty's Ministers will naturally view every political measure adopted in India, as it appears likely to promote the general interests of the Nation, more than as it immediately affects the separate interests of the Company: to which the attention of the Directors will, on the other hand, be almost exclusively turned: and it must be difficult to conciliate their approbation to any political measure, which has the least injurious operation of even a temporary nature upon their commerce or finances.

The Court of Directors must, from it's constitution, always be composed of liberal and respectable persons; but that body can seldom have any members, who have a large and detailed knowledge of the political interests of the Company. The motives which lead men to seek a place in the Direction, and the duties which they have to perform as Directors, are chiefly suited to those, whose lives have passed in the commercial service of the Company, or in commerce at home. The general exceptions to this rule, are Officers, or civil servants, who have acquired some fortune and reputation in the service of the Company, and who desire to obtain a place in the Direction, on account of it's patronage; and, from a feeling as natural as it is laudable, are ready to enter into active life again, with the object of providing for their families.

That a body so constituted and composed, and which always acts in a great degree under the check and control of it's constituents, the proprietors of India stock, should often take a very limited and partial view of large political questions, cannot be a matter of surprise. The fact is, that very few of the Directors have had the slightest opportunity of studying the political affairs of the Company before they entered the Direction. The complete occupation of every civil as well as every military servant* of the

* Those few servants of the Company, who have been employed in any distinguished manner in the conduct of political affairs, are, from nearly the same causes, probably ignorant of the commercial interests of the Company. This unfits them, in a certain degree, for the Direction; and their minds are, from acquired habits, unsuited to the bustle and occupations of such a life. When they return to England, they have no public employment before them, and they retire to private life. Some years afterwards, perhaps, when embarrassing questions occur relative to India, a President of the Board of Control, or a Chairman of the Court of Directors, seeks them out, as having a high and a just reputation for their political knowledge of India; but changes have occurred, since the persons applied to were in employ; their minds have not gradually gone along with those changes; they cannot alter opinions, of which they are tenacious, in a moment; and their respectable names are often thus obtained to the side of error. To give the State, in some shape or another, the advantage at home of those talents, and that experience, which has benefited it's interests abroad, would appear a great object; but it is one, which, under the present form of the Indian Government in England, would seem difficult, if not impracticable, to attain.

Company in his particular line of service, combined with the secrecy observed in all political transactions in India, is such, that a most able and respectable public Officer may pass the greater part of his life in the commercial or military line in that Country, and return to England with as little, or less, knowledge of the real state of it's political affairs, than an Under-Secretary at the India House.

From what has been stated regarding the character of the Board of Control and the Court of Directors, and from all experience since the first introduction of this form of Government, it appears unlikely that these public bodies should ever cordially agree regarding the political Administration of India; and as their frequent disagreement must produce the worst of consequences, some means will probably be devised, of making the authority, which is actually to direct and control the political affairs of India, more efficient to it's large functions; and of avoiding a collision at the very source of authority, which must, while it continues, spread weakness and distraction among all who are subject to it; and the effect of which will be always more dangerous, from the character of party-spirit in England, and the distance and nature of the Indian Government.

It is a principle of the British Constitution

to leave the executive Administration of the Country free and unembarrassed in the employment of it's principal Officers, and the execution of those measures which it may deem wise, and advantageous to the State; for which, however, the Administration of the day become strictly responsible to the public. It's applause, or condemnation, determines their title to fame and the period of their power: and this forms, perhaps, as great a check as it is possible to have upon human action. This check has been found sufficient to the management of the affairs of the Empire of Great Britain, and would appear equal to the conduct of the political Government of the possessions of that Power in India. It may be questioned, therefore, how far it is either wise, or consistent with the constitutional principle here stated, to fetter and embarrass the Administration in the execution of every measure which they adopt respecting that Country. It will be said, that, under the act of Parliament, the Board of Control have the power, and that they must ultimately prevail in any contests which they have with the Court of Directors of a political nature: but the very privilege of an official expression of contrary opinion, which the form of the act warrants, has the effect of throwing these questions into discussion; and that effect produces delays, destroys confidence in the local Government of India, and renders the whole system of our rule in that quarter, weak, wavering, and distracted.

The Court of Directors cannot claim, under the act, political power in the Administration of British India, as a matter of right; but they should be debarred from seeking it through the means of their influence or patronage: and that can never be done, unless by some modification of the present system, which, by a strange contradiction, often compels, as a matter of form, a committee of this body to an official expression of sentiments upon a political subject, which have afterwards been declared to be at complete variance with the judgment of those by whom they were officially stated.

This apparently prominent defect in the political Administration of British India, has been shortly noticed: but it is not meant to go further into a subject, which involves so many intricate and important questions, and with which I am only acquainted through an observation of it's effects in India. With regard to the exact nature and shape of that Government in England, which may be found best calculated to promote the prosperity of our Eastern possessions, I cannot presume to speak. It appears of little consequence what men, or body of men, are the instruments through which Great Britain rules India, provided the medium used for that purpose is shaped and constituted for the object; and that care is taken, that the public should neither suffer from incompetency, nor a continual clashing of opposite and unequal interests.

Though the general pursuits and habits of the Court of Directors, and the strange anomaly of their constitution, may be urged, and with reason, against their competency, as a body, to the exercise, in any shape or mode whatever, of political power; it would appear, that, as long as it is judged wise to continue the monopoly of the Company, the patronage of the Indian Empire could not be in safer or more honourable hands,* than those of that respectable Corporation; who, though they may not be equal to exercise the functions of Sovereignty † over

* The description of persons selected as Writers and Cadets, is the best proof of the just manner in which this patronage is exercised; and the late public inquiries into it's abuses have had a result very honourable to the Directors.

† The Company's Government in India has a serious disadvantage, from not, in itself, inspiring that awe and respect, which make such impression upon mankind. It is, of course, no more than a body through which the Government of England rules India: but all it's liberality (and no Government was ever more liberal) cannot make amends to it's servants for those wounds, which their pride suffers, by even a supposed inferiority

an extended Empire, must, from the greatness of their concerns, the liberality upon which those are conducted, and the general characters of the individuals elected to the Direction, be always deemed the first mercantile body in the world.

There can be no doubt, but that Mr. Pitt's Bill for the better Administration of India, (which, from the regard it paid to established form, weakened, as has been before stated, it's own principle, and left the power in England, which was to direct and control the political Administration of India, shackled and embarrassed,) gave ample powers to the Governor General of India, who was by it clothed with all the authority which the execution of his large duties could require, subject to a direct personal responsibility for the exercise of the great trust committed to his charge.

It has been ascertained, from the whole experience of this system, that the internal security of our possessions in India, as well as their

in rank and consideration to persons of the same class in life, who more immediately serve the King; and in being (from the character of the Indian Government) almost virtually debarred from all hope of those honours and rewards, which they see showered upon others, whose rank in life, or whose zeal and success in the service of their common Sovereign and Country, they cannot think greater than their own.

defence against external attack, has been in the greatest degree promoted by a measure, which, by giving one head to our wide territories in that quarter, has assimilated them in the same system of rule and management, subdued all contentions of subordinate authorities, and given a combination to the distant resources of our Indian Empire, which has made them easily applicable to every object of general interest.

There, perhaps, never was any public measure, which remedied more real evils, than the change of system with respect to the powers lodged in the Governor General of India; and it's beneficial effects have been universally acknowledged. It would be a further improvement upon this system, if it was possible to make an arrangement, by which this high public Officer could be relieved from that load of business with which he is now oppressed, in consequence of having charge of the details of one of the separate Governments of British India; which not only occupies his time with matter of inferior consideration, but makes it more difficult for him, than it otherwise would be, to visit* the different parts of the Empire under his charge. It might, however, be difficult to make such a

* A point of essential importance to their good government and general improvement.

change in this part of the system, without affecting the influence or patronage of the Governor General: and the efficiency and consideration of his high station can never be touched in the slightest manner, without serious danger to the public interests: for the subject, who is raised to an office where he has sovereign functions to perform, requires, while he enjoys it, regal powers. He represents, in his person, the Government of his Country; and he receives from other States that rank and character which are naturally associated, in the estimation of the world, with the possession of extensive power, and ascendency in the scale of political influence: that respect, which belongs to the real supremacy of the British dominions in India, is necessarily transferred to the person exercising it's authority; and to weaken his influence, or degrade his dignity, is to diminish the consequence, and impair the power, of the Government.

The same political causes, which dictated these great powers being vested in the Governor General, do not apply, with equal force, to the Governors of the inferior Settlements of Madras and Bombay; who have in fact, under the present constitution of the Indian Government, few, if any, political duties of importance to perform; all points of a political nature being subject to the immediate direction and control of the Supreme Government. These powers are useful, however, as they add to the consideration of these high public Officers, and free them, in a certain degree, from the embarrassment and opposition to which they might otherwise frequently be subject.

The limits of the territories of the local Governments of India have undergone great changes since the act of 1784 was passed. These may make some modifications in the shape of the system advisable; and if such are made upon principles, which simplify the forms of Government, and which, without withdrawing necessary checks, add to the strength and efficiency of the local authorities, they will prove beneficial.

The former parts of this work have sufficiently elucidated the nature of those political principles upon which our territories in India have been hitherto governed. I shall now venture to give some opinions respecting those leading principles which should form the object of our rule of this Empire in it's present extended state.

However opinions may differ with regard to the advantages which Great Britain has derived, or may derive, from it's possessions in India, there can be no doubt in the breast of any man, that, if we mean to retain our Empire in that quarter, it is equally our duty and our interest to govern it in a manner which will promote the prosperity of the Country and the happiness of it's inhabitants. To effect this, no laws, no established principles of policy, or regulations for internal rule, will ever be sufficient, unless those authorities, by which these edicts, precepts and rules, are to be carried into execution, are in every respect competent and efficient to their great duties. This fact makes the selection of persons to fill the Governments of India, and particularly the great station of Governor General, an object, beyond all others, of importance in the future Government of British India.

The power exercised by the Governor General has none of that impression in it's favour, which often supports, even at a period of decline, hereditary Monarchies and national Governments. It can only obtain respect by the intrinsic qualities of the person by whom this high station is filled. Great talents and virtues, and the able and active exercise of them, will always obtain the suffrage of both the European and native subjects of our Indian Empire, and, in all human probability, preserve that in peace; or, at all events, suppress danger: but moderate abilities, however combined with information, will be found unequal to the great task in any times; and if the Supreme Government of India ever passes into weak or unequal hands, the high station will fall into disrepute, and all the dangers that flow from the contempt of a governing authority will be generated.

It appears quite impossible ever to introduce any system of Government into our possessions in India, which will render them secure for a day, except under the management of an able and firm Ruler;* and, if this is admitted, there is no part of the duty of Government in England so important, as the selection of a person to fill that high office. If a succession of men of great talents and virtues cannot be found, or if the operation of any party-principles prevents their being chosen, we must reconcile ourselves to the most serious hazard of the early decline, if not the loss, of the great Empire which we have founded in India.

These observations apply to other stations besides that of Governor General (though with a lesser degree of force); but particu-

* The only safe view that Great Britain can take of it's Empire in India, is to consider it (as it really is) always in a state of danger, and to nominate persons to rule it, calculated, from their superior energy of character, to meet every emergency that can arise.

larly to the high offices of Governor of Fort St. George and Bombay.

There has been much speculative opinion on the subject of such selections. Some have conceived that military men were best qualified for these stations: others, that they should be exclusively filled by those who had risen in civil life. It has been argued, that noblemen (who carried with them the impression of high rank and birth) should alone be appointed to them: while many believed they would be best filled by servants of the Company, who had local knowledge, and a large and detailed acquaintance with their affairs.

Any principle which excludes distinguished talent and eminent virtue, in whatever rank or condition of life these qualities are found, from such fair and legitimate objects of honourable ambition, must have an operation unfavourable to that competition which is necessary to form men for such elevated stations as the Governments of British India. Whether these be filled by a military or a civil character, provided such be qualified for the great task, appears to be a matter of indifference. Perhaps there is an advantage, (as was experienced in the case of Lord Cornwallis,) when that rare mixture of talent for civil rule, and military command, can be found in one person. That the rank and birth of the person employed, as it gives in some degree that impression which these high stations require, is of great consequence, cannot be denied: but that consequence can never be sufficient to supersede the claims of superior talent, or to remedy the defects of inefficiency: and as to the servants of the Company, their local experience, and knowledge of details, is, unless attended with higher qualifications, but a poor recommendation to stations, which do not so much require that the person holding them should have that description of information which is to be obtained from many subordinate Officers of the State, as that they should possess that large knowledge of human nature, active energy of character, and that commanding talent for rule, which has in all ages distinguished those who have exercised power in a manner calculated to benefit their Country and mankind.

Whatever person is nominated to either the high station of Governor General, or to the Governments of Madras or Bombay, should receive a full and liberal confidence from the authority by which he is appointed: nor should he be continued in station one moment after that is withdrawn. The dangers which assail our Empire in India from internal weakness, are much greater than we can ever apprehend from external attack; and these will always increase in an alarming degree, when the Administration abroad has not the decided support of the Government at home. That period is past at which it might have been safe to have fettered the local Governments of India with jealous restraints; and to lessen their power, by a petty and vexatious interference with their exercise of it. Our Empire in that quarter is now too large, and too complicated, to be exposed to the operation of a system of mistrust. The reliance placed on those to whom it is confided, must be of that complete nature, which will enable them to fulfil so great a duty.

On the political principles which should regulate our future intercourse with the native Powers in India, I have before stated an opinion, to which I can only add, that such intercourse is likely to be marked by events and contingencies, which will disappoint, as has been the case heretofore, all hopes that we can ever form of the local Government in India being able to follow any exact rules, which are laid down for it's guidance. The neutral system of noninterference, and of trusting in a great degree for our security to the contests of our neighbours, has been proved, by experience, to be equally unwise and impracticable. We shall therefore best maintain the peace and prosperity of our own territories, by using our established influence and power towards the great object of preserving, as far as we have the means, the general tranquillity of India. It will not, perhaps, be easy to effect the complete accomplishment of this object; nor are we called upon to interfere in every case of quarrel between States with whom we have no engagements; but, if we shape our general policy towards this end, we shall, from the commanding state of our power, gradually promote peace, without much danger of involving ourselves; and we shall receive our share of those benefits which this system will bring to others.

It is, however, certain, that with whatever care we cultivate our external relations, and however much we endeavour to avoid future wars, we cannot expect to escape altogether an evil, which is among those conditions on which human dominion is enjoyed. But, as we can only hope for a comparative exemption from this evil by the complete efficiency of our military force, that will always, in the reduced state of the present Powers of India, enable us to defeat it; and we can, on it's occurrence, if circumstances connected with the local situation of the Countries which we conquer, or any other consideration, forbid us annexing conquests to our own territories, confer them upon some of our Allies on such terms as we deem proper: and every such act of liberal policy will give life and strength to the exercise of that large influence and power, through which we may hope to establish the permanent tranquillity of India.

It is not meant to notice any of those distant political relations, which it appears wise to improve, with a view to our permanent security against the attack of an European Power. This is a subject not immediately connected with the political Government of India: and, if that is administered upon wise and enlarged principles, our strength will be too much consolidated, to admit of our having any alarm at invasion.

The question of our political Administration of India, is not of more importance, than the civil Government of our possessions in that quarter: for there can be no doubt, that the real and intrinsic strength of a State depends chiefly on the loyalty and attachment of it's subjects; and there is no means of creating or securing the continuance of that attachment, but by the action of a just and steady rule, which rests upon established principles, and gives security to the lives and properties of those who are under it, and grants to them the enjoyment of as much personal liberty as is consistent with their habits and the character of the Government established over them.

The greatest effort which has been made towards the improvement of the civil Government of British India, is the permanent settlement of the revenues, and the introduction of that judicial system* which is now general throughout all our territories. Though the success of these measures has not, perhaps, been so complete as enthusiasts might have expected, it has been sufficient to prevent disappointment to those who take a rational and comparative view of that good which can be produced by any human institution.

It is an acknowledged truth, that there is no branch of Government which requires such attention to fixed principles, and will less admit of alteration, than a code of laws, or civil regulations. These it will always require labour to understand; and, if they were constantly changing, a knowledge of them would never be

* I have not entered into any discussion of those principles upon which his Majesty's Courts in India are established, as it is a subject to which I do not conceive myself competent.

attained. It is also to be observed, that they acquire respect with age: and our veneration, at last, almost extends to their defects, which we are often more willing to tolerate, than to incur the hazard of alteration. It must, from these causes, be the most arduous task which human wisdom can attempt, to form laws; and very hazardous to change them, when formed: and this difficulty must be greatly increased, when the Empire, for which we legislate, is one of so various and extraordinary a nature, as that we have founded in the East.

Whoever, therefore, takes a large view of this subject, will find greater reason for surprise at the success, than regret at the failure, of the system which we have adopted. It is true, that it has in it's operation given a shock to the authority of military Officers, and, to a certain degree, weakened the impression of a character, which it is politic to hold high among the natives of India. It has been hastily introduced into Countries neither calculated to estimate it's benefits, nor understand it's object. It has effected a revolution in the state of society, by raising the lower orders into an independence of their superiors, in a manner inconsistent with the established usages of the Country; and it's delays have been so intolerable in many instances, as to leave to the inhabitants little but the name of justice. But it must, on the other hand, be remembered, that this system, at it's introduction, superseded another, under which the happiness of the community was guarded by few general regulations and laws; and consequently exposed to all the changes and hazards incident to a rule, which required, that great, and almost uncontrolled, power should be vested in an individual during the period of his temporary authority; that the evils, which have arisen from it's precipitate introduction into Countries unprepared for it's reception, can but be of short duration; that the revolution, which it has effected in society, though of a nature calculated to excite, during the operation of change, great discontent, if not disturbance, has the ulterior effect of giving that society a shape more congenial to our Government, and is, perhaps, necessary to it's security: and, with regard to the great delays which have been found to attend the administration of this system, it is an evil which certainly requires a remedy; but, if it is capable of being remedied, it never can be adduced as a proof against the excellence of the system itself.

There can, I imagine, be no doubt in the mind of any man, who reflects seriously on the subject, but that the permanent settlement of the revenues, and the introduction of the judicial regulations, have already been attended with great benefit, and that the character of this system is progressive improvement. Many objections may be urged against it; and it has, no doubt, many defects; but it appears better than any other yet tried. It's principles are such as will admit of gradual amelioration. We should apply ourselves, therefore, with ardour, to that purpose; and if we can either alter, abridge or simplify, the regulations and forms of our Courts in a manner that will accelerate the trial of causes, and defeat, to a certain degree, that artful chicanery and litigious disposition, which characterize a great proportion of our subjects in India, we shall attain a great end. Every advance towards so desirable an object, will be an additional security for the permanence of our Empire in India; which rests chiefly upon the allegiance and attachment of our native subjects; and which nothing can secure but their feeling a constantly recurring sense of benefit from our rule.

If we examine the history of the English Government in India, we shall discover, that it has been founded in a spirit of attention and respect to the usages and religion of the different tribes in India; nor can it ever be maintained upon any other principles. It has been recently urged, and by some whose characters entitle their opinions to great regard, that the introduction of the Christian religion, through the means of it's influence and power, was not only a sacred duty, but an object of policy to the British Nation. This is a delicate question to discuss; but it is one I cannot evade. With respect to that part of it, which relates to the duty of a Christian to convert others to his faith, I am too ignorant to presume to offer an opinion. The few remarks I shall make upon this subject, will be confined, therefore, to a consideration of the manner in which such a proceeding would affect our political interests.

The experience we have of those converts to Christianity, which have been made since the first intercourse between Europe and India, does not afford much encouragement to make us persevere in this design. These converts are but little acquainted with the purity of the faith which they profess; and so far from being that example in their lives, which, if they were sincere and enlightened followers of our religion, they ought to be; they would appear to a common observer (who was uninformed of their conversion) to be a set of men, who had agreed to separate themselves from the other natives of India, in order that they might be freed from a number of restraints, with regard to diet and morality, by which the different tribes of both

Hindoos and Mahomedans are bound. There are, no doubt, exceptions to this observation; but it is applicable to the great mass of Christians in India, who are, in consequence, the very dregs of the community; not only from their station in life, but their morals and conduct. Under such circumstances, it must occur, that knowledge should precede Christianity; and if we were at liberty, from our political obligations to those whom we govern, to give the authority of Government in support of the attempts made to convert our Indian subjects, and at the same time perfectly secure that those attempts would not endanger our safety, we are not yet arrived at the point where our labours ought to commence. But there would appear objections to our adopting this measure, connected with the very constitution of our Empire in that quarter, which it is at least necessary to examine.

The Portuguese, who were the first European settlers in India, hastened, if they did not cause, their downfal by that bigoted spirit with which they endeavoured to introduce their religion. They surrounded themselves in their towns and settlements with native Christians: but, by doing so, they drew a line of separation between those natives, who adhered to them, and all others; and thereby deprived themselves of that aid, which they might otherwise have received; and rendered themselves an object of general dread to all the natives of India out of the pale of their church; who opposed their advancement in power, not only with a view of preserving their independence, but their religion. The French, though neither so bigoted nor so superstitious as the Portuguese, adhered in some degree to their unwise policy in this respect; and the native inhabitants of their settlements, and the servants in whom the principal Officers of Government reposed trust, were almost all Christians: and it was remarked, that when their power was at the highest (in the days of Dupleix and Lally), they were so far from showing a scrupulous attention to the prejudices and religious usages of the Hindoos, that the most sacred of those were sometimes violated.* From the career of the English in India, a person would suppose, that, at every stage of their progress, they had looked for

* It must have been this abuse of power, connected with the conduct of the French adventurers in the service of native Princes, that gave an impression of the character of that Nation, which I have repeatedly heard expressed by one of the most intelligent natives that I have ever known, Meer Allum, the late Prime Minister at the Court of Hyderabad; who used to say, "That the French were bad masters, but good servants; intolerant and tyrannical in the exercise of power; but cheerful, mild, and obedient, when under authority."

success, from avoiding the great errors of their rivals. The Government, and all it's servants, have not only withheld their aid from the efforts made to convert the natives of India; but have, as far as depended upon their measures and conduct, discouraged it; upon a principle, no doubt, of inspiring confidence; in which they have succeeded in a degree which cannot be calculated; and the extent of which may never be discovered, till the charm is broken by which this great Empire is held. In proof of the systematic discouragement which the English Government has ever given to the conversion of it's native subjects, it will suffice to mention a few facts, which will fully illustrate the principle. It has always shown the most marked indulgence and attention to the civil habits, and religious prejudices and usages, of it's Indian subjects; and, in conformity with this fundamental principle, Government has not only contributed to the support of their different religious establishments, but has regulated itself, in the employment of the natives under it's rule, with attention to the different pretensions which they derived from the rank they held under those religious institutions which they venerate; and has abstained, in so cautious a manner, from giving any alarm to the natives of India, by encouraging or even countenancing any attempt to convert them, that there is hardly one instance of any native (among the many who have become Christians) being employed in a situation of trust or responsibility by any one of the public servants of the Company in India.

When we add to this, that the English Government have, in the introduction of that judicial system, by which it is fixed, that their different native subjects shall have the same laws, which were established by their former rulers, improved, ameliorated, and tempered by the mild spirit of English jurisprudence, but unaltered and untouched on every point connected with their religious usages; it may be assumed, that State has given every pledge, by which a Nation can be bound, not only to withhold every active interference of authority for the conversion of it's native subjects, but not to give the weight of it's influence, or the support of it's encouragement, towards that object. Should the dictates of a conscientious, but heated zeal, ever lead it to break this pledge; the alarm among it's subjects will be great; the consequences may be fatal to it's power; and a good Christian would regret to see an effort made to promote his religion, by means so unsuited to it's character and divine origin; and would deprecate the exercise of an influence and authority for that object, which had been obtained on a confidence, which had been studiously inspired, of it's never being so used.

Under such circumstances, it is to be hoped that the British Government will never be so deluded by well-meant but misguided representations, as to adopt measures, which are likely to fail in effecting the object of promoting the Christian religion; but will be certain to destroy our reputation, and probably our power, in India. Let every proper attention be paid to our church establishment in that Country: let the clergymen sent thither be men of exemplary conduct and character; and let their numbers be sufficient to secure to the European part of the community, the means of learning and practising the duties of their religion; but the clergymen in the employ of Government, whether as Ministers of religion, or head Professors of Colleges, should be prohibited from using their efforts to make converts; which task might be left, as it hitherto has been, to the labours of the humble missionary; whose habits and zeal give him more prospect of success, and whose unnoticed and unsupported efforts will prevent his exciting any alarm; and consequently not expose Government to those seditious tempests, which, if they pursued another course, would, in all human probability, be raised against them by an artful and bigoted priesthood; whose fear, at the progress of Christianity, is equally grounded on the love of spiritual and temporal power.

Colonization seems one of the most likely means by which knowledge of the Christian religion and civilization may be hereafter disseminated throughout India; but that appears to be so much dreaded, from the political consequences by which it is thought likely to be attended, that a long period must elapse before it's operation can be seen. It is not meant to discuss the policy of this question. The example of America, by which it is often tried, cannot, it is presumed, be a correct criterion for deciding it: but there is, no doubt, great force in many of those reasons, which have led the Legislature to adopt every measure which was calculated to discourage the settlement of Europeans in India. Notwithstanding these, the cities of Calcutta, Madras, and Bombay, and the fertile Provinces of Bengal and Bahar, contain a number of English mechanics, tradesmen, and planters, who may be almost considered as colonists; and who have, by their industry and skill, taught many of the inhabitants of India the improved arts of civil life.

The advance of the natives of India in every branch of useful knowledge, will be exactly proportionate to the means and examples which we afford them: and this consideration gives a great value to that class of industrious British subjects, who are willing to pass the greatest part, if not the whole, of their lives in India, subject to those strict restraints and limitations, which the peculiar constitution of the Government of that Country renders necessary.

The half-casts (as they are generally termed), or children of Europeans by native women, form a considerable class of British subjects in India, who certainly merit more of the attention of Government than they have hitherto received. They may be considered a distinct class; and one which is gradually rising into importance, from it's increasing numbers. They have not the robust frame of their fathers; but they are in general equal, if not superior, in strength to the natives of those parts of India where they are born. They are remarkable for their docility and intelligence; and only require the care of the State, to become valuable subjects. This race are at present considered as inferior to the European part of the community, and do not enjoy that consideration, to which their qualities are often entitled, from the natives. Yet, under these circumstances of depression and discouragement, they lose few opportunities of making themselves useful and respectable in the various walks of life to which their pursuit is directed; and all the seminaries, which have been founded for their education and improvement, have fully succeeded. This class have, in short, been found, from all the experiments yet made, to possess a disposition and talents suited to all the occupations of civil life; and there can be no doubt, that, under a proper system of encouragement, they might be employed in our army. They would form a distinct corps, on whose fidelity and attachment every reliance might be placed; and, if military feelings and habits were early inculcated, there can be no ground to conclude, that they would prove deficient either in courage or hardihood. As it is impossible to adopt any measures which will prevent the rapid increase of this part of the population of our Indian territories, it becomes our duty to try every means of rendering them useful. They are a distinct, but that is no cause why they should be a depressed, class in the community: and it appears both humane and politic to take every step, which will raise them in their own estimation, and that of others. We should cultivate their moral and religious principles; and, while we instituted and encouraged seminaries for their instruction upon an extended scale, we should provide the means for their future employment in the conditions of life best suited to their respective situations and qualifications.

If the justice of this proposition is admitted, the means of carrying it into execution will not be found difficult. These require no change in those salutary restraints, on which the constitutional principles of both the civil and military services in India are now grounded. The object is not to impair our present, but to lay the foundations of future, strength; and to render, by the care which we bestow upon them, a numerous and increasing class of our population useful and attached subjects.

It would appear necessary, if we contemplate any serious and great improvements in the condition of our possessions in India, that we should dismiss that principle, which requires that these should be ruled with an exclusive view to the immediate profit and advantage of England. A more liberal exercise of the great power, which we have acquired, while it advances the happiness of our Indian subjects, and promotes the prosperity of our dominions, will tend ultimately much more, than the pursuit of this limited system, to the permanent benefit and strength of Great Britain. In introducing civilization—by the promulgation of knowledge, the cultivation of the liberal arts, and by the construction of such public works as are necessary to the real and essential improvement of our eastern territories—we shall find an occupation worthy of a great Nation, and calculated to establish our power over India on the firmest basis. The arts of peace cannot be carried too far. On the natives of India acquiring a love for them depends, in no slight degree, the future tranquillity of that Country.

It will, however, be vain to contemplate those great objects, unless we maintain that commanding military power which we now enjoy. The British Government in India has been established, and must be supported, by the sword: and this consideration gives the utmost importance to every question connected with our military establishment in that Country; which, though the only means by which we can preserve India, is too likely, if mismanaged, to prove our ruin. This is a position, which has been too fully elucidated by events, to require support from either evidence or argument.

It will not be necessary to make any remarks upon the constitution of his Majesty's troops employed in India, as that force is solely composed of Europeans, and differs in no respect from the British army, of which they are a detachment. I shall therefore proceed to examine the organization and principles of the Company's army, which consists (besides three regiments of European infantry, and five battalions of artillery) of one hundred and eighteen battalions of native infantry, and sixteen regiments of cavalry;* making, in all, an effective army of nearly one hundred and fifty thousand men.

I shall first offer a few general observations on the subject of the European Officers, by whom this large body is commanded; and next enter into a consideration of the rise and progress of the native part of our army, and of the means best calculated to secure the lasting fidelity and attachment of the men, of whom this branch of our force is composed.

Many beneficial changes have been made in the condition of the Company's Officers: but radical defects still remain in the constitution of that body; and these must be altered; or that, which forms the strength of the British Government in India, will become it's weakness, if not it's danger.

The Officers of the native army in India should have their attention uniformly directed to the study of that service to which they are attached; and should (not as a matter of choice, but as an obligation of duty) be compelled to

* Several corps of horse artillery, gun lascars, and pioneers, are not included; and a very large invalid establishment.

learn the language, and make themselves acquainted with the customs and prejudices of the men whom they command. Their promotion should depend upon their possessing these indispensable qualifications: and it should, upon the same principle, be made as impossible for a man to attain any rank or charge in the native army, without a knowledge of the vernacular dialect of his men, as it is for an Officer to be placed in the command of a vessel, who is ignorant of navigation.

There is, perhaps, no service in the world, where so much is required from Officers, as in the native army of India; or one, in which it is of such importance, that they should possess military qualifications, combined with a correct and just sense of the particular nature of their situation; as a small body of Officers in an army of foreign troops, whom it is not more their duty to discipline, than to attach to their Country, by every attention to their civil and religious usages.

There never was a period at which this subject required more consideration. On the efforts of the European Officers in the native army, the permanent fidelity and excellence of that corps must depend: and if this is admitted, can there be a question of more importance, than the future constitution of that part of the establishment of our Indian army? It involves, if I am not greatly mistaken, the very existence of our Empire in India, and with it the greatness of England.

This branch of the service no longer enjoys those pecuniary advantages, which formerly made it so desirable to the European Officer; and it is fortunate for the honour, as well as the real interest of the service, that it does not. Emolument from an indirect and unavowed (though, perhaps, not a corrupt) source, must have a progress towards abuse, and should never be allowed to exist: but, when the operation of a just and necessary reform demanded that a powerful motive to action, which had existed for a long period, should be withdrawn, another should have been substituted; and a body of men, on whose talents, temper, and courage, the safety of the British Empire in India must always in a very great degree depend, should be stimulated to exertion by every means within the power of the State which they served. If it cannot afford to give high pecuniary rewards, it should purchase the services of men of birth and education; and remunerate the great sacrifices, which they make in entering the native army of India, by approbation, rank, and honours; and, instead of leaving them in a state of comparative obscurity, depressed by the consideration, that they are in an inferior service, and that military fame, and the applause of their King and Country, are objects placed almost beyond their hopes; their minds should be studiously elevated to these objects; and they should be put upon a footing, which would make them have an honourable pride in the service to which they belong. This they never can have, (such is the nature of military feeling,) while they consider themselves, one shade even, below another army, with which they are constantly associated.

There is, perhaps, no other efficient remedy for this great evil, than the adoption of a measure, by which the whole of that army, which Great Britain employs in India, should be consolidated into one. The distinctions, which now exist, are pregnant with every mischief to our rule. They are the source of constant irritation, and are calculated to produce an opposition of feeling among those, whose complete union is the pillar of strength on which Great Britain must depend for the safety of her possessions in India. It has been suggested, that such divisions might be useful, as they maintained a salutary check: but this limited and unwise suggestion can never merit a moment's attention. It is founded on a distrust of ourselves, which is quite incompatible with the permanent preservation of our eastern possessions. Besides, this opinion has it's only grounds on the occurrence of events,* chiefly caused by the very evils, which those invidious distinctions, and clashing feelings and interests, have produced.

It is in this place worthy of remark, that in no stage of those unwarrantable proceedings, to which a part of the Officers of the Company's army have at different periods resorted, has there been the most remote suspicion entertained of their loyalty to the King, and attachment to their Country; and it is evident, that the existence of such a doubt could alone justify the policy or necessity of maintaining any check upon their future conduct. All military bodies require to be raised, and made important, in their own estimation. In no situation will they bear depression or degradation; and certainly not in one like India, where their minds require the utmost spring to bear up against the influence of the climate, and the killing reflection of being banished, almost for life, from their native Country. It is from this cause clear, that no measure can be successful in removing the evils of the present system, but one which

* Commotions in the army of Bengal in 1794, and in the coast army in 1809.

makes it as proud a distinction for a British Officer to serve his Country in India, as in England, or in any other quarter. It is not sufficient, that a small increase of pay should enable him to live apparently better in a Country, where the climate makes what are termed luxuries, necessaries of life; but the feelings of his mind must be, that the service in which he is employed is as honourable as it is arduous; and that he will receive, in the respect and admiration of his countrymen, a just reward for the sacrifices which he has made to support the fame and interests of his Country in a distant and ungenial climate.

If the leading principles of this great change are once fixed, it's execution will not be difficult; but upon the principles on which it rests the fate of India may depend. The strictest regulations will be required, with regard to the promotion of Officers of the native infantry. No step above the rank of Ensign ought to be attainable, without qualifications as to period of service in that branch of the army, and knowledge of the language of the troops; and the road to employment in the staff of the army of India should be the same. The regulations meant to protect this branch of the service should be made permanent, and be defended by an act of the Legislature. This arrangement, if ever it be made, should be grounded on the most enlarged and liberal principles; and must reject those limited considerations of party-views and personal interest; which, from the operation of one of the chief defects of our admirable constitution, too often supersede the public good. If it does not, it will bring injury, instead of relief; and ruin that service, which it proposes to improve.

Among the many political considerations, which are likely to affect the future prosperity and security of that Empire which Great Britain has established in India, there appears hardly one of such magnitude, as that of improving and maintaining the attachment of the native army, on whose fidelity the existence of our power must always depend. For the population of England (supposing the revenues of India would bear the load of expense) cannot afford an army of sufficient numbers to protect it's extended territories in this quarter of the globe.

The most sanguine admirer of that civil code of regulations, which has been lately introduced over all the possessions of the Company, cannot expect that it will do more, in it's immediate operation, than attach to our rule those classes of our subjects, who are, from their civil and religious institutions, devoted to peaceful occupations; and consequently to a certain degree unable, if they were willing, to defend that Government, to which they may have become, from a sincere and strong sense of benefit, well affected. That our laws may ultimately change the habits of even the military classes of India, is to be expected. But this change must be gradual; and, before it is completed, we must lay our account with some of those convulsions, which are the too frequent attendants on all great changes in the condition and character of large classes of society. Against those convulsions it is our particular duty to provide; otherwise we may (such is the peculiar nature of the constitution of our power in India) lose our dominions, before we have laid those deep foundations of equity and justice, upon which it is our wise and liberal intention, that our rule should rest. If this conclusion be just, it must follow, that the realization of those great hopes of permanent dominion, which we have allowed ourselves to indulge, as the certain consequence of the wisdom and justice of our liberal policy and civil institutions, must greatly, if not solely, depend upon our success in obviating one of the greatest dangers to which our Empire is exposed, "the disaffection of our native army:" and if this be admitted, that object of our attention must become paramount to all others. Should any plan be suggested, by the action of which we can promise ourselves to improve and confirm the attachment of the military classes in India, and particularly of those employed in our ranks, (at the same time that we accelerate the period at which they shall occupy themselves in peaceful pursuits, and become good, instead of dangerous subjects,) we ought to hasten it's adoption. Both the rigid principles of economy, and the usual forms of our civil rule, should yield to the establishment of this corner stone of our strength; as, without it, the vast fabric, which has been raised with such pains, must totter to it's base at every tempest with which it is assailed.

Before we examine the nature of those causes, which appear in their operation likely to weaken, and perhaps altogether to alienate, the attachment of our native troops; and to state those principles upon which we ought to adopt remedies of a preventive nature against this great evil; it will be necessary to take a short and general view of the history of the native army; as it would appear indispensable to bear in mind it's progress, and the various changes which it has undergone, from it's first origin, to the present moment, before we can come to any just conclusions on those measures which are essential to maintain and improve it's fidelity and attachment.

When the British Government first established itself in India, military tactics in Europe were in a comparatively rude state; and the caution with which a few Europeans, endeavouring to conciliate the natives of India to fight their battles on a foreign shore, were obliged to act, prevented the introduction of any part of those tactics (imperfect as they were), which could in the least interfere with the prejudices, habits, or religion, of the natives. A jacket of English broad cloth, made up in the shape of his own dress, the knowledge of his manual exercise, and a few military evolutions, constituted the original sepoy: and with this art, and his English fire-arms, he was found to possess an incalculable superiority over the other natives of India, who, ignorant of the first principles of discipline, (which enable men to act in body,) were easily defeated, however great their numbers, by a small corps of their brothers, armed, disciplined, and directed, by the art, intelligence, and spirit, of their European leaders.

It was natural, that the early sepoy should share in that feeling of pride, which his superiority in discipline obtained him over his countrymen; and the native Officers in the employment of the Company were gratified not only by the opportunities which they had of acquiring military distinction, but of improving their fortunes. There were in the first sepoy battalions but few European Officers. A Captain, an Adjutant, with a Serjeant to each Company, was the original establishment. Commands frequently fell to Soubahdars and Jemadars: and the comparative laxity of discipline, as well as the general corruption of the times, enabled the whole of the native army, from the Soubahdar to the sepoy, to derive pecuniary benefit from the nature of those services on which they were occasionally employed. To this advantage, which rendered the service of the Company desirable, and often lucrative, was added a still more powerful attraction, in the kind treatment which they generally received from the European Officers; the number of whom to each battalion was so small, that they, from necessity, if not from inclination, acted as much upon principles of conciliation, as of coercion; and their authority in their corps rested more on affection than fear. They were most particular in their conduct to the native Officers, towards whom they behaved with a regard and respect proportionate to the responsibility of their situations. One of those native Officers, who held the rank of native Commandant, often possessed an influence in the corps nearly equal to the European Commander. As a strong and convincing proof of this fact, it is only necessary to mention, that many of the oldest battalions in the native army of the coast, are known to this day by the name of one of their former native Commandants.

This system, which had undoubtedly many defects, had also much to recommend it. For, though the European commanding Officer, who acted without check in the exercise of a great trust, generally made his corps a source of pecuniary advantage, in which he was aided by the native Commandant, (to whose principles such a practice was congenial, and who, in his turn, no doubt derived every advantage from his power and influence); yet both had a strong interest in the character and conduct of the corps, to the men of which they were almost always kind and generous. It is to this disposition, to the respectability and advantage which attached to the rank of native Officers, and the comparative relaxation in their military duties, to which we must ascribe the native corps having been, during the continuance of this system, filled by men of the highest cast, and of the best families of the military classes, in those Countries in which they were raised.*

The first material changes which took place in the constitution of the native corps, was an increase of the European Officers, a great alteration in their dress, and improvement in their discipline. This was occasioned by several causes. The native Princes had trained sepoys in European tactics; and, to maintain a superiority over them, it became necessary that the native army of the Company's Government should make further advances in the military art; which they were not only enabled to do, from the great improvements which had taken place in that science in Europe, and from the example that they had in some regiments of Europeans, which had been sent to India; but from the number of Officers of liberal education, and respectable character, whom a prospect of advantage had at this period drawn to the service of the Company.

It is the opinion of many able Officers, that it was under this system that the native army attained the greatest state of efficiency which it has yet known. The Captains were selected

* This remark applies more to Madras than Bengal, where the sepoys have always been of the same class as they now are.

to the command of battalions;* and that command was an object of sufficient emolument, to limit the views of Officers of that rank (which was then one of the highest in the service) to it's attainment. These Officers were almost invariably selected from their reputation as sepoy Officers; that is, Officers who united to all the military qualifications of a soldier, a particular knowledge of the prejudices, habits, and characters, of the men whom they were appointed to command. It was remarked, under this system, that though many of the corps were brought to a great perfection of dress and discipline, there was hardly an instance in which this was done at the expense of the temper of the men: on the contrary, those corps, which were most remarkable for their discipline, were almost uniformly most attached to their commanding Officers, whom they found as liberal to their wants, and attentive to their prejudices, as they were anxious

* These selections were made from the Captains in the regiments of Europeans in the service of the Company: and it often happened that Officers, who had neglected to attain the Country languages, and who, from violence of temper, were judged unfit to command natives, remained subordinate in an European corps, till they reached the rank of Field-Officers. Ten subaltern Officers were, under this system, attached to every battalion.

for that superiority and excellence in their appearance, discipline, and attachment, upon which they grounded all their hopes of reputation and preferment in the service to which they belonged.

The native Officers continued, under this system, to enjoy great respect and regard. This circumstance, which was chiefly owing to the European commanding Officer, who, from his superior rank, and the emoluments of his station,* enjoyed a consideration and consequence, which enabled him not only to confer distinction by his personal favour and regard, but to keep in complete check and control the younger Officers of the service, and to direct their minds to a moderate and indulgent conduct towards all the natives; but particularly to those, who, from their gallantry or long services, were entitled to respect and attention, and to whom it was proper, on every ground of policy, as well as of generosity, to show it.

In the year 1796 the native service underwent a great change; when those new regulations were introduced, which a train of events, connected with the comparative rank of the Company's Officers with those of his Majesty

* He had the off-reckonings of his corps, and in general the advantage of the command of a station.

serving in India, had rendered indispensably necessary. By these regulations, two battalions of native infantry were formed into one regiment; to which the same number of Officers* were allowed as to a regiment in the King's service. Regimental rise to the rank of Major was introduced at the same time: and this, by attaching the Officers to corps, would, it was hoped, confirm and strengthen that reciprocal confidence and connexion between the European Officers and the sepoys, which had ever been deemed the most essential principle in the constitution of the native army. It was also expected,† that the increased number of Euro-

* One Colonel, two Lieutenant-Colonels, two Majors, seven Captains, one Captain-Lieutenant, twenty-two Lieutenants, and eight Ensigns.

† On the establishment of Madras, with which I am best acquainted, the result of this great change has not been so favourable as was expected. The conduct of the sepoys has, no doubt, been very distinguished during the late wars with Tippoo Sultaun and the Mahrattas; but not more so, than it was on former occasions: and that good understanding and confidence, which before subsisted between the European Officers and their men, and which was the acknowledged basis of our strength in India, has been recently much shaken, and in some instances almost wholly destroyed.

The mutiny at Vellore gave a shock to that complete reliance on the attachment and fidelity of the native troops, from which it will be long before the Officers of the coast army perfectly recover. There can be no doubt but that horrid event was the

pean Officers would greatly add to the efficiency of the native corps, as the smallest parties that could be detached would be commanded by an

result of treason and intrigue, which artfully took advantage of other circumstances to forward it's daring designs; and found in the minute improvements of dress, (which, though long in progress, had at that moment been carried, by an unfortunate zeal, to an extreme,) the means by which it was able to inflame the ignorant multitude, and to excite them to excesses of the most violent nature. We must not, however, deceive ourselves so far as to ascribe this melancholy event solely to those causes. Had those ties, which ought to unite the European Officers and native troops under their command, existed in full force, such an event could hardly have occurred. Had there been one of those native Officers, who were concerned, or who knew what was going on, whose mind had been alive to a sense of gratitude for the distinction with which he was treated, or the favour and respect which was shown him by the Government which he served, or who could have looked with confidence to further honours and advancement, he would either have exercised his influence to the total suppression of the desperate designs of his countrymen, or have informed his European Commander of their plots. But that no such sentiments existed, is proved not only by what happened at Vellore, but by the conduct of the native Officers in almost all the corps which were suspected of disaffection about that period. These became the general objects of the suspicion of their superiors; and, if guilt was not fixed upon them, they were often convicted of a sullen indifference of conduct, which seemed to proceed from a feeling of disgust, which was produced by such a stagnation of their views, as left them almost without a motive of action. In attempting to check a spirit of turbulence, they saw some danger; and they were not encouraged to meet it by any certain hopes of reward

European Officer, and have the advantage of his knowledge and example.

The first effect of the regulations of 1796, was a great and sudden promotion of all the older Officers of the Company's service, and the arrival of a vast number of young Officers from England, to complete the establishment.

By those changes, a great proportion of the old Officers of the service were at once promoted to a rank, which removed them from regimental charge, and enabled them to return to England by the provision made for them; while the native corps were suddenly filled with young Officers: and as the command of a corps had ceased, about this period, to be attended with either advantage or distinction, it bestowed but little influence and consideration on those by whom it was held. It was, in fact, no longer an object of military ambition, as it had been formerly. It had become a station of

and preferment. They had attained all they could look to; and that all was but a comfortable subsistence during their lives. Their families were left in penury. They had therefore little to lose by a change, and some prospect of gain; and their behaviour under these feelings was, I believe, in general shaped with a view of saving themselves from personal risk in the event of the failure of the designs of the discontented, and of having some merit in having been passive, on that of their success.

trouble, without adequate emolument; and every Officer of interest or reputation in the service exerted himself to avoid it, and to obtain a Government command, or a situation on the general staff. From these causes it has often happened, since the introduction of the new regulations, that the native corps have been commanded for a period by young Captains and subaltern Officers; who, from their rank, condition and age, could not inspire that awe and respect, which is indispensable to keep in order the junior European Officers of a sepoy corps.

The German school of tactics has, for more than twenty years, been the favourite model of the English; and many Officers of rank,* who have been sent to India within that period, have been deeply imbued with the principles of that school: and these have, of course, endeavoured to introduce them into that service, which they conceived themselves specially deputed to improve; and much has, no doubt, been effected by these zealous endeavours. The

* The Generals sent to India, whether to the stations of chief command, or on the staff, should invariably be Officers of talent and reputation. Their charge is always great; and may often, from accident, become very important; and the evils which must be produced in India, by the inefficiency of those who exercise high military command in periods of difficulty, are not to be calculated.

appearance of the native army has been greatly altered for the better; they look more like soldiers, and are, perhaps, more precise in their exercise and movements: but it may be questioned whether those advantages will counterbalance the bad consequences of too exclusive an attention having been given to these points. The European Officers of the native infantry, who have naturally been led to study the disposition of the head-quarters, have, in their anxiety to merit that praise and distinction which they saw bestowed on those who succeeded in these points, not only neglected many more essential duties, but, in some instances, practised a severity and harshness* altogether unsuited to the character of the men under their command.

I entertain the highest regard and respect for both the public and private characters of several of those distinguished Officers who have fallen into this error; and am sensible, that it was hardly possible for them to avoid it. Their knowledge was limited to his Majesty's service,

* I never knew an instance of unkind and gross behaviour to the natives of India in a person acquainted with their language and manners: and it would appear, from this fact, that, to secure their being treated with that indulgence and regard, which both humanity and policy require, we have only to take care that those placed over them have that knowledge which is indispensable for such a charge.

to the usage of which they were naturally attached; and when they arrived in India they were surrounded by Officers in the Company's army, who, however high their reputations, were too desirous that the service, to which they belonged, should emulate in appearance and discipline the troops of his Majesty, to offer objections to this system of improvement in the external appearance of the native troops;* and, for a period, all those qualities, such as a knowledge of the languages and customs of the men under their command, a kindness of manner, and solicitude for their comfort, and a frequent and intimate intercourse with the native Officers, appeared to be in a great degree forgotten, or neglected. The minds of the most enlightened were perhaps never fully sensible of the importance of that chain of confidence, which had been allowed to rust till it was nearly broken. They then discovered, that, heated by a spirit of emulation, they had concurred in attempts to imitate too closely a service, opposite in it's very nature to that to which they belonged; and had lost sight, for a moment, of those principles on which the native army was formed; and by attention to which,

* These remarks apply chiefly to the native establishment of Madras.

it's fidelity and efficiency can alone be preserved.

The Officers enjoying chief command in India, should direct their attention to the solid, instead of the superficial, improvement of the native army. They ought to look more to the internal economy, than to the external appearance, of the different sepoy corps; and, instead of lavishing praises on those Officers whose only merit consists in a skill in dress and a minute knowledge of drill, they must exclusively distinguish, by their approbation and reward, those who are acquainted with the language and customs, and preserve the temper and attachment of their men, at the same time that they maintain their discipline.

The condition of the native Officers of our sepoy corps has often been the subject of the most serious attention of Government: but, though their allowances have been at times a little increased,* no measures have yet been taken on which we could ground a just and well-founded reliance on their continued fidelity and attachment. In an army of nearly one

* The most beneficial measure of this nature was that adopted by the Government of Fort St. George, which gave an increase of pay to Soubahdars, in classes formed according to length of service: but, though this regulation was good, it was too limited to have much effect.

hundred and fifty thousand natives, the highest pay which a Soubahdar of infantry can attain, is twenty pagodas (under one hundred rupees) per month; and he enjoys no consideration, after attaining that rank, which can save him from the harshness of an European Officer; a boy, who has just joined that corps, to which he has perhaps belonged for forty years. He has, in barracks and in camp, no other accommodation than that provided for the sepoys; and, on his retiring to the invalid list, he has his pay; but that is become, from habit, necessary for his support: and his children, whom a sense of personal honour, and a fear of that indiscriminate severity lately introduced, has prevented him from bringing up in the army, are generally left poor, proud, and discontented.

There are, no doubt, a few instances in the army, where a small pension has been given to a native Officer; and part of it has, in some very rare cases, been continued to his family. But such instances have seldom occurred; and only when the person, to whom the reward was granted, had an opportunity of distinguishing himself beyond all the common chances of the service; and, even then, it has not been bestowed without the greatest exertion of all the interest and influence of those Officers under whom the fortunate native Officer had acted. Under such circumstances of difficulty and discouragement, others have looked with despair for similar distinction.

It has been the opinion of many individuals, that it would be an act of wisdom to abolish the rank of native Officers altogether in the native army of the Company; and this measure was, I believe, actually recommended by the Officers of the Bengal establishment, at the period when the regulations of 1796 were under discussion.

The arguments used in support of this opinion, by it's advocates, were as follow :—

First. That since the appointment of so many European Officers to sepoy corps, the native Officers were not required to command those detachments which had been formerly intrusted to their charge, as all parties, above a Havildar's guard, would be under an European Officer; and that, in consequence, a native Officer had no duty.

Secondly. That having no duty to perform, he was of course unnecessary in a mere military point of view; and therefore the pay to this class was a great and useless expenditure of the public money.

Thirdly. That the native Officers, from having little or no duty, generally become idle and indifferent, and were alone anxious (particularly after they attained the rank of Soubahdar) to get invalided, and enjoy their full pay in perfect ease during the remainder of their lives.

Fourthly. That, from having commissions, they were, to a certain degree, independent of the regimental commanding Officer; and, in consequence, often showed little regard to his authority, contenting themselves with a mere cold discharge of their duty, in a manner which put it out of his power to bring them to a General Court Martial.

Fifthly. That the native Officers possessed a great, and in some respects a dangerous, influence; and that, elevated to a condition in life, which, from their birth, they had no right to expect, they were apt to adopt new sentiments in their promotion; and we might find, that we had not only given men a power, but infused into their minds an ambition, which they might be tempted to turn against us.

Sixthly, and lastly. It is argued, that on the abolition of the native commissioned Officers there would be no danger from the non-commissioned, as these were too near the sepoys ever to possess any great influence over their minds. That their zeal in the performance of their duty, and their obedience to their immediate commanding Officer, would be completely secured by the authority which he possessed of reducing them on the instant to the ranks; and that this system would be more approximated to that of the army of England, in which no man, who enlisted as a private, could indulge a rational hope of raising himself to any rank higher than that of a non-commissioned Officer.

The objections, which must appear to every reflecting mind, to the measure of abolishing the rank of native commissioned Officers, are so numerous, so strong, and so founded upon the result of experience, the peculiar constitution of the native army, the character of the men of whom it is formed, and upon every consideration which refers to the feelings of a large mass of society; that the very mention of such an idea having been contemplated, must excite surprise and astonishment. But as this idea has been often urged, and has had the countenance of some respectable names, it will be proper to offer a few observations in answer to those which are adduced by the advocates of this measure. It may be assumed as a fact of general experience, that in no Country has an army ever been improved by the adoption of a principle, which limited the action of emulation, and repressed that military fire and ambition, which has ever been deemed the greatest essential of a soldier; and least of all would such a rule appear applicable in a case, where it was admitted by those who wished to adopt it, that the rank they desired to abolish, was an object, from it's consequence, and the influence which it gave, of universal ambition from the youngest recruit to the oldest non-commissioned Officer in the corps.

They say, a native Officer has little or no duty: but is he not one of the chief links between the European Officer and the sepoy? And when it is considered, that he has been promoted to the rank he holds, in consequence of long and approved services, what man can be a more proper object of trust?

They state, that the native commissioned Officers become indifferent to their duty, and anxious alone to retire on their pay, the moment they reach the rank of Soubahdar: but does it never occur, that this desire proceeds more from a stagnation of hope, than a spirit of discontent? Are we not to consider, that the same spirit of emulation, which has actuated the native Officer's breast, till his exertions under it's impulse have raised him to that rank, would continue to operate, if he could look to further reward or distinction? And would not his increased rank and consequence, and the enjoyment of that very influence which is dreaded, be, in such case, actively employed to recommend himself to those superiors from whom he expected notice or preferment?

If the limited allowance given to native Officers, and the stagnation of their hopes, be the causes of that apathy and discontent which is remarked among them; would these causes cease to operate in a sepoy corps when those ranks were abolished? Would not the Havildars and Naigues then become the principal natives in the corps, with a pay smaller, and with hopes still more limited? But these, it is supposed, would not entertain the same sentiments, because they would move in a more subordinate rank, have consequently less influence, and be more dependent upon the regimental commanding Officer. Such reasoners forget, that the great existing cause of their present zeal and activity, that of recommending themselves for promotion to the rank of commissioned Officers, would be gone. They assuredly cannot expect any reflecting man to think, that because they had reduced the pay of the principal natives in a corps of sepoys, and rendered their situation more precarious, by withdrawing from them the protection of Government, placed them at the mercy of every European commanding Officer, whom chance put for a few days at the head of their corps, that they had, by such means, taken a securer pledge for their increased fidelity and attachment. Such a conclusion is contrary to all experience of the human character. The more men have to lose, the greater disinclination they will ever have to change: and the more limited and uncertain their means of subsistence and rank in life, the less they will hesitate in exposing themselves to those hazards by which they may lose both.

It cannot be intended by those, who advocate this change of system, that the pay of the Havildars and Naigues should be increased; as such a measure would tend to give them that consequence, which it is their wish to depress. Could it then be expected, when five pagodas a month become the highest pay, which a sepoy could attain, after the longest and most meritorious course of service; and when that, even, unaccompanied by either the name or the reality of rank, was, in fact, a most precarious tenure, dependent in a great degree upon the caprice and temper of every commanding Officer to whom he was subject; that any man, who, from his appearance or character, could obtain a pay nearly equal, the moment he entered the public service under a civil Officer, or embraced menial employment under an European gentleman, would ever think of entering the regular army?

We are also to consider, that the different native Powers will always maintain sepoys; and these men will rise to the rank of Soubahdars and Jemadars with more authority, and often with more pecuniary perquisites, if not higher fixed pay, than in the Company's service: and we are mistaken, if we conceive, that the solid advantages of our native army, such as regularity of payment, and the invalid and pension lists, would counterbalance such allurements. Benefits, when made too general, often cease to have a strong effect in exciting emulation. The best recruits who enter our service, are young men of spirit and ambition, whose chief view, in entering as soldiers, is to rise to the highest ranks. Abolish those, or strip them of their advantages and respectability, and men of high cast and proud feelings will turn with disgust from our army; and, if determined upon a military life, will enter into that of some other State, however unstable, which continues to hold out a hope of their attaining those objects by which their imaginations have been captivated.

There can be no analogy between the native corps of India and regiments of Europeans. In the former there must ever be a strong line of separation, marked by difference of habits, of language, of Country, and of religion, between the Officers and men; and their feelings, interests, motives of action, and rewards, must consequently always be considered on distinct grounds. In the latter, they have common Country language and religion: and the Officers are, from birth or merit, of a higher class in that society to which they both belong; and have, in consequence, a kind of prescriptive right to the respect, obedience, and attachment of those whom they command.

In estimating the consequence of the native commissioned Officers of it's army to the English Government, it seems first necessary to state, that the existence of this rank is coeval with the establishment of that Government in India. The first sepoys of the Company were raised and commanded by native Officers, acting under the authority and direction of an European Officer; but still exercising great influence and power over their men, whom they brought to the service. Those Officers long continued to be the medium on which we relied for the fidelity and attachment of the sepoys, who saw in them men of high cast and superior character, of their own Country, at whose call they had embraced the service of strangers. Even since the original consequence of this class of men has been diminished, the sepoys have continued to regard them as the most distinguished of their own body; and have given them a ready respect and obedience, not only from a feeling of what was due to their stations, but from a dutiful concurrence in the judgment of their European Commander, by whom the native commissioned Officers had been elevated to that rank, which all were anxiously struggling to attain. But supposing that the State derived no benefit, in a military point of view, from the existence of the rank of native commissioned Officers; it is of the greatest importance to have in our native army a class of men, (comparatively few in number,) by our attention to whom we can stimulate and attach the whole mass; and whose merit and valour we can reward with an assurance, that we will excite, by so doing, throughout all ranks, that spirit of hope and emulation, which is the vital principle of every military body.

In the native army, as it is at present constituted, no native can rise to the enjoyment of any military command: that is, he cannot, unless in extraordinary cases, when the European Officers are sick, or absent, expect to have under his orders a body of more than thirty or forty men; and he cannot attain a pay beyond twenty pagodas per month; and no rank which he obtains gives him any particular privilege or consequence in that civil community, from which he came, and to which he in general returns, when disabled by age, wounds, or infirmity, from continuing the active duties of a soldier.

The nature of our power in India requires this exclusion of the native Officer from the exercise of military command, which should, no doubt, be always kept in the hands of Europeans. But if that gate is barred by policy, others should be opened. In the strictest conformity to those principles upon which the native army is formed, we might lead the minds of those troops to expect comfort and distinction in civil life, as the reward of approved military service: and by directing their ambition to the natural and seductive object of acquiring importance in their own tribe, and enjoying some privileges, however trivial, which might (under certain regulations) descend to their children, we should not only discover a motive sufficiently powerful to supply the place of that, which a jealous but wise policy obliges us to withhold, but place their fidelity beyond the power of corruption.

The native service would become, if such measures were adopted, popular and respected; and would be embraced with eagerness by men of the first families in the Country;* and, in

* It has been suggested, that we might enlist men for limited service in India: and this practice, which in some degree obtains

the course of years, we might expect, that the attachment of our subjects would be greatly improved by that spirit of active allegiance, which would be generally diffused by veterans and their descendants, whose claim to their rank or land was founded in the gratitude of a State, whom they had served with fidelity and distinction.

The men, who form the native army of the Company, are almost all sober, and of good conduct in private life. Drunkenness, as a general vice, is indeed unknown: and notorious immorality is rare. But their virtues are more of a passive, than an active nature. They consist more in forbearance, from fear of offending against their civil institutions and the rigid tenets of their religion, than from any sense of the beauty of virtue, or the deformity of vice. These men would appear hardly to consider themselves as free moral agents, and blindly resign their judgment, in almost all cases, to the law of usage, the dictates of their priest, or the influence of their superiors in cast or station. And it is from these causes, that we observe them in an instant change their mild, inoffensive, and indolent character, for that of the most savage obstinacy, and active ferocity.

in Bengal, might perhaps be adopted with great advantage. It is, at all events, a subject that merits consideration.

All the natives of India, but particularly those of military classes, are fond of show, and of high titles; and they often seem to prize the external, beyond the reality of power. It is, indeed, surprising to see the consequence which they attach to every mark of outward respect, particularly when bestowed by their superiors: and, partaking of the character of his countryman, the native soldier of the Company, intelligent and quick in his conception, full of vanity and a love of pre-eminence, if not of glory, is of all men the most sensible to the effect of attention, or neglect. Though the climate disposes him to inertness, and his frame is seldom very robust,* he may be flattered and encouraged to make the most extraordinary exertions; while harshness or cruelty serves only to subdue his spirit, and sink him into apathy, if it does not rouse him to resentment, which is too often the case. It may be adduced in proof of this, that there never has been (as far as I am informed) a mutiny in the native army, in which the men did not pursue, as an object of their marked vengeance, some particular European Officer, who had treated them with injustice or severity.

An army so constituted, and formed of men

* The Bengal native soldier is an exception.

of such tempers, may appear very susceptible of being corrupted, and made instrumental to the destruction of that Power which it is employed to protect; but of this there is no danger, unless in the improbable case of our becoming too presumptuous in what we may deem our intrinsic strength; confiding too exclusively in our European troops, and altogether undervaluing and neglecting our native army. From the day of that fatal errour we may date the downfal of our Eastern Empire.

It will be useful in this place to enter into a short recapitulation of what has been stated, and to advert to that description of measures which would appear best calculated to preserve and maintain the native army in it's full efficiency, and to secure it's fidelity under all emergencies. This, for the sake of perspicuity, will be best divided under different heads.

First. We should watch, with incessant vigilance, the sentiments and disposition of this great body, which will of course be liable to fluctuation and change: and, while we temper the strictness of discipline with those indulgencies which the climate and the habits and character of the native soldier may require, we should be most careful to remove, by a preventive policy, every cause of complaint: for, in all instances, (but particularly one like the present,) the difference between a wise foresight, which prevents demand, and that weakness which meets it with concession, is immense. The former is the characteristic of a rising and vigorous, the latter, of a fallen and expiring Government.

Secondly. The Officers, who are intrusted with the general command in India, should be made minutely attentive to the manner in which discipline is carried on in the native corps; and they ought particularly to discountenance and discourage that rudeness of language to the native Officers, and that harsh severity to the sepoys, which, experience has shown, is not at all necessary to their perfection in discipline: on the contrary, that it retards that object, by making them disgusted and discontented with the service.

Thirdly. Arrangements should be made, either by striking the staff off the strength of the army, or by adding more Officers to a sepoy battalion, to secure it's being always complete with European Officers.

Fourthly. It appears of the last importance to the efficiency of this branch of the army, that the native corps should be always commanded by Officers of rank and experience. Every measure should be adopted, which can promote the accomplishment of this essential point;

which never can be effected, till the command of a native battalion is made an object of ambition to the best qualified Officers in the service.

Fifthly. Every means should be adopted, which can have a tendency to raise the pride, stimulate the zeal, or improve the minds, of the European Officers of the sepoy corps. It is upon their conduct that Government must place it's chief reliance for the continued discipline and fidelity of the native army; and their distinction, as a body of Officers, should be suited to the great national trust reposed in them. No Officer of this class, as I before stated, should be permitted to rise to rank, or charge, in this branch of the service, without an adequate knowledge of the customs and language of the men whom he commands. And both the Commanders-in-Chief and the Governor in India should be restricted, by law, from giving an appointment, or staff situation,* to any Officer in India, who had not acquired a competent knowledge of the native language. These regulations might be considered by some as too severe; but they are indispensable for the public good: and, after all, where is the hardship in insisting upon

* If such a regulation existed, Officers of European corps, as well as of native, would early qualify themselves for such situations.

Officers possessing themselves of qualifications, without which they can never perform their duty in an efficient manner?

Sixthly.. As there can be no doubt, that the most serious danger is likely to occur from any spirit of discontent among the native commissioned Officers; and as this can only arise from the stagnation of all hope in the minds of men, who, whether we consider their services, or the influence which they exercise over the sepoys, appear proper objects of the attention of Government; we should endeavour to keep alive the zeal and attachment of this valuable class, and through them to give life and animation to the whole of our native army, whose minds should be studiously directed to the object of attaining civil privileges through the medium of military service. We may pursue this object with a confidence, that, if we succeed in it's attainment, we may defy all those attempts, which can be hereafter made, either by rival European or native Powers, to corrupt the fidelity of our troops in India.

In concluding this important subject, it will be necessary to state in a general manner those means which would meet this great object. They will be found such, as will neither violate the principles of our civil or military rule, nor cause any serious increase to our disbursements,

When a native Officer has obtained a commission, he ought, upon principle, to be treated with the most marked respect by the European Officer; who should, from that instant, consider him as a person who has, from merit and long services, stepped from the rank which he before held, to one more permanent and dignified; and to have received, with his commission, a sacred pledge of the favour and protection of the Government he serves, which nothing, but established crime or misconduct, can forfeit.

There can be no motive to action more powerful in the breast of a soldier, than a conviction, that his superiors will never pass without notice any remarkable act of gallantry or good conduct. The commanding Officers of all native corps, employed on service, should be required to report such, as soon as they occur, to the head-quarters of the army; and medals, of a value suited to the rank of the person and the nature of the action, should be immediately given. These medals should entitle the man (if not a Soubahdar) on whom they were bestowed, to the first vacancy in his corps in the rank above that which he held; and they should also increase his general claims upon the service. If to a Soubahdar, his claims to those rewards, which were instituted for the most meritorious of that rank, should be greatly strengthened.

There is no subject of more common, or of more reasonable, complaint among the native commissioned Officers, than that their pay is never sufficient to allow them to make a provision for their families; and that no action, which they can perform, entitles their sons to any consideration in that service to which their fathers' lives have been devoted: and it is chiefly on this account, that they seldom allow their sons to be sepoys. Among other expedients, which have been suggested with a view of remedying this evil, and of restoring to the service a race of men who ought to have an hereditary attachment to our Government, it has been proposed to allow the sons of native Officers to enter as volunteers, and to rise to the rank of commissioned Officers when vacancies occurred. Such a regulation would strike at the root of the constitution of the native service, and is therefore altogether inadmissible: but there is no objection whatever to our giving some distinction, in their course through the service, to the sons of veterans, who have, from their valour or good conduct, attained a rank, which it is the policy of the Government he serves to render as valuable as possible; but which those holding it must think of little use, if it only raises them to a station, such, that they cannot, without suffering some degradation in general opinion, place their sons in that army in which they have passed their lives; and yet does not enable them to save any thing for their future support.

The sons* of native commissioned Officers ought, when boys of the specified age, to be received in the corps to which their fathers belonged on the full pay of a sepoy;† and, when of an age and stature to carry arms, they should be made sepoys, with one pagoda a month more than regular pay: and this increase should be given till they attain, by their services, the rank of a commissioned Officer. It should be a regulation of the service, that they were, on account of their fathers, to be treated with consideration by the European Officers; and should not suffer corporal punishment, unless in cases of great enormity: and when their conduct was generally bad, or they committed any crime which called for notice, they should be discharged the service; which, considering

* This regulation should, of course, be made with some limitation to numbers.

† The sons of an invalid Officer should be entitled to this indulgence, as well as of those who were effective.

the indulgence with which they are treated, would be itself a sufficient punishment. Such attention to the sons of commissioned Officers, while it affected no principle of the service, would gratify all ranks of the army: and the sepoys would see with satisfaction, instead of jealousy, the sons of men, whom they had so long obeyed and respected, enjoying advantage from their birth, which, while it gave increased value to the object of all their ambition, did not interfere with them in it's attainment; as the sons of commissioned Officers would depend, like every man in the corps, upon their own merit for promotion.

Though this regulation would, no doubt, be of great benefit to the service; yet that powerful principle of action, which is so essential to fix the allegiance, and excite a proper feeling in the higher ranks of the native army, can only be produced by more liberal arrangements, which, suited to the constitution of the army, and the character of those of whom it is composed, should lead the veteran from the hardships of a long and active military life, to the enjoyment of that ease and distinction on his native soil, which is in all Countries the noblest reward for the declining age of those, whose youth and manhood have been devoted to the defence of the State. These rewards should be calculated on a higher scale, than would appear, on a consideration of the actual pay or duties of those to whom they were allotted, to be necessary; because they are not only meant to compensate to the minds of distinguished individuals for being cut short in those hopes of military distinction in which they were educated, but to strengthen the attachment of a numerous army to the Government which it serves.

As one great measure for effecting this desirable purpose, an arrangement* might be made, by which a certain number of the most meritorious Soubahdars should be advanced to the rank of Commandants (as a general, not regimental rank), and made Killadars, or Governors of petty posts or dismantled forts; and they might, in rare cases, be gratified with such titles as were suited to their merits, and the tribe or religion to which they belonged. This would gain them the respect of the community among whom they lived: and to secure it from possible injury, as well as to save men, who had done their duty faithfully to the State, from the control of those who, from their habits, must be unacquainted with mili-

* A plan of this nature was proposed by Sir John Craddock, but not adopted.

tary rules, they should not be required (as a matter of course) to perform any particular duties under the civil Magistrate; but be allowed to reside in their native district, or where they chose; and not to have any station, military or civil, unless they desired it, and were thought by Government peculiarly fitted for the discharge of it's duties.

The salaries attached to such stations should be liberal, as they are meant to place those by whom they are enjoyed in the first rank of that community in which they live; and, by doing so, to give popularity and respectability to the native service. A greater and better effect would be produced upon the feelings of the whole army by a few distinguished rewards than by a small increase of pay to a number. We might also expect, that the efforts made by native Officers to attain such rewards, would be in proportion to the magnitude of their value: and when a native Officer of superior character could raise himself so high, in point both of comfort and respectability, under the Government which he served, it would hardly be possible to tempt him from his allegiance.

The most particular respect should be paid by Government to the few native commanding Officers whom it distinguishes by such marked favour. They should receive the grant, which was made to them, with every form and ceremony that could add to it's value; and it should be accompanied with a rich medal; and, to the first class, with an honorary dress. The European civil and military Officers in the Country where they settled, should treat them with particular respect and attention. This, indeed, is quite indispensable to give effect to the measure recommended.

By such an institution of honourable rewards, the native service would be greatly elevated; men of the best families in the military class would enter it, in the hope of attaining distinction;* and, by their employment, the Government would be freed from the most dangerous of it's discontented subjects.

In addition to such distinguished rewards; which, though calculated to have an effect on all, could only reach a few; it would appear of great importance to adopt some plan, which would lead the veteran from the camp to the

* Native Officers of distinction might be employed as native aides-de-camp to General Officers on the staff. Generals Floyd, Campbell, and Wellesley, had native Officers in their suite, and found them very useful. If an increase of pay was attached to native Officers so employed, it would operate in some degree as a stimulus to exertion to men of that class; and might in many other respects be attended with beneficial effects.

soil, and give him not only an object to support him through the hardships of a military life, and to fix his attachment to his foreign masters, but a deep interest in the permanency of the Government which he served: and such can only be done by giving him lands on terms of an advantageous nature.

The Tannah Establishment in Bengal is a noble instance of what may be done in this way. It's constitution has been greatly altered from the original plan; but it's history must furnish a volume of experience. Many objections have been made to this Establishment: but these have always referred to the difficulty of managing it; the interference with the civil regulations; and a small temporary loss of revenue; and must sink to nothing, when we contemplate the happy and important results of this great national measure. I have beheld with more patriotic pride, than has ever been excited in my mind by any other act of British policy in India, a tract of Country more than an hundred miles in length, upon the banks of the Ganges, which had a few years before been a complete jungle, (abandoned for ages to tigers and robbers,) covered with cultivated fields and villages; the latter of which were filled with old soldiers and their families, who spoke of that State, which had rewarded their services, in a manner which showed their deep gratitude and attachment* for the comfort and happiness they enjoyed.

When we consider the immeasurable quantity of waste land in the dominions of the Company, it appears extraordinary that this plan has not been adopted, in every part of British India, upon a more liberal and enlarged scale. The fact is, that we have hitherto been startled at a few practical difficulties, which would yield, the moment they were met with spirit and resolution. It must be evident to every man, who reflects upon the subject, that the accomplishment of this object will add, in an incalculable degree, to the ties which we have upon the permanent fidelity of those by whom our

* The native soldiers of Bengal are almost all cultivators; and a reward of this nature was peculiarly calculated to attach them. General Perron, in Scindiah's service, had established one of very nearly a similar nature, which the liberality of the English Government (when the Duab was conquered) directed to be kept up; and it fell to my lot to adjust the claims of most of the men who were entitled to it's benefit. From what I at that time observed, I am convinced that the Establishment for a few old and wounded soldiers (for it was then in it's infancy, and on a limited scale) was one of the great causes of that extraordinary fidelity and attachment which Scindiah's sepoys showed to their Government, even after they were deserted by their Officers.

dominion in India is likely to be preserved or lost.

It appears that we might also connect with such a plan the employment of some of the most meritorious commissioned and non-commissioned Officers, who had been invalided (but were still capable of exertion) in the higher stations of the Police Establishment. The additional pay, which a veteran would receive upon this account, while it rewarded his services, and gave encouragement to the whole army, would not put Government to any expense whatever; as it would only be a disbursement of the same, or probably a less pay, than that which is given, under the present system, to some inhabitant of the Country, who has little or no claim to the favour of Government; and the rewarding of whom only makes men of the military class, fitted for soldiers, withhold themselves from the army, in the hopes of attaining, in the police of their native district, a station of nearly as great pay, and of as much respectability, as they could expect to reach by twenty years' service in the regular army.

It is, in short, necessary, if we desire to attach the native troops to our Government in such a manner as will defy all corruption, to place them on a higher and more favoured footing than any part of the population. It is sufficiently obvious, that while we are secure of their attachment we have nothing to dread from others: and we should, from this consideration, make it a fundamental principle of our rule, that all employments and situations of profit and honour in the civil Administration, which were filled by natives of the military class, should only be attainable through the means of approved service in the regular army. The number of men qualified for such employment by their character and services, would be always sufficiently great to secure an ample field for the choice of effective instruments to the Magistrate, who would probably soon discover, that the habits of the soldier peculiarly fitted him for the duties of an Officer of police.

We should, on the same principle, grant civil privileges to the commissioned Officers, and those non-commissioned Officers and privates, who had obtained medals, and were retired from the service. They should have a right, when they were complainants in a civil suit,* to have their cause put first on the file. They should also have precedence in their ceremonies,

* This is, I believe, a regulation in Bengal.

and remissions of particular small duties; or, in short, any thing which marked that attention, which Government paid to those who had served it with valour and fidelity; and which separated them, by distinctions that gratified their feelings, from the mass of the population.

No part of those arrangements, which have been suggested, would interfere with the fundamental principles of that judicial system which has been introduced into our territories; but they might, from many causes, be found, at their first introduction, repugnant to the feelings and wishes of those by whom that system is carried into execution. The patronage of individuals would be in some degree affected; usages infringed; and, for a period, some inconvenience might be experienced. But if the truth of what has been urged is granted; if the operation of this plan is likely to prove an essential and permanent source of strength and security; all petty difficulties ought to be surmounted: less considerations must give way; and the civil Officers of Government must be taught to consider the promotion of the full success of this measure, as one of the most important branches of their public duty.

The subject of the native army of India has been treated in more detail than the general character of this Sketch perhaps warranted; but it is one of deep interest to the State; and the observations made upon it, are the result of long experience and mature reflection; and, as such, they cannot be deemed altogether unappropriate, at the close of a work, in which the author has anxiously endeavoured to contribute all he was able towards that fuller knowledge of the real interests of the British Government in India, which seems requisite for the information of those on whose virtue and wisdom the future fate of that great Empire must depend.

APPENDIX.

APPENDIX.

TRANSLATION of a FIRMAUN *from* FUTTEH ALI SHAUH, *King of Persia; and of an annexed Treaty concluded by* HAUJY IBRAHIM KHAN, *Prime Minister, on the Part of the King of Persia, by whom he was fully empowered: and by Captain* JOHN MALCOLM, *on the Part of the English Government; by virtue of Powers delegated to him for that Purpose by the Most Noble the Marquis* WELLESLEY, *K. P., Governor General of India, &c. &c. &c.*

FIRMAUN.

In the name of the beloved and great God.

The King
of
Persia's Seal.

The Earth is the Lord's.

Our august commands are issued, that the high in rank, the exalted in station, the great Rulers, Officers, and Writers of the ports, sea-coasts and islands, of the

Province of Fars and Khoozistaun, do consider themselves as particularly honoured and advanced by the royal favour. And whereas, at this period, the foundations of union and friendship have been cemented, and the habits of amity and intercourse have been increased, between the Ministers of the (Persian) State of eternal duration, and the Ministers of the high Government of the refulgent sun of the sky of royalty, greatness, and eminence, the Sovereign of the Countries of England and India; and as various engagements and treaties, calculated for duration and permanence, and for mutual good understanding, have been contracted; therefore, this command from the palace of glory, requiring obedience, has been proclaimed; that you, high in rank, do cheerfully comply, and execute the clear sense and meaning of what has been established. And should ever any person of the French Nation attempt to pass your ports or boundaries, or desire to establish themselves either on the shores or frontiers, you are to take means to expel and extirpate them, and never to allow them to obtain a footing in any place; and you are at full liberty, and authorized, to disgrace and slay them. You are to look upon it as your duty, to aid and act in a friendly manner to all traders, merchants, and men of rank, of the English Nation. All such you are to consider as possessing the favour of the King; and you must act in conformity to the conditions of the annexed treaty, that has been concluded between the trust-worthy of the high State, the bracelet of the graceful Government, Haujy Ibrahim Khan; and the high in rank, Captain John Malcolm. View this as obligation. Dated the 12th of Shaubaun, in the year of the Hejree 1215; corresponding with the month of January, anno Domini 1801.

Sealed, in the usual form, on the back of the Firmaun, by the following Ministers :—

Seal of HAUJY IBRAHIM KHAN.

MEERZA SHUFFEE.

MEERZA REZA KOULI.

MEERZA ASSUD OOLLAH.

MEERZA REZY.

MEERZA AHMUD.

MEERZA MOORTIZA KOULI.

MEERZA TAZULLAH.

MEERZA YOOSUF.

TREATY ANNEXED.

PREAMBLE.

Praise be unto God, who said, " Oh you, who believe, " perform your contracts, perform your covenant with " God, when you enter into covenant with him, and " violate not your engagements after the ratification " thereof." After the voice is raised to the praise and glory of the God of the world, and the brain is perfumed with the scent of the saints and prophets, to whom be health and glory! whose rare perfections are perpetually chaunted by birds of melodious notes,* furnished with two, three, and four pair of wings, and to the Highest seated in the Heavens, for whom good has been predestinated, and the perfume mixed with musk, which scenteth the celestial mansions of those that sing hymns in the ethereal sphere, and to the light of the flame of the Most High, which gives radiant splendour to the collected view of those who dwell in the heavenly regions; the clear meaning of the treaty, which has been established on a solid basis, is fully explained in this page, and is fixed as a prescription of law, that in this world of existence and trouble, in this universe of *creation* and concord, there is no action among those of mankind, that tends more to the perfection of the human race, or to answer the end of their being and existence, than that of cementing friendship, and of establishing intercourse, communication, and connexion, betwixt each other. The image reflected from the mirror of accomplishment is a tree fruitful and abundant, and one that produces good, both now and hereafter. To illustrate the allusions that it has been proper to make, and explain these metaphors, worthy of exposition at this happy period of auspicious aspect, a treaty has been concluded between the high in dignity, the exalted in station, attended by fortune, of great and splendid power, the greatest among the high Viziers, in whom confidence is placed, the faithful of the powerful Government, the adorned with greatness, power, glory, splendour and fortune, Haujy Ibrahim Khan, on being granted leave, and vested with authority from the Port of the High King, whose Court

* Metaphorically, Angels.

is like that of Solomon, the asylum of the world, the sign of the power of God, the jewel in the ring of Kings, the ornament in the cheek of eternal Empire, the grace of the beauty of sovereignty and royalty, the King of the universe, like Caherman, the mansion of mercy and justice, the phœnix of good fortune, the eminence of never-fading prosperity, the King powerful as Alexander, who has no equal among the Princes exalted to Majesty by the Heavens in this globe, a shade from the shade of the Most High, a Khoosroo whose saddle is the moon, and whose stirrup is the new moon, a Prince of great rank, before whom the sun is concealed.

ARABIC VERSE.

Thy benevolence is universally dispersed! every where drops are scattered! Thy kindness shadows cities; may God fix firm the basis of thy dominion, and may God fix and extend thy power over the servants of the Almighty! And the high in dignity, the great and able in power, the adorner of those acquainted with manners, Captain John Malcolm, delegated from the sublime quarter of the high in power (seated on a throne the asylum of the world, the chief jewel in the crown of royalty and sovereignty, the anchor of the vessel of victory and fortune, the ship on the sea of glory and Empire, the blazing sun in the sky of greatness and glory, Lord of the Countries of England and India; may God strengthen his territories, and establish his glory and commands upon the seas!) in the manner explained in his credentials, which are sealed with the seal of the most powerful and most glorious, possessing fortune, the origin of rank, splendour and nobility, the ornament of the world, the accomplisher of the works of mankind, the Governor General of India.

This treaty between these two great States shall be binding on race after race; and the two Governments must ever, while the world exists, act in conformity to what is now settled.

ARTICLE I.

As long as the sun, illuminating the circle of the two great contracting parties, shines on their sovereign dominions, and bestows light on the whole world, the beautiful image of excellent union shall remain fixed on the mirror of duration and perpetuity. The thread of shameful enmity and distance shall be cut, conditions of mutual aid and assistance between the two States shall be instituted, and all causes of hatred and hostility shall be banished.

ARTICLE II.

If the King of the Afghauns should ever show a resolution to invade India, which is subject to the Government of the Monarch (above mentioned), the Prince of high rank, the King of England; an army, overthrowing mountains, furnished with all warlike stores, shall be appointed from the State of the conspicuous and exalted, high and fixed in power, (the King of Persia,) to lay waste and desolate the Afghaun dominions, and every exertion shall be employed to ruin and humble the above-mentioned Nation.

ARTICLE III.

Should it happen, that the King of the Afghaun Nation ever becomes desirous of opening the gates of peace and friendship with the Government of the King (of Persia), who is in rank like Solomon, in dignity like Jumsheed, the shade of God! who has bestowed his mercy and kindness on the earth; when negotiations are opened for an amicable adjustment, it shall be stipulated in the peace concluded, that the King of the Afghauns, or his armies, shall abandon all design of attack on the territories subject to the Government of the King above mentioned, who is worthy of royalty, the King of England.

ARTICLE IV.

Should ever any King of the Afghauns, or any person of the French Nation, commence war and hostilities with the powerful of the ever-enduring State (of the King of Persia), the Rulers of the Government of the King (of England), whose Court is like Heaven, and who has been before mentioned, shall (on such event) send as many cannon and warlike stores as possible, with necessary apparatus, attendants, and inspectors, and such (supply) shall be delivered over at one of the ports of Persia, whose boundaries are conspicuous, to the Officers of the high in dignity, the King of Persia.

ARTICLE V.

Should it ever occur, that an army of the French Nation, actuated by design and deceit, attempts to settle with a view of establishing themselves on any of the islands or shores of Persia, a conjunct force shall be appointed by the two high contracting States, to act in co-operation for their expulsion and extirpation, and to destroy and put an end to the foundations of their treason. It is a condition, if such event happens, and the conquering troops (of Persia) march, that the Officers of the Government of the King (of England), who is powerful as the Heavens, and has been before mentioned, shall load, transport, and deliver (for their service), as great a quantity of necessaries, stores, and provisions, as they possibly can ; and if ever any of the great men of the French Nation express a wish or desire to obtain a place of residence, or dwelling, on any of the islands or shores of the Kingdom of Persia, that they may there raise the standard of abode or settlement, such request or representation shall not be consented unto by the high in rank of the State encompassed with justice (the Government of Persia); and leave for their residing in such place shall not be granted.

While time endures, and while the world exists, the contents of this exalted treaty shall remain an admired picture in the mirror of duration and perpetuity ; and submission to the fair image on this conspicuous page shall be everlasting.

Seal of ▱ HAUJY IBRAHIM KHAN.

▱ Captain JOHN MALCOLM.

(Signed) JOHN MALCOLM, Envoy.

A true translation.

(Signed) JOHN MALCOLM, Envoy.

TRANSLATION of a FIRMAUN *from* FUTTEH ALI SHAUH, *King of Persia; and of an annexed Treaty concluded by* HAUJY IBRAHIM KHAN, *Prime Minister, on the Part of the King of Persia, by whom he was fully empowered: and by Captain* JOHN MALCOLM, *on the Part of the English Government; by virtue of Powers delegated to him for that Purpose by the Most Noble the Marquis* WELLESLEY, *K. P., Governor General of India, &c. &c. &c.*

FIRMAUN.

In the name of the beloved and great God!

The King
of
Persia's Seal.

The Earth is the Lord's.

Our august commands are issued, that the high in dignity, the exalted in station, the refuge of power and glory, the noble and great in authority, the chiefs of high nobles, the Beglerbegs, the Haukims, the Naibs, and Mootsuddies of the Kingdom under our protection (who are raised by our royal favour), become acquainted; that, at this period, the dignified and eminent in station, the prudent, able, and penetrating, the greatest of the exalted followers of the

Messiah, Captain John Malcolm, deputed from a glorious quarter, (from the Government of the King of England, whose Court resembles the Firmament, an Emperor in dignity like Alexander, possessing the power of the globe, and from the repository of glory, greatness, and ability, endowed with nobility, power, and justice, the Governor General of the Kingdom of Hindoostan,) for the purpose of establishing union and friendship between the two great States, has arrived at our threshold, founded on justice, and has been honoured by admission to our royal presence of conspicuous splendour, and has expressed a desire, that the *foundations* of amity and union should be laid between the two States, that they should be connected together in the bonds of friendship and harmony, and that a constant union, and reciprocal good understanding, should exist: We, from our august selves, have given our consent, and have granted the requests and desires of the high in rank above mentioned; and a treaty, sealed with the seal of the Minister* of our ever-enduring Government, has been given to him: and you, exalted in station, are positively enjoined of the necessity (after you become informed of our royal and august order) for all of you acting in strict conformity with the conditions of the treaty concluded and exchanged between the high in rank, the exalted in station, the great and glorious in power, near to the throne, in whom the royal confidence is placed, Haujy Ibrahim Khan; and the high in rank, the Envoy (Captain John Malcolm), whose titles have

* Literally, one in whom confidence is placed.

been before enumerated. Let no one act contrary to this high command, or to the contents of the annexed treaty. And should it ever be represented to us, that any of the great nobles conduct themselves in opposition to the stipulations of this treaty, or are in this respect either guilty or negligent, such will incur our displeasure, and punishment, and be exposed to our royal anger, which is like fire: and let them view this as an obligation.

Dated in the month of Shaubaun, in the year of the Hejree 1215; corresponding with the month of January, anno Domini 1801. Sealed in the usual form on the back of the Firmaun, by the following Ministers:—

Seal of ▱ Haujy Ibrahim Khan.

▱ Meerza Shuffee.

▱ Meerza Reza Kouli.

▱ Meerza Assud Oóllah.

▱ Meerza Rezy.

▱ Meerza Ahmud.

▱ Meerza Moortiza Kouli.

▱ Meerza Tazullah.

▱ Meerza Yoosuf.

TREATY ANNEXED.

PREAMBLE.

Praise be to God, who has said, "Perform your "covenant, for the performance of your covenant "shall be inquired into hereafter." As establishing the obligations of friendship between all mankind, is a charge from the Almighty, and is a most laudable and excellent institution; and as the Creator is pleased, and the happiness and tranquillity of his subjects consulted by it; therefore, at this happy period of auspicious aspect, a treaty has been concluded between the high in dignity, the exalted in station, attended by fortune, of great and splendid power, the greatest among the high Viziers, in whom confidence is placed, the faithful of the powerful Government, the adorned with greatness, power, glory, splendour, and fortune, Haujy Ibrahim Khan, on being granted leave, and vested with authority from the Port of the high King, whose Court is like that of Solomon, the asylum of the world, the sign of the power of God, the jewel in the ring of Kings, the ornament in the cheek of eternal Empire, the grace of the beauty of sovereignty and royalty, the King of the universe, like Caherman, the mansion of mercy and justice, the phœnix of good fortune, the eminence of never-fading prosperity, the King powerful as Alexander, who has no equal among the Princes exalted to Majesty by the Heavens in this globe, a shade from the shade of the Most High, a

PREFACE.

THE Author of the following Sketch has passed twenty-five years in India; during a great part of which time he has filled stations which gave him a near and full view of the Political Administration of that Country. He conceives, that to lay before the Public the opinions which he has formed, and the arguments which have produced them, on some parts of this extensive subject, is a continuation of that public service to which his life has been devoted: he therefore steals a short time, for that purpose, from the occupations of a busy and hurried life. At a time when discussions have commenced in England likely to terminate in fixing for a long time the political constitution of British India, he hopes that he shall be able to furnish some materials, which may assist the judgment of those who are to pronounce on some of the most momentous questions of policy which have ever employed the attention of a Government.

The relations of the Indian Government to the Constitution of Great Britain; the influence of the present system of conducting the Indian trade, on the prosperity of the Company, of Great Britain, and of British India; are extensive and important branches of the subject, which the Author leaves to those, who, from their habits of life, are more familiarly conversant with them. He has been chiefly employed in the political service of the Supreme Government of India, and principally in it's negotiations with native States.

His great object will be, to illustrate, by an appeal to experience, the nature of the powers, which the condition of India requires to be vested in the Supreme Government; and of those general maxims of policy, which seem to him prescribed, by the nature of things, in their intercourse with neighbouring States.

Other subjects of great importance, both civil and military, will be considered; but the chief object of the Author, is to discuss those subjects on which his own experience is the most extensive.

The situation of a dependent State, with a population of fifty millions, at the distance of ten thousand miles from the principal State, and surrounded by Governments without faith, or even long-sighted prudence, is unparalleled in the History of the World; and the application of the common maxims of political morality to the management of such a dependence, is, from the very singularity of the case, likely to require much caution, and to be subject to considerable mistake.

The opinions of the Author are likely to be so different from those of many, perhaps of most, of his readers, that he is under the necessity of bespeaking their candour, and of requesting, that no man will reject his opinions without a calm consideration of his reasons. He will probably be charged with Indian prejudices; and, as he does not pretend to any exemption from the common frailties of human nature, he willingly admits, that he must be prepossessed in favour of measures which he has contributed to carry into execution.

The merely English reader will, however, do well to recollect, that there are also English prejudices: and that those, who never saw a Country so distant, and so unlike every thing in Europe, as India, must acknowledge at least one great inferiority in such discussions.

From all the partialities of the internal politics of England the Author must necessarily be exempt. His life has been passed at too vast a distance to be reached by their influence. He cannot therefore write with any view to gratify resentments, or to advance himself, or to exalt or depress any English Statesman, or Parties. He may be prejudiced or mistaken; but he can have no other object, than that of contributing towards a right judgment on the Government of India.

The most valuable authorities, for the greater part of what follows, are the records of the several Governments of India; which the constitution of these Governments render the depositaries of the reasons for and against every public measure. Most of them have already been published in Europe: perhaps many more than the Author is aware of. At this distance he finds it difficult to ascertain what paper may remain unpublished. If, in consequence of his ignorance, he should have made extracts from any hitherto unpublished documents, he trusts, that he may be excused for employing, for merely public purposes, records, which, from the liberal access allowed to them, may almost be considered as, after a certain time, becoming virtually public.

CHAPTER I.

INTRODUCTION.

CONTENTS.

General Preliminary Observations on the Acquisition of British India.—Errors in the Theory of it's Government.—Reflections on that Subject.—Probable Changes.—Principles upon which they should be made.—Object of the Author of this Work, to furnish Information.—Concise Abstract of the History of the Company, from their Origin in 1600, till the Failure of Mr. Fox's Indian Bills in 1783.

THE great Empire, which England has established in the East, will be the theme of wonder to succeeding ages. That a small Island in the Atlantic should have conquered, and held the vast Continent of India as a subject Province, is in itself a fact, which can never be stated without exciting astonishment. But the surprise will be increased, when it is added, that this great Conquest was made, not by the collective force of the Nation, but by a Company of Merchants, who, originally vested with a charter of exclusive commerce, and with the privilege and right to protect their property, and to retaliate attack, were in a few years hurried, by the enterprise and ambition of their agents; the hostile and rival spirit of the other nations of Europe; and the weakness and perfidy of the Princes of Asia, to whom they became, from their encroachments or their riches, an object of jealousy or plunder; into the possession of Royal power; and actually found themselves called upon to act in the character of Sovereigns over extended kingdoms, before they had ceased to be the mercantile directors of petty factories.

Those, who look deep into the causes of great revolutions, and find them, not in the successful issue of the complex schemes of ambitious Statesmen, but in the simple operation of natural and obvious causes, will perhaps discover, that the means by which India was rendered subject to England (however inadequate they might at first glance appear), were of all others the best calculated to effect that great object. Force, and power, could not have approached the shores of India, without meeting with resistance; but to the unpretending merchant every encouragement was offered: and when the spirit with which the early settlers defended their property from spoliation showed they were as superior in their military as their commercial character, they became more an object of admiration than of jealousy to the principal Powers of India; who in process of time courted their alliance and aid against each other.

For the agents of the Company to have refused such aid, was perhaps in many cases impossible, or at least would have been dangerous to their immediate security; and by granting it, additional immunities and privileges, calculated to benefit and increase their trade, were often obtained; and thus the desire of promoting the security, and improving the prosperity, of their commercial establishments, first led them to political connexions. From that moment, the substance, though not the form, of their Government was altered: and they were involved, beyond the power of retreating, in all the complicated relations of a Political State. This important change was reluctantly admitted by the managers of the Company's concerns in England, as the advantages, which had attended the early commerce with India, made the proprietors of that capital by which it was carried on, view with anxiety and alarm a revolution, which they thought increased their risk, without a prospect of adequate return; they consequently denounced, at every step, that progress, which their agents made to territorial power in India;

and, with a view of checking this spirit of aggrandizement, they at last called for the aid of the legislative power of the Kingdom, which readily seconded their efforts, and gave the authority of law to their orders. But had those proprietors, or the administration of the Government of England, been more fully informed, or had they drawn their conclusions more from plain practical reasoning, combined with a correct view of human nature (as it existed in the Country for which they legislated), than from abstract principles of general policy, they might, perhaps, have been more moderate, and less dogmatical in their efforts to correct the system; and they might have discovered, that, though they might regulate, it was a vain attempt to endeavour to stop altogether the career of a State, which was rising rapidly into greatness, under the influence of causes, that were irresistible in their force, and which it was not possible to control. The truth is, that from the day on which the Company's troops marched one mile from their factories, the increase of their territories and their armies became a principle of self-preservation; and at the end of every one of those numerous contests, in which they were involved by the jealousy, avarice or ambition, of their neighbours, or the rapacity and ambition of their own servants, they were forced to adopt measures for improving their strength; which soon appeared to be the only mode by which they could avert the occurrence of similar danger.

Such, in a few words, is the History of the Progress of the East India Company to power in India: but in the separation of that body of merchants from the Nation of Great Britain, we may discover many other causes, which, while they gave a peculiar character to their system of Government, tended greatly to promote that general success, which has raised this Company to such an eminence of political power.

The servants of the Company had a great field open for the exercise of their talents in India; and, in the early part of their History, the advancement of individuals to wealth and authority, depended in a great degree upon the advancement of the Government which they served. Under such circumstances, and acting in a scene too distant to admit of much check or control, it was natural that they should apply all the knowledge and ability, which they possessed, toward the latter object, with that ardour, which such a combination of personal interest and patriotic pride was likely to produce: and there cannot be a doubt, but that the comparative smallness of their numbers contributed more than any other cause, or perhaps than all others put together, to their success. For that circumstance, while it lulled the jealousy of the different States in their vicinity, forced them to the adoption of the only means by which such a revolution could have been effected. It made them bend their superior and commanding knowledge to the conciliation and management of the natives of India, whom they literally employed to conquer each other. The actual condition of that vast continent greatly facilitated the execution of this plan.

The East India Company began to rise into political power and consequence, as a State, about the period of the downfal of the Imperial House of Timour; when the different Princes of India were contending for the fragments of the broken Empire, every province of which was distracted by their petty wars, or groaning under their temporary oppression. It cannot be a matter of surprise, that, at such a period, the inhabitants of that country rejoiced at the introduction of a Government, which gave toleration to their religion, security to their property, and which, from it's character, promised to them and their descendants a durable tranquillity beyond what they had ever enjoyed.

To men tired out as they were with wars and contentions, and who had long (from the repeated conquests to which they had been subjected) been lost to all feeling of national pride, the very permanency of usurpation was a blessing; and it was natural for them to forget their prejudices against their European masters, in a contemplation of that superior regard to justice, good faith, and civilization, by which they saw their rule accompanied.

The Princes and Chiefs of India, who have been the great, and indeed the only sufferers by the rise of the East India Company, saw too late the error which they had committed, in allowing it to attain a strength, which they could not shake; and had the mortification to find that their efforts for it's destruction tended but to confirm and enlarge it's power; which they not only saw improve by success, but rise still higher from misfortune. And this latter circumstance made a deeper impression, as it was effected through the means of resources which were drawn from a distant land, which were unseen, and therefore conceived by the nations of India to be inexhaustible. "I am "not alarmed at what I see of the force and "resources of the Company, but at what is "unseen,"* was the emphatic speech of one of

* This observation of Hyder Ally Khan was repeated to me by Purneah, the present Dewan of Mysore.

their most able, powerful, and inveterate enemies; and it faithfully represents the impression, which was made upon ignorant nations, of the power of a State, which they observed to draw support at pleasure from a country with whose means they were unacquainted, and whose power they had only been able to judge of by it's effects; which in India have been of a nature calculated to make them form the most exaggerated opinion of it's magnitude.

These general reflections upon the causes of our rise to power in India, have been suggested by a sense of their importance. It is only by continually reverting to the past, that we can hope for success in the future. For if, in the pride of power, we ever forget the means by which it has been attained; and, casting away all our harvest of experience, are betrayed by a rash confidence in what we may deem our intrinsic strength, to neglect those collateral means by which the great fabrick of our power in India has hitherto been supported, we shall with our own hands precipitate the downfal of our authority. But that event is still more likely to be accelerated by the opposite error, which should lead us to disown our greatness, and, under an affected and unwise humility, (ill suited to our condition,) to pursue a policy, calculated to discourage friends, and give confidence to our enemies, and in it's consequences to involve us in those very wars and conquests, which it pretends to disclaim.

There is a mean between these extremes, which we must follow, if we desire that our Empire in India should be durable; and that mean must combine the unshaken firmness and dignified spirit of an absolute, but tempered rule, with the most unceasing attention to the religious prejudices and civil rights of our Indian subjects; whose condition it must be our continual study to improve, in the conviction, that our Government, on the great scale upon which it is now established, cannot be permanent, but by their means; and that it is not in nature, that they should contribute their efforts to it's support, unless they are, by a constantly recurring sense of benefit, made to feel a lively and warm interest in it's prosperity and duration.

The British Legislature has hitherto but slowly followed the progress of the power of the Company in India. It had legislated for factories on a foreign shore, when that Corporation was in the possession of provinces; and when the laws were completed to govern those, it had obtained kingdoms. That the present system of Government is inadequate, and the laws, under which it exists, defective, and not calculated for the greatness of the Empire, every one acquainted with the subject must acknowledge; and the time probably approaches, when some great change must take place. But, at all events, our interests in India have become at this moment an object of the most serious consideration: and whether the present constitution of Government be confirmed or changed, it is of importance to examine all those facts, which can enable us to judge of it's merits and defects; as such alone can qualify those, on whom that duty must devolve, to form plans for it's future security and improvement.

What appears the most prominent error in all the laws and regulations, which have been passed in England relative to the political government of India, is, that dogmatical principle on which they proceed, in the endeavour to fix that, which is constantly changing. This principle is perhaps too natural to those by whom these laws and regulations must be framed, ever to be wholly eradicated. It arises out of a warm interest in what immediately affects the mother country, and a feeling, which approaches to indifference toward our distant possessions. This produces a continual desire to mould the latter into that shape and character, which will best suit the former; but, unfortunately, empire is a substance, which cannot be shaped and moulded. It is by the laws of Nature mutable; and this character, which our Empire in the East has in common with all Empires in the world, has hitherto, and must always continue to disappoint those expectations, which are formed, of limiting the precise extent of the dominions, or of fixing the exact power, of the British Government in Asia.

That this consideration renders our connexion with India as awful as it is important, no person can deny. Human wisdom cannot foresee the consequences, which the possession of such an extended Empire may produce; but we must not allow our plans of amendment to be arrested, because we are threatened with distant and uncertain evils. We should rather appreciate justly the great advantages which Great Britain has already derived from her Indian possessions, and the benefits which may be anticipated from their preservation and improvement, while we reflect most seriously on the dangers which would result from those possessions being lost, or passing into the hands of an European rival.

Reflections of this nature ought to dispose the legislative wisdom of our country to adopt measures for placing the administration of British India upon the basis, which it judges best calculated to preserve that country to Great

Britain; and, in the accomplishment of this purpose, while it respects just and established rights, and rejects every crude and hasty plan of rash innovation, it will no doubt proceed, on the most enlarged and enlightened principles, to fix the Government of our Empire in India on a foundation, which is commensurate with it's present magnitude; and which reconciles, as far as the two objects can be reconciled, the most vigorous and efficient system of local Government for India, with an observation of those important principles of check and control, which form the soul and essence of the Government of England.

It has been observed by one of our great Statesmen,* that any plan, which could be suggested for the Government of a country so situated as the British Empire in the East, must be inadequate; that in such a case no theoretical perfection could be imagined, much less executed; and that the option of a form of Government was only a choice of inconveniencies. But a conviction of the truth of this general observation should rouse, instead of discouraging, the minds of those to whom this great and difficult work is assigned; and while it reconciles them to the necessity of changes in a

* Mr. Pitt.

system, which was declaredly * deemed by those even by whom it was established, as an experiment, it ought to elevate them to efforts proportionate to the performance of the most arduous task, which has perhaps ever been attempted by human wisdom.

It is the object of this work to afford information to those upon whom this important labour must devolve, and to elucidate (as well as the author can) the political principles upon which the Government of British India has been conducted since the introduction of Mr. Pitt's Bill in 1784. But it will be necessary to preface this account with a general and concise view of the proceedings of the Company, from the first date of their union as a Corporation, to that, on which the more detailed history of their progress commences.

Though the merchants of Great Britain, after the discovery of the passage to India by the Cape of Good Hope (A. D. 1497), made early efforts to share with the Portuguese in the rich trade, which was carried on by the newly discovered channel between Europe and that quarter of the globe, more than a century elapsed before they were in any degree successful. Individual capital, after several attempts,

* Vide 'Plans for British India.'

was found too limited for a trade, which, however lucrative, was attended with great risk, and required force to protect it.

It is to these causes, that we must trace the original association of that body of wealthy merchants, who petitioned Queen Elizabeth to grant them encouragement, and exclusive privileges, for the purpose of carrying on the trade with India. That Princess, alive to every project which promised to increase the wealth and greatness of her country, sent an Embassy to the Emperor of Dehly (Ahbar), to solicit him to extend his favour and protection to her subjects, trading with his dominions. Elizabeth, however, when she adopted this measure, did not wait for it's result, which was not very successful, but granted a Charter on the 31st of December 1600, which erected the Merchants,* who had petitioned her, into a Body or Corporation, under the title of "*Governors and Company of Merchants of London trading to the East Indies.*" By this Charter they were vested with the power of purchasing lands without any limitation; their commerce was to be directed by a Governor and twenty-four persons in committees. Their first Governor, Sir

* The Petition was signed by the Earl of Cumberland, and two hundred and fifteen persons. The Earl's name is specified in the Grant.

Thomas Knight, was named in the act. The Company, their sons when of age, their apprentices, servants and factors in India, were vested, for a period of fifteen years, with the privilege, to use the words of the Charter, of an exclusive trade "into the countries and parts of Asia and "Africa, and into and from all the islands, "ports, towns, and places of Asia, Africa and "America, or any of them, beyond the Cape of "Bona Esperanza, or the Straits of Magellan, "where any traffic may be used, and to and "from every of them."

The General Assemblies of the Company were vested with the power of making any laws and regulations for the conduct of their concerns, which were not at variance with the laws of the realm; and their exports were made free of custom for a term of four years. They were empowered to fit out and send six good ships and six pinnaces annually to India; and to export, under some restrictions, thirty thousand pounds in foreign coin or bullion.

This Charter concludes with a proviso, by which the Crown, in the event of it's operation not being profitable to the State, had the right, upon giving two years' warning, to resume the Grant, which in the same clause it pledged itself to prolong for fifteen years beyond the first period, in the event of it's proving advantageous to the country.

Such was the first Charter under which the merchants of England commenced their commerce with India. Their original capital was seventy-two thousand pounds, divided into shares, each of which was fifty pounds.

The first fleets which the Company sent to India were successful, but particularly the third, which was commanded by Captain Keeling, who returned to England in 1610, after a prosperous though long voyage, with his ships richly laden, and without the loss of a man in his fleet.

Notwithstanding these successes, the trade to India was inconsiderable and uncertain. It's prosperity depended upon the good-will and honesty of the natives of the countries to which the Company traded, and the address of the local agents by whom their concerns in India were managed.

Destitute of settlements or forts, they had neither accommodation nor security for their servants or property; and were consequently subject to every insult or injury, which the jealousy or hatred of European rivals could stimulate the inhabitants of the ports, which they frequented, to offer; and they had early to

Khoosroo whose saddle is the moon, and whose stirrup is the new moon, a Prince of great rank, before whom the sun is concealed.

ARABIC VERSE.

Thy benevolence is universally dispersed! every where drops are scattered! Thy kindness shadows cities: may God fix firm the basis of thy dominion! And the high in dignity, the great and able in power, the adorner of those acquainted with manners, Captain John Malcolm, delegated from the sublime quarter of the high in power, (seated on a throne the asylum of the world, the chief jewel in the crown of royalty and sovereignty, the anchor of the vessel of victory and fortune, the ship on the sea of glory and empire, the blazing sun in the sky of greatness and glory, Lord of the Countries of England and India, may God strengthen his territories and establish his glory and commands upon the seas!) in the manner explained in his credentials, which are sealed with the seal of the most powerful and most glorious, possessing fortune, the origin of rank, splendour and nobility, the ornament of the world, the accomplisher of the works of mankind, the Governor General of India. This treaty between these two great Powers shall be binding on race after race; and the two Governments must ever, while the world exists, act in conformity to what is now settled.

ARTICLE I.

The merchants of the high contracting States are to travel, and carry on their affairs in the territories of both Nations, in full security and confidence; and the Rulers and Governors of all cities are to consider it their duty to protect from injury their cattle and goods.

ARTICLE II.

The traders and merchants of the Kingdom of England or Hindoostan, that are in the service of the English Government, shall be permitted to settle in any of the sea-ports or cities of the boundless Empire of Persia (which may God preserve from calamity,) that they prefer; and no Government duties, taxes, or requisitions, shall ever be collected on any goods that are the actual property of the Governments, the usual duties on such to be taken from purchasers.

ARTICLE III.

Should it happen, that either the persons or property (of merchants) are injured, or lost, by thieves or robbers, the utmost exertions shall be made to punish the delinquents, and recover the property: and if any merchant or trader of Persia evades, or delays, the payment of a debt to the English Government, the latter are authorized to use every possible mode for the recovery of their demands, taking care to do so in communication and with the knowledge of the Ruler or Governor of the place; who is to consider it as his duty to grant, on such occasion, every aid in his power. And, should any merchants of Persia be in India attending to their mercantile concerns, the Officers of the English Government are not to prevent them carrying on their affairs, but to aid and favour them: and the above-mentioned merchants are to recover their debts and demands in the mode prescribed by the customs and laws of the English Government.

ARTICLE IV.

If any person in the Empire of Persia die indebted to the English Government, the Ruler of the place must exert his power to have such demand satisfied before those of any other creditor whatever. The servants of the English Government resident in Persia, are permitted to hire as many domestics, natives of that country, as are necessary for the transaction of their affairs; and they are authorized to punish such, in cases of misconduct, in the manner they judge most expedient, provided such punishment does not extend to life or limb: in such cases, the punishment to be inflicted by the Ruler or Governor of the place.

ARTICLE V.

The English are at liberty to build houses and mansions in any of the ports or cities of Persia that they choose; and they may sell, or rent, all such houses or mansions at pleasure. And should ever a ship belonging to the English Government be in a damaged state in any of the ports of Persia, or one of Persia be in that condition in an English harbour, the Chiefs and Rulers of the ports and harbours of the respective Nations are to consider it as their duty, to give every aid to refit and repair vessels so situated: and if it happens that any of the vessels of either Nation are sunk, or shipwrecked, in or near the ports or shores of either Country; on such occasions, whatever part of the property is recovered shall be restored to their owners or their heirs, and a just hire is to be allowed by the owners to those who recover it.

FINAL ARTICLE.

Whenever any native of England or India, in the service of the English Government, resident in Persia, wishes to leave that Country, he is to suffer obstruction from no person, but to be at full liberty to do so, and to carry with him his property.

The articles of the treaty between the two States are fixed and determined. That person who turns from God turns from his own soul.

Seal of ▱ HAUJY IBRAHIM KHAN.

▱ Captain JOHN MALCOLM.

(Signed) JOHN MALCOLM, Envoy.

ADDITIONAL ARTICLE.

It is further written in sincerity, that on iron, lead, steel, broad cloth, and purpetts, that are exclusively the property of the English Government, no duties whatever shall be taken from the sellers, a duty not exceeding one per cent to be levied upon the purchasers; and the duties, imposts, and customs, which are at this period established in Persia and India (on other goods), are to remain fixed, and not to be increased.

The high in rank Haujy Khutteel Khan, Malick or Tijjar, is charged and intrusted with the arrangement and settlement of the remaining points relative to commerce.

Seal of ▱ HAUJY IBRAHIM KHAN.

▱ Captain JOHN MALCOLM.

(Signed) JOHN MALCOLM, Envoy.

A true translation.

(True Copy.) (Signed) JOHN MALCOLM, Envoy.

FINIS.